W. W. Norton & Company has been independent since its founding in 1923, when William Warder Norton and Mary D. Herter Norton first published lectures delivered at the People's Institute, the adult education division of New York City's Cooper Union. The firm soon expanded its program beyond the Institute, publishing books by celebrated academics from America and abroad. By mid-century, the two major pillars of Norton's publishing program—trade books and college texts—were firmly established. In the 1950s, the Norton family transferred control of the company to its employees, and today—with a staff of four hundred and a comparable number of trade, college, and professional titles published each year—W. W. Norton & Company stands as the largest publishing house owned wholly by its employees.

W9-CEL-822

Governing California in the Twenty-first Century

SECOND EDITION

Copyright © 2009, 2008 by W. W. Norton & Company, Inc.

The text of this book is composed in Berlin with the display set in Interstate.
Composition by TexTech, Inc.
Manufacturing by Victor Graphics.
Book design by Sandra Watanabe.
Production manager: Eric Pier-Hocking.

ISBN: 978-0-393-93291-1

W. W. Norton & Company, Inc., 500 Fifth Avenue, New York, N.Y. 10110
www.wwnorton.com

W. W. Norton & Company Ltd., Castle House, 75/76 Wells Street, London W1T 3QT

3 4 5 6 7 8 9 0

Governing California in the Twenty-first Century

THE POLITICAL DYNAMICS OF THE GOLDEN STATE

SECOND EDITION

J. Theodore Anagnoson
CALIFORNIA STATE UNIVERSITY, LOS ANGELES

Gerald Bonetto
CALIFORNIA STATE UNIVERSITY, LOS ANGELES

J. Vincent Buck
CALIFORNIA STATE UNIVERSITY, FULLERTON

Richard E. DeLeon
SAN FRANCISCO STATE UNIVERSITY

Jolly Emrey
UNIVERSITY OF WISCONSIN-WHITEWATER

James J. Kelleher
COLLEGE OF THE CANYONS

Nadine Koch
CALIFORNIA STATE UNIVERSITY, LOS ANGELES

 W. W. NORTON AND COMPANY
NEW YORK ★ LONDON

Contents

Preface

Welcome to California politics and government. For entirely too many of California's citizens, our state's politics are unfathomable. Our premise in this book is that ordinary citizens can understand the fundamental forces and factors governing California politics, and that they need to do so to be better citizens, to communicate with public officials more effectively, and to help improve government by supporting positive changes to legislation and constitutional amendments. By understanding what is beneath the surface in California's politics and government, citizens can avoid the curse of indifference—the attitude that "everything is a mess, and no one can do anything about it." We hope this book helps the reader in that journey.

We cover the basics of California's politics and government with some special emphases:

- the Progressive movement and its legacy of rules and norms that so strongly influence us today;

- the image, and sometimes the reality, of interest groups' domination—and conflict;

- the reality of endless campaigns and of a system that seems structured to keep compromise from happening;

- a legislature that so often is at the center of things and is so often bypassed by groups seeking to make state policy on their own;

- local politics, often neglected in California government texts, and the fundamental factors that govern local politics in California;

- the factors and issues that are in the news today, things like term limits, Indian gaming and casinos, California's perpetually unbalanced budget, the poor condition of the state's highways, and more.

We divided the job of creating this book in the following way. Ted Anagnoson was the overall coordinator. Each chapter was primarily written as follows:

1. California Government in Crisis—Anagnoson (tanagno@calstatela.edu)
2. The Constitution and the Progressive Legacy—Anagnoson / Bonetto (gerry@piasc.org)
3. Interest Groups and the Media in California—Bonetto
4. Parties and Elections in California—Koch (nkoch@calstatela.edu)
5. The California Legislature—Buck (vbuck@fullerton.edu)
6. The Governor and the Executive Branch—Buck
7. The California Judiciary—Emrey (emreyj@uww.edu)
8. The State Budget and Budgetary Limitations—Anagnoson
9. Local Government—DeLeon (rdeleon@sfsu.edu)
10. Public Policy in California—Anagnoson

Acknowledgments

Tom Higgins and Tim Hodson were particularly helpful in thinking about the legislature and executive branch. Corey Cook read several chapters and submitted helpful and insightful comments. Many of us read each other's chapters and commented as well.

We would like to hear from you about this book. Use the e-mail addresses above to communicate with us.

J. Theodore Anagnoson
Professor of Political Science
California State University, Los Angeles

Governing California in the Twenty-first Century

SECOND EDITION

1   California Government in Crisis

WHAT CALIFORNIA GOVERNMENT DOES AND WHY IT MATTERS

Which of the following actions does not involve the use of an object or action regulated by the federal, state, or local government?

★ Driving on the freeway

★ Driving on a tollway

★ Driving across a bridge

★ Walking to the grocery store

★ Buying fruit at the grocery store

★ Going to school at any level, public or private

★ Working for the California Highway Patrol

★ Working for a private security guard service

★ Working for a grocery store

★ Eating dinner in a restaurant

[Answers at the end of the chapter.]

The California Dream?

For almost 200 years, the dream of California has attracted immigrants from the United States and abroad. Even Governor Schwarzenegger in one of his State of the State speeches (2004) said that California represented "an empire of hope and aspiration," a place where "Californians do great things." To some, the California dream is sun and surf; to others, the warm winter season; to still others, a house on the coast in the redwoods and acres of untrammeled wilderness or three or four cars per family. Many of these dreams can be summed up in the phrases "freedom from restraints" or "freedom from traditions." These are typical themes in statewide elections and gubernatorial state of the state speeches—bringing back the glories of a California that everyone seems to be seeking.

The reality is that *some of the dream is attainable for many*—we live in a place with winter weather that is the envy of most of the rest of the nation—but much of it is not. One of the themes of this book is the conflict between the dream and the reality, between the ideals that we set for ourselves and the reality of our everyday lives. One conflict particularly vivid to politicians is the conflict between the expectations we have for them and the reality of the constraints and incentives we saddle them with, so that they cannot possibly meet our expectations. Think about the desire we have for balanced budgets and the reality of the programs we all desire that cause those budgets to be thrown out of balance.

The Crisis of California Politics

The period from 2003 to 2009 will long be remembered in California not only for the stalemate and lack of progress on crucial state issues, but also for the beginnings of change. Consider:

- The voters voted overwhelmingly in 2003 to recall an incumbent governor, Gray Davis, who had been elected by a substantial margin just a year earlier, the first recall of an incumbent governor in any state since North Dakota in 1921.

- The new governor, Arnold Schwarzenegger, overwhelmingly elected from a field of 163 candidates, had not run for office before or held any position in the public sector. In 2004, he convinced both the legislature and the voters to reform the workers' compensation system, something that neither group had been able to do for many years, but he balanced the state budget the same way that Governor Davis had, by borrowing against the future and papering over other differences with accounting changes.

- In 2005, the new governor called a special election so that the people could enact his "reform plan," consisting of several initiatives to change the way California functioned. All were rejected.

- But in 2006, the governor and the legislature placed before the voters a $40+ billion infrastructure re-building plan, a first step toward restoring California's "greatness." All six bond issues passed, and Governor Schwarzenegger was re-elected by a substantial margin.

- In November 2008, Proposition 11, which took the power to establish the districts of the Assembly and State Senate away from those bodies and gave it to a citizens' commission, passed. At the same time, neither the legislature nor the governor could find the two-thirds majority necessary to increase fees or reduce expenditures sufficiently to balance a budget that went from a $10 billion deficit to a $15 billion deficit to projections of as much as $40 billion over a two-year period (compared with an approximate $100 billion general fund "base").

- In the November 2008 election, Proposition 8 passed, defining marriage as existing only between a man and a woman. The movement to pass the proposition stemmed from the May 2008 decision of the California Supreme Court allowing gay marriage. Some 18,000 gay marriages were held between May and the passage of Proposition 8 in November. The issue produced more rancor and a seemingly lasting argument between strong interest groups.

California state government thus faces a series of paradoxes. On the one hand, the two-thirds rule required to pass the budget and increase taxes has kept the governor and legislature from agreeing on long-term changes that might stabilize state expenditures, ensuring a budget crisis for months at a time almost every year. On the other hand, some progress has been made in starting to rebuild California's aging infrastructure and, after several attempts, passing an initiative to reduce the amount of gerrymandering that has existed regarding California's legislative districts. Whether the Obama administration is more sympathetic to California's calls for help with undocumented immigrants or other problems than the George W. Bush administration was remains to be seen.

Is the state close to paralysis? It would seem so on budget and taxation issues, between the Democratic majority that seems to be willing to countenance small tax increases to balance the budget and the Republican minority that will countenance no tax increases under any conditions, plus the taxpayer groups that promise to sue the instant any tax increase is passed. And yet, in other areas, progress seems to have been made. And historically, there have been times when California was more partisan and just as paralyzed as it is at present.

Here are some reasons why we seem to have a continual crisis in California state government:

The Two-thirds Requirement for Passing the State Budget

California's constitution requires a two-thirds vote of the total membership—not just those present and voting—in each house of the legislature in order to pass the budget. The intent of the two-thirds requirement is to ensure that a larger majority than 50 percent agrees on the size and distribution of the budget, on the assumption that this number reflects a consensus in the society at large. However, since neither party has had a two-thirds majority in either the Assembly or the State Senate in decades, the majority party must make accommodations with some minority party legislators in order to obtain the necessary votes. The price these legislators have demanded in the past has been support for programs and projects of interest to them. The irony, according to many observers, is that the requirement designed to produce a budget that reflects a strong consensus in society and is smaller than what a simple majority would pass in fact results in a bigger budget. Meanwhile, when offered the opportunity to reduce the two-thirds requirement to 55 percent or a majority, the voters have opted to stay with the two-thirds requirement.

Only two other states, Arkansas and Rhode Island, require this strong a majority—a two-thirds vote of the total legislative membership—to pass the budget. Some observers consider this requirement alone responsible for the negative perception of state government among the public. Willie Brown, former Speaker of the California Assembly and recently mayor of San Francisco, said, "It's the 100 percent reason why we're in the mess we're in."[1]

Lack of Consensus in Fundamental Questions

How can a political system overcome the inertia generated by narrow interests in order to make decisions that benefit the broader general interest of the public as a whole? In a large complex state like California, this issue will persist, but in the past, California politicians have been able to overcome the lack of consensus to make progress on significant questions. Has California changed? Why do interest groups cause impasse now, after 2000, when they did not back in the 1970s and 1980s? After all, we had interest groups back then, and we have had the two-thirds decision rule for adopting the budget or raising taxes in the legislature since 1935. Dan Walters suggests that the blame heaped on the legislature is inappropriate:

> In fact, California's governance maladies stem from the complex, often contradictory nature of the state itself. With its immense geographic, economic, and cultural diversity, California has myriad policy issues, but those same factors also have become an impediment to governance. The state lost its vital consensus on public policy issues, and without that civic compass, its politicians tend to ignore major issues and pursue trivial ones. . . . The real issue is whether the public's anger at Gray Davis will morph into a new sense of civic purpose or whether California is destined to be . . . ungovernable.[2]

Term Limits

The term limit movement found fertile ground in California in the 1980s and 1990s. Proposition 140 in 1990 imposed the severest term limits in the nation on the legislature and the elected officials of the executive branch, and the voters in many cities in California enacted term limits as well. Part of the statewide anger was directed against Willie Brown, then Speaker of the California Assembly, whose flamboyant lifestyle and prolific fundraising raised the ire of voters.

The theory of the term limits movement is that if term limits are imposed, members of the Assembly and State Senate will pay more attention to their jobs and raise less money for future campaigns, and the system will be opened up to minority and female candidates. Since term limits have been imposed, the proportion of Latino legislators in particular has indeed risen, but, paradoxically, members have much less expertise on the matters they vote on and many—perhaps most—members of the legislature spend a good deal of their time worrying about their next position and raising funds for those campaigns.

The result is that most observers think that term limits have worsened the legislature, not bettered it. By the time legislators acquire the expertise to make good decisions, they are term-limited out. One of the reasons our limits are the most strict in the nation is that there is a lifetime ban on running for the same position again. Voters, however, strongly support term limits, and a proposal in 2002 to allow four extra years to legislators who reached their term limit maximum if they got the signatures of 20 percent of the voters, failed 58 percent to 42 percent. A February 2008 proposal from the legislature to allow legislators twelve years in one house also failed to receive voter approval.

The Safe-Seat Reapportionment

Every ten years, after the census has been taken, state legislatures realign their seats in accordance with the census numbers. This process traditionally has been highly partisan. In some reapportionments, the legislature comes together across party lines to form a coalition in which most incumbent seats become safe seats—that is, seats where the incumbent generally wins by more than a 10 percent to 15 percent margin (a 55 percent to 45 percent win is a 10 percent margin). Short of a surge in voter anger, most incumbents are safe, meaning that their votes in the Assembly or State Senate are not restricted by considerations of what their opponent will say about the vote in the next election campaign.

Here are the results from the 2008 legislative elections, combining congressional, State Senate, and Assembly seats:

WON BY	<10%	10-19.9%	20-29.9%	30-44.9%	45-99%	100%
Total of 153 districts	21	24	10	43	41	14
Percent	14%	16%	7%	28%	27%	9%

SOURCE: Compiled by the author from the Secretary of State's web site.

Almost 10 percent of the districts face no opposition at all, and some 36 percent are won by more than a 45 percent margin. Almost two-thirds, 64 percent, are won by margins of more than 30 percent—a percentage generally denoting a landslide. Either almost all Californians are living with people of similar political views or the level of gerrymandering in California is severe indeed!

The combination of the safe seats and the disproportionately liberal Democrats and conservative Republicans who tend to vote in primary elections mean that our legislators tend to be more conservative than the Republican Party as a whole or more liberal than the Democratic Party as a whole. Proposition 11, passed in November 2008, will substitute a citizens' commission for the legislature itself in drawing up the Assembly and State Senate districts (but not congressional districts). It should reduce the proportion of extremely safe seats after the 2010 Census.

The tendency toward ideological extremism in both parties, combined with the effects of term limits on legislators' knowledge and the need to obtain a two-thirds majority to pass the budget, has led to a late budget every year but four since 1990—and two of the on-time budget years were those with budget surpluses.

Reform Ideas

Numerous reforms have been suggested. Box 1.1 shows one example of a program to help reform California politics and government. This proposal is from State Senator John Vasconcellos (D-Santa Clara), a liberal who served in the Assembly

1. We owe it to ourselves to recognize that we Californians have the power within us to rise to this occasion.

2. Public financing of campaigns.

3. Assuring independent voters the right to vote in the primary of their choice.

4. Moving our primary elections to September.

5. Requiring all major candidates to engage in several very public debates, all terms to be entirely set by an utterly independent third party; plus all campaign TV ads to be only face and voice of the candidate him/herself.

6. Provision for "none of the above" on initial ballot, plus requiring a majority to win, plus instant runoff.

7. Reducing two-thirds vote required for budget to a simple majority.

8. Immediately proceeding toward enacting a state of California comprehensive economic recovery and sustained prosperity strategic action plan.

9. A bipartisan reapportionment commission.

10. Modifying term limits to six terms in the Assembly, three in the Senate.

11. Providing for expandable houses in the legislature—per population growth.

12. Restoring trust to politics via the politics of trust.

and State Senate since 1967 and was term-limited out in 2004. Many reformers from both sides of the political spectrum would agree with some, and perhaps most, of his ideas.

Why Study California Politics?

We know the obvious answer—the course meets some requirement for graduation or your major. The State of California decided that every college student should know something about the California Constitution and California government and politics. But more importantly—why?

- You are *the citizens and voters of the future*—or the present, except that younger adults tend to vote in strikingly smaller percentages than their elders.

- California politics is plagued by *low levels of participation and turnout*. Your vote and participation can make a difference.

- California politics also suffers from *too much interest-group participation and not enough citizen participation*. The general interests of large groups of citizens need to be represented at the table.

That's the narrow answer. A broader answer as to why we study California politics is that California's government and politics are distinctive and thus worthy of study. How are we different?

- We have much *more cultural diversity* than other states, including a much higher proportion of Latino and Asian residents in California than the other states. By some measures, we are the multicultural trendsetter among states (see the table on page 9).

- We have *the fifth or sixth largest economy in the world*. We are much larger than other states and larger than most entire countries. The 38 million citizens of the state of California produce as much in goods and services as France or Great Britain. However, we need to be cautious about statements about the economy—not only are there different ways to measure the size of the economy, but governors and state government have much less control of that economy than nations do. Nations can run deficits and print money; governors and states can't, at least in the long run. Nations can influence the money supply through their reserve banks; governors and states cannot.

- We are *the most populous state and we have grown more quickly than other states*. In 1960 New York had forty-one members in the U.S. House of Representatives; California had thirty-eight. Today California has fifty-three seats, and New York has fallen to twenty-nine, in third place. Texas is in second place with thirty-two seats.

- We are *more majoritarian than other states*, meaning that we like the measures for direct democracy—the initiative, the referendum, and the recall—that were added to the state constitution by the Progressive movement in 1912. Every state uses majority rule for most decisions, but when we use the term *majoritarian*, we mean that the public makes policy decisions, rather than our elected representatives. Consider the following continuum:

   Majoritarian   Republican
   |————————————————————————————————————|

   A *majoritarian* government is one that is highly influenced by the public at large through public-opinion polls that politicians take and through such measures as the initiative, referendum, and recall that enable the public to decide government policies directly.

   A *republican* government is one in which we elect representatives to make our decisions for us, very much on the Madison model for the federal government.

   California government has moved much more toward the majoritarian model than other states. Not only are initiatives to amend the constitution routine, but interest groups often begin collecting signatures for an initiative just to pressure the legislature into voting on their legislation. Californians like being majoritarian: surveys show that most don't want to restrict use of the initiative, in spite of its extensive use by interest groups.[3]

What Determines the Content and Character of California's Politics?

Three factors shape the content and character of California's politics:

1. The underlying demographic and sociopolitical trends that affect California and the other states;
2. The rules of the game, as set out in the federal and state constitutions and in state laws; and
3. The decisions of voters and politicians.

In Chapters 1 and 2 we will discuss the underlying demographic and sociopolitical trends and the rules of the game. What voters and politicians do in different areas is the subject of the rest of the book.

Underlying Socioeconomic Trends

Socioeconomic trends have driven many of the problems that have faced California voters and politicians. Some of these are:

POPULATION GROWTH Except for the four years from 1993 to 1996, California's population has grown by approximately 450,000 per year for more than two decades. In 1960, California had almost 16 million people; in 1970, 20 million; 1980, 24 million; 1990, 30 million; in 2000, about 34 million; and in 2008, 38 million. This strong and consistent growth has shown itself in political controversies over issues such as the following:

- *Housing and Transportation*—Even with the declines of 2007 and 2008, housing prices in many middle-class areas have skyrocketed since the short downturn of the early 1990s. Many lower- and middle-class people must live in the Central Valley and commute to work in the San Francisco Bay Area or in Riverside and San Bernardino Counties and commute to the Los Angeles area. In both of these places commutes of one to two hours—and even more—each way are not uncommon. Our transportation systems have not kept pace and reflect a much smaller population.

- *Schools*—Population growth means more schoolchildren, and there is a high demand for teachers across the state, along with a lack of fully qualified or credentialed teachers in many urban areas.

- *Immigration*—California has had high levels of immigration since the 1950s, so high in some areas that candidates for the presidency of Mexico have campaigned in the Los Angeles area. Between 1970 and 2006 the number of immigrants in the California population increased from 1.8 to 9.9 million; 27 percent of the state's current population was born somewhere else, a much higher proportion than in any other state. Most immigrants in California are from Latin America or Asia, with 4.4 million from Mexico, some 44 percent of the total immigrant population in California. Immigrants live in all parts of California, with those from Latin America more likely to live in Southern California and those from Asia in Northern California. Immigrants are younger than nonimmigrant Californians and more likely to be poor, and while some have relatively high levels of education, most immigrants are less educated than the native population.[4]

- *Undocumented Immigration*—There are approximately 2.8 million illegal immigrants in California's population of 38 million, estimates the Urban Institute, using the census figures on the foreign-born population and subtracting the numbers we know are naturalized or here on legal visas and work permits.[5] Illegal immigrants are a continuing political issue, ranging from Proposition 187 in the mid-1990s, which would have refused public services to anyone who could not show documentation, to the politically volatile driver-license bill that would have granted driver's licenses without reference to immigration status in 2003 to the presidential election of 2008, where some of the candidates in the primaries took strong stands against immigration.

RACE AND ETHNICITY The *U.S. Statistical Abstract*, a product of the Census Bureau and the most reliable guide to population statistics, projects California's 2007 population as the following, compared with the U.S. population:

	CALIFORNIA	U.S.
White alone	77%	80%
Black/African American alone	7%	13%
Asian alone	12%	4%
American Indian/Alaskan Native alone	1%	1%
Native Hawaiian/other Pacific Islander alone	0%	0%
Two or more races	3%	2%
Total	100%	100%

SOURCE: U.S. Census Bureau, "Annual State Population Estimates by Demographic Characteristics with 6 Race Groups (5 Race Alone Groups and One Group with Two or More Race Groups): April 1, 2000, to July 1, 2007." Release date: May 1, 2008.

Latino or Hispanic is not a racial category in the census, but a separate question asks about Hispanic or Latino origin. About 15 percent of the United States is Latino, but about 36 percent of California is. Almost 60 percent of California's Latino population is of Mexican heritage.

AGE California's population is relatively young, mostly because of immigration. Immigrants tend to be younger and to have larger families than those who have been residents for longer periods.

EDUCATION Californians are highly educated. A greater proportion of Californians have gone to college or completed a bachelor's or higher degree than in the United States in general.

MOBILITY AND FOREIGN-BORN Sixty percent of all Americans live in the state where they were born, but only 50 percent of all Californians were born in California. One-quarter, in fact, were foreign-born, a much higher percentage than in the United States as a whole (12 percent). Most foreign-born residents are not

U.S. citizens; only 40 percent of the foreign-born in both the United States and California are citizens. As one might expect with such a large foreign-born population, only 61 percent of those over age five speak English at home in California. In the United States as a whole, 82 percent of those over age five speak English at home. That is a substantial difference by the standards of social science.

INCOME California's median household income of $47,493 in the 2000 census was more than $5,000 greater than the national figure. Compared to the nation, the state has higher percentages of households and families in the income categories above $75,000 and lower percentages in the income categories from $15,000 to $49,000. Whether there is more disposable income after paying for housing costs is quite another question, given how much higher housing costs are in coastal California compared with the rest of the country. These figures are from a state Department of Finance analysis.[6]

Conclusion

In this book we are going to consider the real world and the possibilities, both fascinating and frustrating, of the present, and changes that might make the future more positive for both politicians and the public. We will investigate what makes California different from other states as well as its political problems, including:

- the inability to pass budgets on time or where income equals expenditures
- the malapportioned districts for the California legislature that, in combination with the primary system, produce legislators who are more liberal than the public on the Democratic side and more conservative on the Republican side
- the public's attachment to the strictest term limits in the nation
- the public's attachment to the extreme majoritarianism that produces the longest ballots in the nation as well as some of the lowest turnout rates.

Our coverage includes subjects that the newspapers and bloggers discuss in great detail as well as some, such as the California tax system and the impact of Proposition 13, that are taken for granted but that have kept the state from updating its structure and services. Welcome to the journey.

A Guide to This Book

Chapter 2, "The Constitution and the Progressive Legacy," deals with California's state constitutions and the Progressives, the two crucial factors that defined the shape and direction of today's California government.

Chapters 3 and 4 deal with the bodies outside government that influence what government can accomplish. Chapter 3, "Interest Groups and the Media in California," deals with the groups that are as prevalent and influential in California as they are in our nation's capital. Chapter 4, "Parties and Elections in California," deals with parties and voters, and how both influence government through elections and campaigns.

Chapters 5, 6, and 7 deal with the institutions of government. Chapter 5, "The California Legislature," deals with the legislature, the body we love to hate. We try in this book to understand the legislature and why it functions as it does, rather than simply condemning it. Chapter 6, "The Governor and the Executive Branch," asks whether California has become ungovernable. Chapter 7, "The California Judiciary," deals with judges and the criminal justice system.

Chapters 8, 9, and 10 deal with some policy problems and governmental structures that are particularly relevant today. Chapter 8, "The State Budget and Budgetary Limitations," addresses taxes, spending, and the California budget, asking whether the budget can be controlled in today's political and policy environment with the tools we have available to us. Chapter 9, "Local Government," deals with local government and its dependency on the state, a dependency that localities are taking action to remove in part through the initiative process. Chapter 10, "Public Policy in California," deals with several contemporary public policy problems, illustrating how the institutions and voters have acted in these areas.

FOR FURTHER READING

"California in Crisis." *California Journal*, August 2003, pp. 18–27.

Davis, Mike. *City of Quartz: Excavating the Future in Los Angeles*. New York: Vintage, 1990.

Hofstadter, Richard. *The Age of Reform*. New York: Washington Square Press, 1988.

Horwitz, Sasha. *Termed Out: Reforming California's Term Limits*. Los Angeles: Center for Governmental Studies, October 2007. www.cgs.org.

Legislation by Initiative vs. through Elected Representatives. San Francisco: Field Institute, November, 1999. www.field.com/fieldpollonline/subscribers/COI-99-Nov-Legislation.pdf

Olin, Spencer C. *California's Prodigal Sons: Hiram Johnson and the Progressives, 1911–1917*. Berkeley: University of California Press, 1968.

Public Policy Institute of California. "Just the Facts: Illegal Immigrants." San Francisco: Public Policy Institute of California, June 2008. www.ppic.org.

———. "Just the Facts: Immigrants in California." San Francisco: Public Policy Institute of California, June 2008. www.ppic. org.

———. "Research Brief: How Have Term Limits Affected the California Legislature?" No. 94. San Francisco: Public Policy Institute of California, November 2004. www.ppic. org.

Reyes, Belinda I., ed. *A Portrait of Race and Ethnicity in California, An Assessment of Social and Economic Well-Being*. San Francisco: Public Policy Institute of California, 2001.

Wilson, James Q. "A Guide to Schwarzenegger Country." *Commentary*, December, 2003, 45–49.

ON THE WEB

Center for Governmental Studies: www.cgs.org The Center for Governmental Studies is a think tank that specifically focuses on promoting citizen participation in government.

The Field (California) Poll: Field Institute. www.field.com/

Los Angeles Times (newspaper): www.latimes.com

Public Policy Institute of California: www.ppic.org The Public Policy Institute of California is a think tank devoted to nonpartisan research on how to improve California policy.

Sacramento Bee (newspaper): www.sacbee.com

San Francisco Chronicle (newspaper): www.sfgate.com

SUMMARY

California politics seemed to reach a crisis point with the recall of Governor Gray Davis, the election of Governor Arnold Schwarzenegger, and the inability of the legislature to pass a budget that was either balanced—or even close to balanced—or on time, according to constitutional requirements. The roots of the crisis seem to be from

- the requirement that two-thirds of the total membership of each house of the legislature vote to pass the budget or raise taxes;

- the interest-group impasse reflected in the legislature on many issues;
- the severe term-limits requirement, which has led to a loss of knowledge and interest in staying in the legislature; and
- gerrymandered districts that are safe for most legislators.

There are many reform ideas afloat in California that experts agree on. Long-time state legislator John Vasconcellos has developed a set of reform ideas, which are shown in Box 1.1.

We study California politics for a number of reasons:

- The course is often required.
- California's population is much more multicultural and diverse than that of other states.
- It is the fifth or sixth largest economy in the world.
- It is the most populous state.
- Its people and interest groups are much more likely to use the initiative to pass laws and amend the state constitution than those of other states, a phenomenon we call direct democracy, and that makes the state more "majoritarian" than most.

California, with its huge population, has experienced a multitude of socioeconomic and demographic changes:

- The population soared from 16 million in 1960 to 34 million in 2000.

- The number of immigrants between 1970 and 2000 increased from 1.8 million to 8.9 million.
- The number of illegal immigrants estimated to be in California is 2.4 million.
- The white population in the United States as a whole is 76 percent, while in California it is 59 percent.
- A greater proportion of Californians have gone to college or completed a bachelor's or advanced degree than in the United States in general.
- California's median household income in the 2000 census ($47,493) was more than $5,000 higher than the national figure.

PRACTICE QUIZ

1. The budget must be passed by two-thirds of those present and voting in both chambers of the legislature.
   a) true
   b) false
2. Most states require a two-thirds majority to pass their budgets each year.
   a) true
   b) false
3. What proportion of California legislative seats—those in the Assembly, State Senate, and Congress—are safe, that is, the incumbent wins by a margin of 10 percent margin or more?
   a) 50 percent
   b) 65 percent
   c) 80 percent
   d) 95 percent
4. According to this book, California's extraordinary population growth has had effects in the following policy areas:
   a) welfare, Medi-Cal, and education
   b) schools, immigration, and housing
   c) housing, welfare, and corrections
   d) corrections, Medi-Cal, and higher education
5. California's population, the foreign-born population, and the approximate number of undocumented immigrants, according to the text:
   a) 50 million, 5 million, 2 million
   b) 34 million, 8.8 million, 2.4 million
   c) 25 million, 20 million, 18 million
   d) 36 million, 10 million, 1.5 million

6. Latino or Hispanic is a racial category in the U.S. Census that is taken every 10 years.
   a) true
   b) false
7. The proportion of immigrants in California who speak English at home as compared to the United States as a whole is:
   a) greater.
   b) lesser.
   c) the same.
8. According to this book, the inability of the California legislature to make decisions that benefit the state as a whole is due to
   a) the number of interest groups.
   b) the two-thirds requirement to pass the budget or raise taxes.
   c) California's size.
   d) the loss of consensus since the 1950s and 1960s.
9. California's term limits are
   a) eight years for the governor, four years for the Assembly, and six years for the State Senate.
   b) six years for the governor, six years for the Assembly, and eight years for the State Senate.
   c) eight years for the governor, six years for the Assembly, and eight years for the State Senate.
   d) eight years for the governor, eight years for the Assembly, and twelve years for the State Senate.
10. Undocumented immigrants can obtain a driver's license in California.
    a) true
    b) false

CRITICAL-THINKING QUESTIONS

1. How distinctive is California compared with other states? Are we really that different?

2. California's population differs from that of other states on several levels: what are the two or three most significant, and why are they significant?

KEY TERMS

At this point you should have a general understanding of the following concepts and terms:

California dream (3)

cultural diversity (7)

foreign-born (9)

Latino/Hispanic (9)

majoritarian (7)

racial and ethnic diversity (9)

reapportionment (5)

recall (2)

safe seat (5)

term limits (4)

undocumented immigration (9)

ANSWERS TO QUESTIONS IN "WHAT CALIFORNIA GOVERNMENT DOES AND WHY IT MATTERS"

Every action named involves government at some level and in some way:

- Driving on the freeway: Freeways are built by state government with federal and state funds; traffic is monitored by the California Highway Patrol.

- Driving on a tollway: California has several privately owned tollways; these are freeways built with private funds typically raised by selling bonds, itself a market regulated by government. State government approves the rights of way for these tollways and otherwise regulates their operations.

- Driving across a bridge: Standards for bridges come from both the federal government and the California Department of Transportation; most bridges were constructed with public funds.

- Walking to the grocery store: Sidewalks were constructed with public funds and to local government construction standards.

- Buying fruit at the grocery store: Scales are certified by county government; both imported and domestic fruit must meet U.S. Department of Agriculture and State Department of Agriculture standards.

- Going to school at any level, public or private: States have standards for what must be taught at each grade level, as well as tests to determine whether schools are meeting the standard.

- Working for the California Highway Patrol: The CHP is a state government agency.

- Working for a private security guard service: Security guards must meet local police department standards.

- Working for a grocery store: Wages, hours, and working conditions are governed by the state Department of Employment Security or by union contract.

- Eating dinner in a restaurant: County Departments of Health oversee restaurant food quality and cleanliness.

2 The Constitution and the Progressive Legacy

WHAT CALIFORNIA GOVERNMENT DOES AND WHY IT MATTERS

In Chapter 1, we discussed some of the demographic differences between California and other states. Here are some differences in the political process:

★ The **sheer size of the state** increases the costs of political campaigns and media coverage.

★ The **competing network of interest groups** causes groups to jockey for position and influence.

★ The **extensive use of the initiative** significantly impacts state and local governance and policy.

★ The **divided executive branch**, composed of nine separately elected officials, each with his or her own area of authority and responsibility. Leads to overlapping responsibilities and fragmentation in the execution of state policy.

★ The **widespread, almost universal, use of nonpartisan elections at the local level of government** eliminates a valuable clue for voters to identify the policy positions of the candidates on the ballot.

Aside from the size of the state and the interest-group network, these characteristics are results of the Progressive movement, which flourished from 1900 to 1917. The leaders of this movement focused on one goal: making government more responsive to the political, social, and economic concerns of the people. Their reforms continue to shape California government and politics in ways that sharply differentiate it from other states. To some, these features hamper the political process and should be changed. To others, they are the essence of California, and if they were changed, California would be just another state.

The Rules of the Game: California's Constitution

The California constitution is long and very detailed, with numerous amendments over the years, dealing with both the fundamental principles and powers of government and commonplace issues such as the right to fish on government property, English as the state's official language, and grants for stem cell research. Today California has the second highest number of constitutional amendments, behind Alabama, and the second longest state constitution, behind Louisiana. The California constitution is over one hundred pages long.

The constitution defines the rules under which political actors and the citizenry interact with each other to fulfill their goals as individuals, members of a group, or a population as a whole. Its long and storied history can be divided into four stages:

- **The 1849 constitution**. Written by residents of the territory in anticipation of statehood, this constitution contains many of the basic ideas underlying California government today.

- **The 1879 constitution**. Written by a constitutional convention the previous year, this is the basic document that, with amendments, remains in force today.

- **1900 to 1917**. During this period, the Progressives amended the constitution and passed laws to return government to the people, away from special interests, and make state government responsive to the people's desires and needs. The most prominent reforms of this period were the initiative, referendum, and recall.

- **1918 to the present**. Amendment after amendment lengthened the state's constitution, resulting in a document that at one point was almost 100,000 words long. Several commissions proposed substantive changes, but the only changes adopted came from two constitutional revision commissions, one in the 1960s and the other in the 1990s, that shortened and clarified the language in the constitution but made no substantial changes to its provisions.

The 1849 Constitution

By 1849, 80,000 unruly gold miners had moved to California, giving the area enough people to apply for territorial status, and the settlers of the territory drafted a constitution. Admitting California as a free state, however, would have upset the balance between free states and slave states that had existed in the Union since 1820; therefore, admission as a territory was delayed. In 1849, the newly elected president of the United States, Zachary Taylor, proposed that California draft a constitution and apply for admission as a state directly to Congress, instead of applying as a territory first and moving to state status later. California citizens elected delegates to a constitutional convention; the delegates in turn met and drew up the proposed constitution in forty-three days.

The constitutional convention, forty-eight elected men who met in Monterey in September of 1849, used a book of constitutions that contained the constitutions of the federal government and some thirty states. Several of the provisions were taken directly from the constitutions of New York and Iowa. The basic provisions of the 1849 constitution are still in force:

- The framework of the government rested on the separation of powers—executive, legislative, and judicial—and checks and balances, like the federal government.

- Executive power was divided, as it is today, with the separate election and jurisdiction of the governor, lieutenant governor, comptroller, treasurer, attorney general, surveyor general, and superintendent of public instruction. This division weakens the governor, who cannot appoint—or remove—senior members of his or her own administration. Moreover, each of these statewide officials is a potential competitor for the governor's office, and each can put out statements that contradict what the governor is saying.

- An extensive bill of rights began the constitution, as it still does today.

- The legislature was elected and consisted of two houses, one called the Senate, the other the Assembly.

Features that were different from what we have today include:

- The right to vote at that time was limited to white males twenty-one years of age or older who had lived in California for at least six months.

- The legislature by a two-thirds vote could grant Native Americans the right to vote "in such special cases as such proportion of the legislative body may deem just and proper."

- The judiciary was elected, as judges are today, but they were organized into four levels as Mexico was at the time. All laws and other provisions were to be published in both English and Spanish, since California was a bilingual state.

The first California constitution read very much like any other constitution—it had about 9,000 words, compared with the present U.S. Constitution's 4,500 words, plus another 3,100 words of amendments. Over time, as we shall see, the constitution evolved into a much longer document.

In 1850, the federal government passed a series of bills that made up the Compromise of 1850. These bills admitted California to the Union as a free state, established territorial governments in Utah and New Mexico, allowed residents of those states to decide whether to be free or slave states, settled a dispute over the border between Texas and New Mexico, compensated Texas with $10 million to repay debts to Mexico, abolished the slave trade in the District of Columbia, and put the Fugitive Slave Act into effect.

The 1879 Constitution

Voters approved the convening of a constitutional convention in 1877, but the actual convention was held in 1879. A new political party, the Workingmen's Party, which supported many populist ideas (see below) and which held fifty-one of the 152 seats at the convention, played a significant role in the discussion.[1] The new party supported restrictions on corporations and railroads, and was also strongly opposed to the presence of Chinese workers in California. One of its rallying cries was "The Chinese must go!"[2] The party also opposed centralized governmental power and a powerful legislature, proposing unsuccessfully that California collapse the two houses of the legislature into one, a unicameral legislature, and abolish the lieutenant governor's office.

All kinds of provisions were adopted. For example, stockholders were to be responsible for the debts of a corporation. The railroads could not give free passes to those holding political office; they could not raise rates on one line to compensate for reductions made to compete on alternative lines; and they would be regulated by a Railroad Commission. Other provisions restricted employment of Chinese workers, prohibiting them from being employed on public works projects or by corporations chartered in California.

These additions added words—almost doubling the constitution's size—and policies that read very much like a series of laws rather than a fundamental framework within which laws would operate. By 1948, the California constitution, with amendments, reached 95,000 words.

The new constitution was approved by a 54 percent to 46 percent vote in May 1879, with 90 percent of those eligible to vote participating. In the end, however, most of the reform measures were not put into practice, as corporations and other special interests sued to block their implementation, continuing the domination of the state by corporations and the railroads.

You can get a sense of California's constitution and how different it is from the federal constitution by examining California's bill of rights, called "Declaration of Rights." First, California's bill of rights can be expanded or rewritten as times change. The federal bill of rights consists of the first ten amendments to the U.S. Constitution, and while other amendments may be passed, the first ten will remain the Bill of Rights as they were written. Because of this factor, California's bill of rights reflects the political changes and conflicts that have occurred over time, which means that some of the rights can be much more specific than the corresponding federal right. You can see the result of that specificity in the provisions for freedom of speech as they apply to a newspaper. The federal constitution has the familiar first amendment:

> Amendment 1: Congress shall make no law respecting an establishment of religion, or prohibiting the free exercise thereof, or abridging the freedom of speech, or of the press; or the right of the people peaceably to assemble, and to petition the Government for a redress of grievances.

California's corresponding section has both more detail and more specificity, since it has been amended over time:

> SEC. 2. (a) Every person may freely speak, write and publish his or her sentiments on all subjects, being responsible for the abuse of this right. A law may not restrain or abridge liberty of speech or press.
>
> (b) A publisher, editor, reporter, or other person connected with or employed upon a newspaper, magazine, or other periodical publication, or by a press association

or wire service, or any person who has been so connected or employed, shall not be adjudged in contempt by a judicial, legislative, or administrative body, or any other body having the power to issue subpoenas, for refusing to disclose the source of any information procured while so connected or employed for publication in a newspaper, magazine, or other periodical publication, or for refusing to disclose any unpublished information obtained or prepared in gathering, receiving, or processing of information for communication to the public. Nor shall a radio or television news reporter or other person connected with or employed by a radio or television station, or any person who has been so connected or employed, be so adjudged in contempt for refusing to disclose the source of any information procured while so connected or employed for news or news commentary purposes on radio or television, or for refusing to disclose any unpublished information obtained or prepared in gathering, receiving, or processing of information for communication to the public.

As used in this subdivision, "unpublished information" includes information not disseminated to the public by the person from whom disclosure is sought, whether or not related information has been disseminated and includes, but is not limited to, all notes, outtakes, photographs, tapes, or other data of whatever sort not itself disseminated to the public through a medium of communication, whether or not published information based upon or related to such material has been disseminated.

Note the use of modern language, such as "outtakes," "wire service," "television," and other examples.

California's declaration of rights can also be amended through the initiative process, which allows individuals or groups to put proposed changes before the voting public at any election.

From 1900 to 1917: The Progressive Movement

Pressure for political reform continued. Beginning with the turn of the century, the Progressives pursued three goals: to attack corporate political influence, eliminate the political corruption that went with such influence, and democratize the political process.[3] They understood that these goals had to be accomplished before they could address other equally pressing but more mundane concerns of the time. They accomplished all of this—and much more. Beginning with the 1911 legislative session, these reformers passed dozens of constitutional amendments and statutes that changed the face of California government and politics.[4] The most prominent of the political reforms were the following:

- **Nonpartisanship** This became the norm in local elections, in which no party label is affixed to the candidate's name on the ballot. Of the more than 19,000 elected public officials in California, fewer than 300 are elected in partisan races.

- **Primary elections** Prior to the institution of primary elections, political parties chose their candidates in party conventions, with their stereotypes of the smoke-filled back rooms, or caucuses—meetings of party members at the local level. In a primary election, each prospective party nominee has to obtain more votes than any other prospective nominee to run as the party's candidate in the general election in November.

- **The office block ballot** This is the ballot that we vote on today, with a block for each office and the candidates listed for that office. Prior to this reform, in some elections, the voter cast a ballot by voting for a party, party symbol, or colored piece of paper for the particular party.

- **Direct democracy** These grassroots processes—the initiative, referendum, and recall—give citizens the ability to rein in the abuse of power by elected officials or to ignite those same public officials if they are paralyzed by inaction and partisan bickering.

During this period, the California constitution grew substantially as the legislature enacted dozens of constitutional amendments and statutes. In the first three months of 1911 alone, the legislature approved more than 800 statutes and twenty-three constitutional amendments.

From 1960 to the Present: Later Revisions

In 1963, the legislature created a constitution revision commission as a result of an initiative passed in 1962. The commission, composed of fifty citizens, three State Senators and three Assembly members, submitted two major reports with recommended revisions to the state constitution. The legislature incorporated these recommendations into fourteen constitutional amendments that were submitted to the voters for their approval between 1966 and 1976, and the voters approved ten of these. These amendments simplified, shortened, and reorganized the constitution but made few substantive changes in it.

In 1993, the legislature again established a constitution revision commission that proposed a number of substantial changes to the constitution, provisions reformers had discussed in some cases for generations. For a variety of reasons, many having to do with the two-thirds vote in the Assembly and Senate to place them on the ballot, they were never submitted to the voters.

BOX 2.1	Amending the California Constitution

The California constitution can be amended in one of three ways. In each case, the proposed amendment must be ratified by majority vote in the next statewide election.

1. **A constitutional convention can propose an amendment.** The convention can be called either by the legislature with a two-thirds vote or by a majority vote of the electorate through an initiative. Voters must ratify the amendment by majority vote in the next statewide election.

2. **Citizens can propose an amendment directly through the initiative.** The process requires the proponents to submit a petition with the signatures of 8 percent of the voters in the last gubernatorial election. The proposed amendment is then placed on the ballot for approval in the next statewide election.

3. **The legislature may propose an amendment to the constitution.** The process requires a two-thirds vote of both houses of the legislature. The proposed amendment is then placed on the ballot for approval in the next statewide election.

The Progressive Movement and Its Impact on California Politics

The Progressive movement had its roots in the economic and political changes that swept the United States after the Civil War. It was foreshadowed by the Populist movement, which dominated American politics from 1870 to 1896.

Some of the political concerns and much of the moral indignation expressed by the Populists about the changes taking place in America are reflected in the Progressive movement. One major difference between the two movements is geographic. The Populist movement began in the rural areas of the country; the Progressive movement was urban, born in the major cities.[5] While the Progressive movement was identified mostly with the Republican Party, there were notable Progressive leaders in the Democratic Party as well, such as Woodrow Wilson.

The Progressives perceived many of the same problems as the Populists. From the Civil War on, the United States had rapidly industrialized, and wealth became concentrated in the hands of a new breed of corporate entrepreneurs. Monopoly was the word of the day. These corporate giants dictated economic policy, which in turn had significant social and political consequences. In California, one giant corporation, the Southern Pacific Railroad, stood above all others. It represented a concentration of wealth and power that gave it undue influence not only economically but also politically. To a degree perhaps unparalleled in the nation, the Southern Pacific Railroad and a web of associated interests ruled the state. The Southern Pacific Railroad had the money and resources to influence political decisions. Bribing public officials was not unusual, nor was handpicking candidates for the two major political parties.[6]

The Progressives countered the powerful corporations, specifically the Southern Pacific Railroad, by prosecuting the corrupt politicians who served them. Eventually, this tactic unraveled the railroad's domination of state and local politics, and led to a series of regulatory reforms that loosened the choke hold that they—and especially Southern Pacific Railroad—had on state and local politics.

Local Politics

Progressive reforms began at the local level in the cities of San Francisco and Los Angeles. The battle against the Southern Pacific Railroad, and corporate influence in general, started in San Francisco in 1906 with the reform movement fighting to rid city government of graft and bribery. President Theodore Roosevelt stepped in to help. Working hand in hand with James D. Phelan, the former mayor of San Francisco, Roosevelt sent in federal agents led by William J. Burns to investigate bribery and corruption charges.[7] Public officials were put on trial for bribery, bringing to the public's attention the extent of graft and political corruption in municipal government.

Seventeen supervisors and a number of corporate leaders were indicted.[8] The mayor was forced to resign, and his henchman, Abraham Reuf, who implicated officials of the Southern Pacific Railroad and several utility companies, was convicted and sentenced to fourteen years in jail. While the graft trials largely failed to convict those indicted, they were an important step in breaking the power of the Southern Pacific and its political allies.

In 1906, the Southern Pacific Railroad also dominated Los Angeles.[9] During this time, a group dedicated to good government, the Non-Partisan Committee of One Hundred, was formed. They selected a reform candidate for mayor who was opposed by the two major parties, labor, and the *Los Angeles Times*. While the reform candidate lost his bid for the mayoralty, seventeen of twenty-three reform candidates for other city positions were elected.[10] The nonpartisan reformers were on the way to ridding the city of the Southern Pacific machine.

State Politics

The 1907 legislative session was one of the most corrupt on record, with no action taken without the blessing of the political operatives of the Southern Pacific Railroad. At the end of the session, the editor of the Fresno *Republican*, Chester Rowell, wrote: "If we are fit to govern ourselves, this is the last time we will submit to be governed by the hired bosses of the Southern Pacific Railroad Company."[11]

At the same time, Rowell and Edward Dickson of the Los Angeles *Express* organized a statewide movement to attack the Southern Pacific's power. At Dickson's invitation, a group of lawyers, newspaper publishers, and other political reformers met in Los Angeles. They founded the Lincoln Republicans, later to become the League of Lincoln-Roosevelt Republican Clubs, dedicated to ending the control of California politics by the Southern Pacific Railroad and linking themselves to the national Progressive movement.

The Lincoln-Roosevelt League participated in the statewide elections of 1908 and managed to elect a small group of reformers to the legislature, and two years later it fielded a full-party slate, from governor down to local candidates.

STATEHOUSE VICTORY In 1910, Hiram Johnson became the candidate for governor of the Lincoln-Roosevelt League. He campaigned up and down the state, focusing on one main issue: the Southern Pacific Railroad. He claimed that the Southern Pacific Railroad, acting in concert with criminal elements, had corrupted the political process in California. He defined the battle as one between decent, law-abiding citizens and a few corrupt, powerful individuals who were determined to run the state in their own best interests.

Johnson won the election and met with the leading national Progressives—Theodore Roosevelt, Robert La Follette, and Lincoln Steffens—to discuss a reform program for California. The new administration in Sacramento set out to eliminate every special interest from the government and to make government responsive solely to the people and Johnson. Through a series of legislative acts and constitutional amendments, they went a long way in that direction. In 1911, the voters passed the initiative, the referendum, and the recall. These three reforms, widely known as *direct democracy*, placed enormous power and control over government in the hands of the voters. Now citizens could write their own laws or amend the constitution through the initiative, approve or disapprove constitutional amendments or bond issues passed by the legislature through the referendum, and remove corrupt politicians from office through the recall.

In addition to these reforms, a new law set up a railroad commission with power to fix rates beginning in 1911. Other reforms included the *direct primary*, which gave to ordinary citizens the power to select the candidates of the political parties for national and state offices. Women obtained the right to vote in California in 1911. Legislation was also enacted to limit women to an eight-hour workday, set up a workmen's compensation system, put into practice a weekly pay law, and required employers to inform strikebreakers that they were being hired to replace employees on strike (and thus might face verbal abuse and physical violence).

The Progressives in California more than kept their campaign promises to limit the influence of the corporations and political parties in politics. In the first two years in office, the Johnson administration significantly reduced the power of the Southern Pacific Railroad.[12]

LAST HURRAH The national Progressive Party lost its bid to capture the White House in 1912, with a ticket of Theodore Roosevelt for president and Hiram Johnson for vice president. The failure to win an important national office weakened the party by lessening the enthusiasm of its supporters. It also meant that the party had no patronage with which to reward its followers between elections. Electoral failure was just one of several major problems that plagued the Progressives. Several other factors also contributed to the decline of the party: the public grew tired of reform; there was a major falling out among the leadership in California; the Progressives generally opposed World War I; and the party failed to support reforms that labor so badly wanted.

While the Progressives were hoping that Roosevelt would run again in 1916, he was working to prevent another third-party fiasco. When the Progressives learned that the Republican Party would not nominate Roosevelt, they offered him the nomination, but he turned them down. At a dinner in San Francisco in July 1916, the California Progressive Party disbanded. Hiram Johnson urged his followers to go back to either the Republican or Democratic Party. Later that year Johnson, now a Republican, was elected to the U.S. Senate, where he served for twenty-eight years.

If there was one major flaw in Progressive thinking, it was their belief in the active, informed citizen willing to participate in politics. Progressives believed that given the opportunity, citizens would be happy to support the democratic process and spend whatever time and effort were needed to participate in elections. Since the late 1940s, a host of studies shows that large numbers of people don't vote or pay attention to politics. But the Progressives cannot be faulted for today's diminished interest in politics and government. In the end, they gave the people of California tremendous political power, if or when they choose to use it.

Direct Democracy

The Progressives established civil service reforms, nonpartisan commissions to control key state regulatory functions, nonpartisan elections to cripple local machines, office block voting (a ballot listing all candidates for a given office under the name of that office), and primary elections. If these mechanisms failed to check the power of special interests, they gave voters the power of direct action through the initiative, referendum, and recall. These three processes work in the same way. Citizens circulate petitions to gather a required number of signatures to place the measure on a statewide ballot. The number of signatures, as we shall see, varies depending on the mechanism.

Initiative

THE PROCESS Of the three direct voices in government, the initiative is the most well known and most frequently used. The process, also known as direct legislation, requires the proponent to obtain a title (e.g., "Public Schools: English as Required Language of Instruction") and summary of the proposed initiative from the state attorney general. Upon obtaining the title and summary, the proponents

have 150 days to circulate a petition to gather the required number of signatures to qualify for the ballot—5 percent of voters in the last gubernatorial election for statutes, and 8 percent for constitutional amendments. The secretary of state submits the measure at the next general election, held at least 131 days after it qualifies or at any special election held before the next general election. The governor may call a special election for the measure.

Before 1960, initiatives appeared only on the general election ballot, thus limiting their use to the two-year election cycle. Since 1960, they have appeared on ballots for primary, general, and special elections, which allows more frequent opportunities to qualify and vote on them. The freedom to qualify initiatives in all elections keeps the public aware of them and excited about using them.

FREQUENCY OF USE Initiatives have become a staple of California's political life. From 1912 through 2008, over 1,300 initiatives were titled and summarized for circulation. Of this number, 331 qualified for the ballot, 3 were removed by court order, and 120 were approved by the voters—for an overall passage rate of 36 percent.[13]

Figure 2.1 presents the use of initiative by decade. Note these three points: the increasing frequency of initiatives since 1970; the declining percentage of qualifying

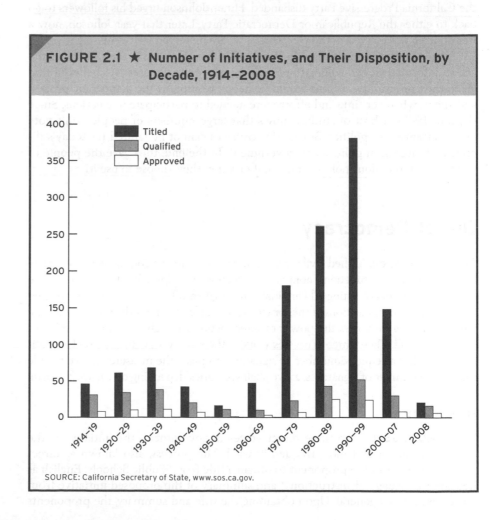

FIGURE 2.1 ★ **Number of Initiatives, and Their Disposition, by Decade, 1914–2008**

SOURCE: California Secretary of State, www.sos.ca.gov.

initiatives for the ballot; and the varying, but generally low, level of success for the measures that made it to the ballot.

For discussion purposes, we can compress the ninety-five year history of initiatives into three relatively equal time periods: 1912–39, 1940–69, and 1970–2007.

1912-39 From the beginning, various individuals and special interests understood that the initiative could be used to forward their special causes. Social and cultural issues, such as outlawing gambling on horse races, professional fighting, prostitution, and land ownership by Asians, drew the highest voter turnout during this period. Labor issues (closed versus open shops) and tax propositions were also volatile issues.

No one issue, however, dominated the initiative process during this period more than the so-called "liquor question."[14] These initiatives were among the most controversial, and they drew high voter turnouts. Twelve measures related to liquor control appeared on the ballot between 1914 and 1936, for and against full prohibition and antisaloon measures, and state regulation versus local control. Voting was consistent throughout this period, with the antiprohibition forces generally prevailing on every measure. The issue, however, wouldn't go away; in 1948, after many failures to qualify an initiative, the antiliquor forces qualified another local option measure, which was rejected by 70 percent of the voters. After this vote, the issue lost its appeal, never to appear on the ballot again.

1940-69 In this time period, use of the initiative declined markedly. Compared with the previous twenty-seven years, a higher percentage of proposed measures failed to gather enough signatures to qualify for the ballot. The subject matter of the initiatives also varied from those of 1912–39. Newer issues came to the forefront: race and civil rights, property taxes, and labor and welfare issues.

Proposition 14 (1964) was the most prominent of a number of initiatives that dealt with fair housing. The initiative was drafted to nullify the Rumford Fair Housing Act, which prohibited discrimination in the rental, lease, or purchase of housing on the basis of race and national origin. The Rumford Act, supporters of Proposition 14 claimed, interfered with their private property rights. Real estate and homeowners' associations led the forces in support of the proposition and a coalition of the Democratic Party's leadership, organized labor, churches, and a variety of other groups led the forces against it. The broader issue of race, specifically African American, lingered in the background of the campaign, and by all accounts, race was the deciding factor in how people voted. Proposition 14 passed by a 2–1 margin in November 1964. Its defeat was a major factor in the Watts riots in the summer of 1965.[15] Over the next two years, Proposition 14 was overturned, first in the California Supreme Court and then the U.S. Supreme Court, because it violated the Fourteenth Amendment.

1970-2008 In this period, initiatives abounded, with over 1,000 being titled, 187 qualifying, and 80 being approved. The subjects addressed social, cultural, and economic issues including the death penalty, gun control, busing, property tax, nuclear power, water resources, air quality, coastal preservation, English as official language, affirmative action, and illegal immigrants.

The most controversial initiatives of this period are Proposition 13, "People's Initiative to Limit Property Taxation" (1978), and Proposition 8, "Eliminates Right of Same-Sex Couples to Marry" (2008). Sponsored by longtime anti-tax activists Howard Jarvis and Paul Gann, Proposition 13 was a reaction to the spiraling appreciation of property throughout the 1970s. For example, in just one year, some properties were reassessed at a value 50 percent to 100 percent higher, and their owners' tax bills jumped correspondingly.

Proposition 13 set a property's assessment at 1 percent of the market value at the time of purchase and capped the increase on the assessment at 2 percent a year until the property was sold. Additionally, the initiative required that all state tax rate increases be approved by a two-thirds vote of the legislature and that local tax rates also be approved by a vote of the people. The proponents of Proposition 13 argued that the people's right to vote on taxes is a key taxpayer protection.

Proposition 13 was a grassroots effort. Nearly every state employee labor union and most Democratic leaders opposed it. The pro side raised $2.2 million and the con side raised $2 million. On June 6, 1978, nearly two-thirds of California's voters passed Proposition 13, reducing property tax rates by about 57 percent.

Now, thirty years later, Proposition 13 is still hotly debated. Critics argue that it creates tax inequities because it treats residential and commercial property the same and assesses similar properties differently based solely on when a homeowner bought a house. Supporters argue that pegging of property tax to the yearly assessed value of the property exposes homeowners to accelerated yearly property tax, which leaves them vulnerable to losing their homes.

In 2008, California voters decided sixteen initiatives in three separate elections. Six passed, including measures on farm animal confinement practices, redistricting the state legislative boundaries, and victims rights and parole procedures.

None of these initiatives, however, was as divisive as Proposition 8—the measure that reversed a State Supreme Court decision that sanctioned the right of same-sex couples to marry. The amount of money spent on the measure was staggering, $73.4 million—$35.8 million for and $37.6 million against.

Proposition 8 drew a range of religious supporters, including the Church of Latter-day Saints, the state's Roman Catholic bishops, Focus on the Family, and a number of evangelical churches. Opponents, however, focused their ire on the Mormon Church for its role in shepherding millions of dollars in contributions from its members for the campaign. But the protest against the church has also triggered accusations of discrimination and of making the church the scapegoat for the defeat when, in fact, post election polls indicate that socio-economic status was also a strong determinant in who supported Proposition 8.

How can we account for the increase in initiatives over the past three decades? The simplest explanation is that it is a consequence of several factors—the complexity of modern society, the growth of the willingness to regulate and specify legally things that had been left to individual citizens in the first half of the twentieth century, and the move from a part-time to a full-time legislature in 1968. As a result of the latter change, politics became a career, more legislation was passed, the budget grew, and decision making and power shifted to Sacramento.

These shifts, coupled with the reforms started by the Progressives to rid the capital of political corruption and an unresponsive legislature—direct primaries, term limits, regulation of campaign contributions, and the various devices utilized to weaken political parties—weakened the influence voters have on elected officials. Accordingly, voters, frustrated by the action or inaction of the legislature, have turned to the initiative to get what they want.

During this time period, special interests have also frequently turned to initiatives to promote policies they can't get through the legislature. More and more, all a group needs is the money to fund an initiative campaign. As a result, an industry of professional campaign managers and signature gatherers is flourishing. In fact, these so-called "policy managers" now identify hot issues and then go out and search for clients who will pay for the privilege of sponsoring the initiative.

Scholars disagree about the influence of money in the initiative process. Some writers, such as journalists David Broder and Peter Schrag, believe that special interests, with their deep pockets, dominate the initiative process at the expense of representative government, with its built-in checks and balances. Other writers, such as academics Elisabeth R. Gerber and Shaun Bowler, take a broader view, arguing that money plays a vital role in defeating initiatives, but not in the passage of initiatives. They argue that successful initiatives are the product of grassroots movements that have more to do with visceral social and economic issues than with well-financed campaigns.

DEBATING THE IMPACT OF THE INITIATIVE ON GOVERNANCE AND DEMOCRACY Journalist David Broder argues that America's founders preferred a system of checks and balances to direct democracy. While ballot initiatives arose late in the 1800s as grassroots efforts to fight government corruption and big business influence, today they are vehicles for special interests. Broder claims that initiatives "threaten to challenge or even subvert the American system of government in the next few decades." He gives the following reasons:

- Initiatives are no longer used as a vehicle to check a corrupt or out-of-control legislature. Rather they have become the vehicle of special interests pursuing a narrow, private agenda.

- Initiatives blur the complexity of many issues and reduce them to clichés or sound bites upon which the voter is asked to make a yes/no choice.

- Initiatives threaten to subvert the American form of representative government by allowing millionaires and special interests to rewrite state laws.

- California is now a multimillion-dollar business in which lawyers, campaign consultants, signature gatherers, and advertising agencies sell their expertise to interest groups or to political activists with private agendas.[16]

On the other side, noted conservative William Niskanen makes the following points in his disagreement with David Broder's thesis:

- Initiatives should be considered "one more check in our system of checks and balances." They should not be viewed as a process that circumvents the system. They act as a check on legislative extremism and irresponsible behavior.

- Most bills, including "pork barrel" bills, involve vote trading. They often succeed only by packaging many different measures, none of which has majority support, into one bill that can be approved by the majority. Thus legislation serves special interests that cooperate with each other to get what they want.

- The legislative process doesn't serve the majority very well.

- While a great deal of money is spent on initiatives, money also permeates almost all other areas of the political process. "Money is pervasive in our political system." The amount spent on initiative campaigns is a fraction of what is spent during any one election cycle.

- Initiatives are not "laws without government." Laws can be made in different ways, either by legislation or initiative. The government is there to enforce laws, regardless of how they are made.[17]

Referendum

THE PROCESS A referendum allows voters to approve or reject statutes or amendments passed by the state legislature. The process is as follows: The measure may be proposed by presenting to the secretary of state a petition with signatures equal to 5 percent of the voters in the last gubernatorial election. The filing of the signatures must take place within a ninety-day period after the enactment of the statute. If qualified to be on the ballot, the measure prevents the law from taking effect until the electorate decides whether or not it should become a law.

FREQUENCY OF USE The referendum is used infrequently. In fact, it has almost faded from use. Between 1912 and 2009, forty-nine referenda have appeared on the ballot. Using the same time period that we used for the initiative, there were twenty-nine referenda from 1912 to 1939, thirteen from 1940 to 1969, and eight from 1970 to 2008.

Voters rejected a law twenty-eight times; they approved a law fifteen times. Moreover, only nine referenda have appeared on the ballot since 1942, one in 1952, four in 1982, one in 2005, two in 2007, and one in 2008. Three of the four referenda of 1982 had to do with the redistricting of congressional, State Senate, and State Assembly district boundaries. The Democratic state legislature had drawn district boundaries for all three bodies that the Republicans believed were unfair. The voters concurred and rejected all three Democratic laws, forcing new boundaries to be drawn, which from the Republican point of view were more reflective of political reality.[18]

Recall

THE PROCESS The recall allows voters to determine whether to recall an elected official before his or her term expires. Proponents first submit a petition alleging the reason for recall. They have 150 days to present to the secretary of state a petition with the required number of signatures to qualify for the ballot. At the same time, if required, a successor is elected if the sitting official is recalled.

For statewide offices, the number of signatures must be equal to 12 percent of the last vote for the office, with signatures from at least five counties equal to 1 percent of the last vote for the office in the county. For the Senate, Assembly, members of the Board of Equalization, and judges, the number of signatures must be equal to 20 percent of the last vote for the office. Upon receiving the petitions, an election must be held between sixty and eighty days from the date of certification of sufficient signatures.

FREQUENCY OF USE Recalls of statewide offices or the state legislature are rare. There have been eight recalls out of 118 filings against state office holders. Seven of the eight were state legislators; Governor Davis was the other. Four of the state legislators were tossed out of office. The recall was put into use almost immediately after its passage against three state legislators—twice in 1913, against Senator Marshall Black for involvement in a banking scandal, which succeeded, and against Senator James Owen for corruption, which failed. The next year Senator Edwin Grant, who represented the red-light district in San Francisco, was recalled for opposing prostitution, which succeeded.

Four other state legislators faced recall votes in 1994 and 1995. The National Rifle Association failed in its attempt to recall Senator David Roberti for his position on gun control. Two Republican members of the Assembly, Doris Allen and Paul Horcher, were voted out of office for supporting Democrat Willie Brown for speaker in a battle between the parties for control of the Assembly. And an attempt to recall Democratic Assemblyman Michael Machado for backing Republicans failed.[19]

The most notorious recall, however, was that of Governor Gray Davis. He is the only governor to have been recalled, although there had been over two dozen previous attempts to gather enough signatures to recall a governor, including three against Ronald Reagan in the 1960s and one against Pete Wilson in the 1990s. During the 2002 campaign for governor, Davis had claimed that the budget deficit was $18 billion, but a week after his election he revealed it was $35 billion. Proponents of the recall immediately accused Davis of misleading voters about the severity of the state's budget crisis during his reelection campaign.

Each of the direct democracy processes—initiative, referendum, and recall—is available in local politics, where they first appeared and where they still thrive today.

California's Constitution: Where Are We Now?

California's constitution has been through three stages—establishment in the mid-1800s, rewriting in 1879, and extensive amendment during the Progressive era. Political scientists and others, most notably the 1996 California Constitutional Revision Commission, have made numerous suggestions to update our constitutional framework. The commission made many suggestions to strengthen the governor and made state government less susceptible to interest-group manipulation:

- The governor and lieutenant governor should run as a team.
- The other elected members of the executive branch should be appointed by the governor.
- The several tax administration agencies should be merged.
- Term limits on the legislature should be lengthened.
- Require a simple majority instead of a two-thirds majority for the enactment of the budget each year.

And many others. Most of these proposals have never come before the voters. Governor Schwarzenegger ran on a platform of governmental reform—he said that instead of moving the boxes around, he wanted to smash them. Now well into his second term in office, Governor Schwarzenegger seems to have lost the momentum he initially had to bring about meaningful governmental reform. In the end it seems like business as usual.

FOR FURTHER READING

Allswang, John M. *The Initiative and Referendum in California, 1898–1998*. Stanford: Stanford University Press, 2000.

Broder, David. *Democracy Derailed: Initiative Campaigns and the Power of Money*. New York: Harcourt Inc., 2000.

California Secretary of State. *A History of California Initiatives*, 2002.

Donovan, Todd, Shawn Bowler, David McCuan, and Ken Fernandez. "Contending Players and Strategies: Opposition Advantages in Initiative Elections," in *Citizens as Legislators: Direct Democracy in the United States*, ed. S. Bowler, T. Donovan and C. J. Tolbert. Columbus: Ohio State University Press, 1998.

Gerber, Elisabeth R. *The Populist Paradox: Interest Group Influence on the Promise of Direct Legislation*. Princeton: Princeton University Press, 1999.

Hofstadter, Richard. *The Age of Reform*. New York: Washington Square Press, 1988.

Johnson, Hiram, First Inaugural Address. January 3, 1913. www.governor.ca.gov/govsite/govsgallery/h/documents/inaugural_23.html

Mowry, George E. *The California Progressives*. Chicago: Quadrangle, 1963.

Olin, Jr., Spencer C. *California's Prodigal Sons: Hiram Johnson and the Progressives, 1911–1917*. Berkeley: University of California Press, 1968.

Policy Forum, "Do Ballot Initiatives Undermine Democracy?" *Cato Policy Report*. July/August, 2000, 6–9. Washington, DC: Cato Institute. www.cato.org/pubs/policy_report/v22n4/initiatives.pdf

Schrag, Peter. *Paradise Lost: California's Experience, America's Future*. Berkeley: University of California Press, 1998.

Starr, Kevin. *Inventing the Dream: California through the Progressive Era*. New York: Oxford University Press, 1985.

Swisher, Carl Brent. *Motivation and Political Technique in the California Constitutional Convention 1878–79*. New York: Da Capo Press, 1969.

ON THE WEB

Ballot Measure Update: www.sos.ca.gov/elections/elections_j.htm

California State Constitution: www.leginfo.ca.gov/const.html This site makes the California Constitution searchable by keyword.

Learn California: www.learncalifornia.org/doc.asp?id=1606 Learn California offers a guide to the history of progressivism in California.

"The Revision of California's Constitution": www.ucop.edu/cprc/documents/caconst.pdf

Southern Pacific Historical & Technical Society: www.sphts.org

SUMMARY

The California constitution has undergone substantial revision and amendment since its adoption in 1849; however, notwithstanding the later inclusion of direct democracy processes, the fundamental organization of government provided in 1849 remains the same.

The history of the constitution can be divided into four stages:

- The 1849 constitution established the basic structure of government, including separation of powers, bicameralism, federalism, and popular elections for most statewide offices.
- The 1879 constitution added nine new articles and some 8,000 words to respond to the concerns of the time.
- The progressive era, 1910–17, added the initiative, referendum, and recall, and passed hundreds of reform laws dealing with important political, social, and economic issues.
- From 1960 to the present time, California voters have authorized significant constitutional revisions recommended by the Constitutional Revision Commission and proposed by the legislature.

The California constitution can be amended in the following ways:

- The legislature can convene a constitutional convention by a two-thirds vote. The convention can also be convened by a majority vote of the electorate.
- The electorate can propose a constitutional amendment through the initiative process.
- The legislature may propose a constitutional amendment by a two-thirds vote.

In each case, the proposed amendment goes on the next statewide ballot and must be approved by a majority of those voting.

The Progressive reformers pursued several major goals: They wanted to

- put an end to the dominance of big corporations, especially the Southern Pacific Railroad;
- reform the corrupt political parties;
- remove from office corrupt politicians at the state and local levels of government;
- return political power to the people.

The Progressives also addressed social problems by ridding the state of child labor, protecting the environment, establishing state parks, and enacting several protections for working people. The most prominent of the Progressive reforms are these:

1. nonpartisan elections
2. primary elections
3. office block voting
4. direct democracy—the initiative, referendum, and recall

The vast bulk of the Progressive reforms are still in operation to this day.

PRACTICE QUIZ

1. The popular democracy process by which citizens can place a constitutional amendment or statute on the ballot is called a(n)
   a) referendum.
   b) initiative.
   c) recall.
   d) nonpartisan election.
2. The individual who served as governor during much of the Progressive period was
   a) Chester Rowell.
   b) Edward Dickson.
   c) Hiram Johnson.
   d) Samuel P. Huntington.
3. The process by which a certain percentage of those who voted in the last gubernatorial election can sign petitions to vote on a law enacted by the legislature is a(n)
   a) referendum.
   b) initiative.
   c) recall.
   d) nonpartisan election.
4. The process by which an elected official is removed from office before his or her term expires is called a(n)
   a) referendum.
   b) initiative.
   c) recall.
   d) nonpartisan election.
5. Progressive reformers pointed to this company whenever they spoke about machine politics and corporate privilege in Sacramento:
   a) Standard Oil Company
   b) Bank of America
   c) Southern Pacific Railroad
   d) Northern Securities Company

6. The only sitting California governor to be recalled from office was
   a) Ronald Reagan.
   b) Jerry Brown.
   c) Gray Davis.
   d) Pete Wilson.
7. Which of the following direct democracy devices allows voters to approve or reject statutes or amendments passed by the legislature?
   a) referendum
   b) direct primary
   c) initiative
   d) recall
8. In which decade has the greatest number of initiatives been titled?
   a) 1960–69
   b) 1970–79
   c) 1980–89
   d) 1990–99
9. Which of the following is not a Progressive Era reform?
   a) nonpartisan elections
   b) primary elections
   c) the office block vote
   d) party caucuses
10. Which of the following is not a legal way to amend the California constitution?
    a) The legislature can convene a constitutional convention by a two-thirds vote.
    b) The governor can sign into law a proposed amendment passed by the legislature.
    c) The legislature may propose a constitutional amendment by a two-thirds vote.
    d) The electorate can propose a constitutional amendment through the initiative process.

CRITICAL-THINKING QUESTIONS

1. The California constitution has gone through a series of revisions. Identify the periods of those revisions, and discuss the contribution that each made to the state's political structure.

2. Suppose you worked for a coalition of interest groups supporting legislation to increase the state sales tax to fund a state-run health care system. The coalition is frustrated by the lack of action in the legislature. They come to you for

advice about the initiative process and the possibility of success. What would you tell them from what you've read in this chapter?

3. Some people argue that direct democracy provides citizens with another way to correct the behavior and decision making of public officials. Others argue that it is merely the instrument of those special interest groups that have enough money to manipulate the political process. Present an argument for each position. Where do you stand in this debate?

4. California is the model Progressive state. The key components, however, greatly weakened the role of political parties in the state. Identify and discuss how some of the reforms of this period have weakened the state's party system. Is this a good or bad thing? Do you think there are any correlations between weak parties and the increasing use of the initiative process?

KEY TERMS

At this point you should have a general understanding of the following concepts and terms:

California Constitutional Revision
    Commission (29)
direct democracy (23)

initiative (15)
Progressive movement (19)

recall (28)
referendum (28)

3 Interest Groups and the Media in California

WHAT ARE INTEREST GROUPS, AND WHY DO THEY MATTER IN CALIFORNIA POLITICS?

Consider the diversity of organizations that try to influence governmental policy or legislation:

★ A **student organization** opposes legislation to raise tuition at state universities

★ A **business trade association** supports legislation that would reform the state's workers' compensation insurance system

★ A **telecommunications company** opposes legislation mandating the use of hands-free telephones in cars and trucks

★ A **citizens' group** supports legislation that would impose stricter penalties on people convicted of drunk driving

★ An **association of county governments** opposes legislation that prohibits the placing of certain juvenile offenders into group homes that are located in residential neighborhoods

★ A **public employees' union** supports legislation that prohibits state agencies from contracting with businesses unless those businesses pay their employees the equivalent of a living wage

Each of these organizations is an interest group. Interest groups have always been part of California's (and America's) political landscape. They are a product of freedom of association that is a First Amendment right under our democratic system of government.

Interest groups are associations of individuals who seek to influence policy decisions primarily in the legislature, at administrative agencies, and through direct legislation (the initiative). They are a way, in addition to voting, for individuals to voice their opinion on issues that concern them.

Interest groups are also called pressure groups, political advocacy groups, special interest groups, and lobbying groups. An interest group can be a political organization or public interest group, such as Common Cause or Citizens for a Better Environment; a company, like The Walt Disney Company or Blue Cross of California; a religious organization, like the California Catholic Conference; or a trade, professional or labor association, like the California Restaurant Association, the California Medical Association, or the California Labor Federation, AFL-CIO.

Since interest groups focus primarily on influencing policy decisions in the legislature, they are often collectively referred to as the third house, a term that describes their standing and influence in the legislative process.[1] The people who do the work for interest groups are called lobbyists, and the work they do is called lobbying.

Lobbyists have played a prominent but often controversial role in California politics. The most controversial figure was Arthur Samish, whose control over the state legislature during the 1930s and 1940s drew national attention. Samish represented the most powerful industries in the state: oil, liquor stores, transportation, breweries, and racing. He maintained his power by first organizing a trade association, if there wasn't one already, and then getting its members to make campaign contributions to legislators who would support the association's interests. Samish was not shy about his influence. He once told a grand jury looking into his lobbying activities, "To hell with the governor of California. I'm the governor of the legislature."[2]

Samish's downfall came as a result of two articles in *Collier's* magazine in 1949 about "the man who secretly controls the state."[3] One article had a photograph of Samish holding a ventriloquist's dummy on his knee and Samish condescendingly saying, "This is my legislature. How are you, Mr. Legislature?"[4] In the article, when asked who had more influence, himself or Samish, Governor Earl Warren responded, "On matters that affect his clients, Artie unquestionably has more power than the governor."[5]

Soon after the articles appeared, the legislature scrambled to shield itself from further ridicule. A committee was formed to study the influence of lobbyists, and Samish himself testified. Governor Warren asked for legislation to regulate lobbyists and require the disclosure of lobbyists' financial activities. The legislature obliged first with the Collier Act and later with the Erwin Act. It also banned Samish from its building. That, however, wasn't a problem for Samish; he just had the legislators come to him. In 1953, Samish was convicted of income tax evasion and served two years in federal prison, thus ending his career as a Sacramento power broker.

Diversity of Interest Groups

The term "interest groups" is an all-inclusive term that covers a wide range of businesses and organizations. The California Secretary of State classifies these groups according to the nature of the interest or point of view they represent.

Box 3.1 lists some groups, along with their Web site addresses, in the major categories. At each Web site, except for those of individual businesses, there is a

BOX 3.1 | **Diversity of Interest Groups in California**

AGRICULTURE

- California Farm Bureau Association   www.cfbf.com
- Western Growers' Association   www.wga.com
- California Poultry Industry Federation   www.cpif.org
- Shamrock Foods Company   www.shamrockfoods.com

EDUCATION/PUBLIC EMPLOYEES

- California Teachers' Association   www.cta.org
- California Correctional Peace Officers' Association   www.cpoa.org
- University of Southern California   www.usc.edu

GOVERNMENT

- California State Association of Counties   www.csac.counties.org
- League of California Cities   www.cacities.org
- Association of California Water Agencies   www.acwa.com

LABOR UNIONS

- California Labor Federation, AFL-CIO   www.calaborfed.org
- California State Council of Service Employees   www.seiucal.org
- California Professional Firefighters   www.cpf.org

LEGAL

- California Applicants' Attorneys Association   www.caaa.org
- American Civil Liberties Union   www.aclu-sc.org
- Milberg Weiss Bershad Hynes & Lerach   www.milberg.com

BUSINESS/TRADE ASSOCIATIONS

- The Irvine Company   www.irvineco.com
- California Bankers' Association   www.calbankers.com
- California Chamber of Commerce   www.calchamber.com

POLITICAL/RELIGIOUS/ETHNIC/MINORITY GROUPS

- California Common Cause   www.commoncause.org/states/california
- California Catholic Conference   www.cacatholic.org
- California Alliance of Child and Family Services   www.cacfs.org

link to a section that discusses the legislative priorities of the group. For each group, as can readily be seen, lobbying or advocacy is a major part of its activity and a principal reason why many individuals and businesses join the group. For example, the California Applicants' Attorneys Association claims to be "the most powerful and most knowledgeable legal voice for the injured workers of California"; the California Labor Federation, AFL-CIO, professes to give "working families a voice in the political process"; and the California Alliance of Child and Family Services lobbies "on behalf of California's most vulnerable children and families."

On the other hand, there is no link to legislative priorities for the individual businesses listed—Shamrock Foods Company, University of Southern California, The Irvine Company, and the law firm of Milberg Weiss Bershad Hynes & Lerach. This omission is understandable and perfectly legitimate. Lobbying is not a primary reason for the existence of these organizations. Profits are. They participate in politics to protect or expand their markets. They are careful not to call attention to their involvement in politics out of fear that they may alienate customers or tarnish their image. Accordingly, information about their lobbying activity must be obtained from newspaper accounts and public disclosure documents.

Many businesses, however, join professional or trade associations to give them a voice on issues that affect their industry. "We're the champion of California businesses, large and small," the California Chamber of Commerce proudly asserts on its Web site. "For more than 100 years, we've worked to make California a better place to do business by giving private-sector employers a voice in state politics." The 14,000-member businesses give the Chamber tremendous clout and stature. In turn, the individual members enjoy several advantages—sharing of cost, strength in numbers, and, perhaps most important, anonymity.

Government also lobbies government. Taxpayer protection groups have come to call these interests—education, health, special districts, local government, state agencies—"the spending lobby," since they are motivated by the desire to maintain or increase their revenue. In 2008, for instance, government was the highest spender among the nineteen categories of lobbyist employers registered with the secretary of state.

According to governmental lobbyists, the passage in 1978 of Proposition 13, which limited the property tax revenues to local government, is what spurred the growth in governmental lobbying and the competition for funds. John P. Quimby, Sr., a former assemblyman who lobbies for San Bernardino County, told the *Riverside Press Enterprise* in 1997: "I wish government wasn't for sale like this, but the fact is you have to hustle to get your share. Local governments without lobbyists see the ones with representation doing better so they say, 'We need to get our butts on board and get one or they're going to steal everything from us.'"[6] Or, to put it another way, government agencies spend taxpayers' money to lobby elected officials for more money to spend on taxpayers.

The Increase in Interest Groups

In California over the last decade, the number of interest groups and the amount of lobbying expenditures have grown steadily. In 1990, lobbyists represented approximately 1,300 interest groups; in 2000, the number had nearly doubled to 2,552;[7] and in 2008, it had increased to 3,100. During the same period, lobbying expenditures also grew substantially, as seen in Table 3.1.

TABLE 3.1 ★ Growth in Lobbying Expenditures

LEGISLATIVE SESSION	LOBBYING EXPENDITURES	PERCENT INCREASE
1989–90	$193,575,480	
1991–92	$233,872,097	20.8
1993–94	$250,119,667	7.0
1995–96	$266,939,559	6.7
1997–98	$292,615,513	9.6
1999–2000	$344,318,650	17.7
2001–02	$386,829,719	12.4
2003–04	$413,376,146	6.9
2005–06	$500,326,710	21.0
2007–08	$533,614,110*	6.7

*Estimate projected from 7 quarters of expenditures in 2007 and 2008 legislative session.
SOURCE: California Secretary of State, "Employers of Lobbyists," various years, http://cal-access.sos.ca.gov/lobbying/employers

California continually ranks first nationally in the number of interest groups and the amount spent on lobbying activities. What Carey McWilliams said about California politics during the 1930s and 1940s still holds true today: "Interests, not people, are represented in Sacramento. Sacramento is the marketplace of California where grape growers and sardine fishermen, morticians and osteopaths bid for allotments of state power."[8] California accounts for one-third of all lobbyist activity in the country. Texas and New York rank second and third behind California, and taken together they spend roughly 60 percent of what is spent in California on lobbying activities.[9]

Several factors have encouraged this proliferation of interest groups:

Weak Political Parties

California has weak parties for a variety of reasons, but largely because of the Progressive reforms of the 1910s. The reforms were directed at the spoils system in government, the control that parties had over which candidates would represent the party in general elections, and the influence of interest groups in the legislature. To balance these influences, the reforms gave voters the direct democracy practices of the initiative, referendum, and recall. These measures, and subsequent reforms such as the direct primary, provided interest groups with powerful tools to circumvent party discipline among elected officials and the electorate.

Growth of Government

California government has grown substantially over the past half century. Californians, like other Americans, initially were suspicious of government. They perceived government as a force whose powers had to be kept in check to protect individual rights. As time passed, however, citizens began to perceive government differently—as a force that could be used to solve myriad social and economic problems. The legislature has eagerly taken up this challenge. With each new law comes regulatory oversight, and, unsurprisingly, groups with a stake in these new programs all need lobbyists to look out for their interests.

Term Limits

In 1990, California voters approved term limits for all state and legislative offices. Term limits, it was argued, would break the cozy relationship between elected officials and lobbyists. Yet this is not what has happened. As legislators with years of institutional memory left office, the capital became more chaotic and less efficient. "Experts say it is this institutional memory that has swung the legislature toward the 'third house' of special interests. In short, the lobbyists have it. Legislators don't." Legislators rely on lobbyists to write complex legislation and counsel them on the flood of complex issues that come across their desks.[10]

Public Interest Groups

The growth of public interest groups, what some call the "new politics" movement, began in the 1970s and continues through today. Examples of such groups are the AARP, the Sierra Club, and the Foundation for Taxpayers and Consumer Rights. As the textbook *We the People* explains, these groups "seek to distinguish themselves from other groups—business groups, in particular—by styling themselves as 'public interest groups,' terminology that suggests they serve the general good rather than their own selfish interest." While these so-called public interest groups claim to represent *only* the public interest, they should be judged critically, for they are sometimes facades behind which narrow private interests hide.

Interest-Group Politics

Interest groups were initially perceived as part of the solution to the problem of irresponsible majority rule. The idea was that a government that nurtures many interests would be one under which no one interest, or combination of interests, would be large enough to gain control of the reins of government. For that to happen, a great number of interests would have to come together and bargain and negotiate with each other; and, through bargaining and negotiating, a majority would emerge that would be both moderate and responsible.

Today such activity takes place under the umbrella of political parties. Although interest groups and their members actively participate in party politics, they generally are much more narrowly focused, often competing with each other on an array of issues and bent on influencing individual officials to support their specific policy goals.

Not all interest groups, however, are equal. Some have considerably more clout than others. The success of an interest group depends on several factors: a clear message, group cohesiveness, the location of active members who know the legislator in as many legislative districts as possible, the alignment of the group's interests with those of those legislators, understanding the political process, technical expertise, and money. As we shall see, money is especially important.

Table 3.2 shows the top employers of lobbyists. This list has remained relatively stable over the past several years, with four or five groups moving in and out of the ranks from one year to the next, depending on their agenda in the legislative session. By most standards, the lobbyists for these groups are some of the most powerful in Sacramento.

Not surprisingly, with the growth of the "lobbying industrial complex" in Sacramento, allegations of influence peddling quickly follow, and the allegations sometimes lead to criminal prosecution. For example, in the late 1980s, the chief lobbyist for the insurance industry, Clay Jackson, was convicted of mail fraud and attempted bribery of Senator Alan Robbins, Chairman of the Senate Insurance Committee, to help defeat a bill that would abolish the state's workers' compensation minimum rate law. As the scheme began to unfold, however, the FBI learned about Robbins's part in the plan. When confronted by the FBI, Robbins agreed to wear a wire to expose Jackson in exchange for a reduced sentence.

In the end, Jackson, Robbins, Senator Paul Carpenter and three other legislators, a former county sheriff, and several legislative staff were either convicted or pled guilty on different charges because of the undercover operation. U.S. Attorney Charles Stevens called it "extraordinarily successful." Yet, he added wistfully, "we don't harbor any illusion that with the conclusion of this case we've eliminated corruption in Sacramento. At the same time, we made a dent. The people at the Capitol are much more reluctant to talk about money."[11]

This incident depicts the blatant sale of votes for money. Most allegations of influence peddling, however, center on the more subtle influence of campaign contributions on legislative votes. Obviously, on many occasions, legislators vote the right

TABLE 3.2 ★ Top 10 Lobbyist Employers January 1, 2007– September 30, 2008

	CUMULATIVE EXPENDITURES
California State Council of Service Employees	$10,118,784
Western States Petroleum Association	9,140,912
Californians for Fire Safety	6,673,216
California Teachers Association	6,632,973
American Chemistry Council	5,625,087
Blue Cross	5,689,731
California Hospital Association	5,462,054
California Chamber of Commerce	4,952,294
AT&T and its affiliates	3,765,508
California Building Industry Association	3,549,638

SOURCE: California Secretary of State, "Employer of Lobbyists," various years, http://cal-access.ss.ca.gov/lobbying/employers

way on issues that are important to interest groups who have contributed funds to them. That doesn't mean that they sold their vote to this or that group. Just as likely, they voted that way because the issue was compatible with the political views from which they judge most political, social, and economic matters—frequently defined by the principles of the party to which the legislators belong.

Lobbyists

Lobbyists are at the forefront of interest-group activity. They coordinate the efforts to secure passage, amendment, or defeat of bills in the legislature and the approval or veto of bills by the governor. Having a good lobbyist is paramount to the success of any interest group.

There are citizen lobbyists and professional lobbyists. A citizen lobbyist is not paid to advocate for a particular issue or set of issues. The citizen lobbyist interacts with his representatives to express his personal views on an issue or set of issues and to attempt to influence legislation on that issue. Citizen lobbyists have the most influence on a legislator when they reside and vote in the elected official's district. Professional lobbyists are paid for their services and must register with the secretary of state. They also must submit quarterly disclosure reports detailing for whom they are working, the amount of money earned, and payment such as gifts and honoraria made to public officials they lobby.

There are two categories of professional lobbyists: contract and in-house. Approximately 50 percent of all the lobbyists in Sacramento are contract lobbyists; the other half are in-house.[12] Contract lobbyists offer their services to the general public; they are advocates for hire and often represent multiple clients on a variety of issues at the same time. For example, KP Advocates and Nielsen, Merksamer, Parrinello, Mueller & Naylor, two of the most prominent contract lobbyist firms in Sacramento, each represent more than seventy-five businesses and organizations and bring in millions of dollars in fees during the legislative session.[13] In-house lobbyists are employees of a trade, professional, or labor association and represent that group's interest only. Many of these interest groups also use contract lobbyists because the group is either involved in too many issues for its in-house staff to handle or it may want to use a lobbyist who specializes in a specific subject area, such as health insurance or transportation, or who has a close relationship with a particular legislator or members of a specific committee whose support is vital to the group's success.

There is no specific course of study or professional examination that one must take to become a lobbyist. The lack of identifiable credentials, however, does not mean that someone can walk off the street and easily get a job as a lobbyist. Most lobbyists come to the profession after they have gained experience working in the legislature as an elected member, on the staff of a member or committee, in a governmental agency in a managerial or public affairs capacity, or in an interest group in some capacity.[14]

The view of lobbyists as cigar-smoking, hard-drinking salesmen is grossly exaggerated. Most lobbyists are college graduates, and a growing number have advanced degrees, often in law, political science, communications, public relations, and journalism. Lobbyists must have knowledge of the legislative and political process, strong analytical and people skills, and the ability to communicate effectively, both orally and in writing. Lastly, they "must be able to understand their clients' issues as well as the policies and law they hope to influence."[15]

Lobbying

Few issues are just lobbied—that is, discussed with a public official or staff during the legislative process. Most issues are managed using a combination of techniques: public relations (marketing), grassroots mobilization, and lobbying.

The first job of the lobbyist is to know the interest group's objective. Is the goal new legislation? Is it to amend existing law? Or is it to stop another business or interest group from passing new legislation or amending an existing law that may affect your group's interest? The goal may not even be legislative. The group may want to amend current regulatory policy or shape the content of new regulations that will affect its members.

Once the lobbyist knows the interest group's objective, he must have a working knowledge of the activity of interest group. For example, he should know the size and scope of the organization: the sector its members represent, how many members the interest group has, how many workers its members employ, the value of its annual sales, its political reputation, and so on.

The lobbyist must also identify the groups that may have an interest in the issue and then assess whether these groups, legislators, the executive branch, regulators, or the general public will support or oppose his group's activity. He can gather this information in a number of ways: talk to the group's management and members; inquire of colleagues, public officials, and legislative staff; and find out if similar measures have previously been introduced and who supported or opposed them.

Moreover, lobbyists who can rely on members of his interest group, especially if they reside in the legislator's district, can more easily influence policy making. The most successful efforts are built around networks of activists who have made it a point to know their elected officials. Just as in personal relationships, elected officials are more likely to support someone they know. These relationships can be built in many ways: working on election campaigns, commending a representative in writing for an action he or she has taken, contributing to political campaigns, and connecting in other ways so as to have a positive relationship with these officials.

With this preparation in hand, the lobbyist has a greater chance of success. Of course, several other factors are also important: knowledge of the legislation process, strong communication skills, established relationships, ability to negotiate, and, above all, honesty.

Campaign Contributions to Candidates

Besides expenditures to influence legislative action, interest groups also make campaign contributions, which enable them to become familiar with and gain access to legislators. They do so through political action committees (PACs).

There is a connection between lobbying success and campaign contributions. Those who invest heavily in lobbying generally also invest heavily in PAC contributions, and vice versa.[16] Table 3.3 shows the top twelve contributors for the 2005–2006 legislative year. The table shows only the amount directly contributed to candidates for the state legislature. It does not include what these organizations may have contributed to the Democratic or Republican candidates for statewide offices, ballot initiatives, or what candidates themselves contributed, which, when totaled, came to $681,867,163.[17] Campaign contributions enable a lobbyist to gain access to legislators. The lobbyist can then make his argument and provide the legislator with important, often technical information.

TABLE 3.3 ★ Top Twelve Contributors to Legislators—2005-06 Legislative Session

AT&T	$941,169
California Teachers Association	847,355
California Medical Association	806,000
California State Council of Service Employees/SEIU	715,600
California Association of Realtors	684,800
California Dental Association	626,852
Pechanga Band of Mission Indians	560,660
California Building Industry Association	509,149
Pacific Gas & Electric	502,375
Service Employees Local 1000/CSEA SEIU	489,650
AFSCME California	457,600
California Correctional Peace Officers Association	431,300

SOURCE: www.followthemoney.org

Jesse Unruh, former Speaker of the Assembly, once said, "Money is the mother's milk of politics." This adage still holds true today. Most interest groups have PACs and carefully target their campaign contributions. They support individuals in positions of power—e.g., incumbent state officers, party leaders in the legislature, committee chairs, and rising political stars. Contributions have little to do with the legislator's or a party's political ideology. The only question is, "Can this legislator help our organization achieve its goals?"

One of the most powerful interest groups in Sacramento today is the California Correctional Peace Officers Association (CCPOA). It has achieved this status through a combination of aggressive lobbying, large campaign contributions, and skillful public relations with such catchy taglines as "Every day they 'walk the line' among some of the toughest, most violent inmates in the world."

Over the past two decades, union membership rose from just over 2,500 to over 31,000, triggered by the rapid growth in the prison population because of tougher sentencing laws, such as the three-strikes initiative that the union helped to launch with a large contribution of funds. As union membership grew, so did union dues—and political influence. In 2002, for example, the union collected $21.9 million in dues from members, $7.7 million of which funded myriad political activities: lobbying services, affiliate groups, public relations, soft money contributions to political parties, and campaign contributions.[18]

Today the union is one of the biggest contributors to candidates running for statewide and legislative office. It contributes aggressively to the campaigns of its supporters, and it contributes just as aggressively to defeat those legislators who oppose its agenda. "If the guards don't like you," former Assemblyman Bill Leonard said, "they're willing to spend money to get you. . . . That certainly adds to their power—you don't want to be considered hostile to them."[19]

The union is one of the few public employee groups to give generously to both Republicans and Democrats. For example, when Pete Wilson ran for governor in 1990, the union gave $1 million to his campaign. Wilson reciprocated with substantial pay increases and stronger sentencing policies. The union, however, really stepped forward with Gray Davis. Besides early endorsement in the primary, which guaranteed his selection as the Democratic candidate for governor, they contributed more than $3 million between 1998 and 2002 to his campaign war chest. During the same period, the union contributed millions of dollars to members of the legislature, with especially large sums going to the leadership of both parties.

The union's strategy has paid off handsomely. Over the past decade, with near unanimous support on each vote, the legislature has given union lobbyists whatever they've wanted as well as ignored the recommendations from bipartisan commissions that called for radical reform of the prison system. As for Governor Davis, he agreed to close three privately run prisons in the state, despite the fact that they were less costly to run than the state-run facilities; signed a 25 percent raise over a five-year period and an increase to 75 percent of their salary at retirement; he also eliminated the requirement to show a doctor's note when claiming sick time, which for the year 2001 led to a 27 percent increase in sick time and an additional 500,000 hours in overtime costs.[20]

These are some of the more publicized victories. CCPOA has negotiated openly, in view of other interest groups, the media, and the general public. The union's success is due to a well-conceived plan that starts with a public relations campaign that provides the basis for a relentless political campaign through lobbying activity, involvement in initiatives, grassroots action, and campaign donations.

With the election of Governor Schwarzenegger, the union has been somewhat on the defensive. The governor, who has not received contributions from CCPOA, wants to overhaul the state's prison system. He has pointed to the need to address such critical issues as guards' compensation, prison overcrowding, and the high recidivism rate of inmates. Moreover, he wants to give the state more power over daily prison operations, including monitoring sick leaves, limiting grievance policy, reducing overtime, and defining who determines when inmates visit medical clinics. Obviously, the guards oppose most of these proposals. Contract talks with the governor continue to stall, and in September 2008 the corrections employees launched a drive to recall the governor. One month later the union dropped its recall, while claiming that the governor's written response to the recall was false and misleading. On the other hand, the governor accused the union of using bully tactics in an attempt to extract $1.3 billion in contract concessions. The struggle has yet to play out. In the end, however, it will probably be the state legislature that has the final say in the matter, and the state legislature is much beholden to the guards for campaign contributions.

Regulating Interest Groups

With the passage of the Political Reform Act (PRA) of 1974, California lobbyists and interest groups are required to report campaign and lobbying expenditures. At the same time, the PRA shifted the filing of lobbying statements from the state legislature to the independent Fair Political Practices Commission.

Since its passage, the PRA has undergone numerous amendments, the most significant being in 2000 with the passage of Proposition 34. The following rules now govern interest groups and lobbyists:

- A lobbyist or lobbying firm cannot present a gift to a state elected official or legislative official in aggregate of more than $10 a month. Anyone who is not a registered lobbyist can give up to $250 in gifts in any calendar year.

- A lobbyist cannot contribute to state candidates or officeholders if he or she is registered to lobby that candidate's or officeholder's agency. However, the various interest groups that employ lobbyists have no such restrictions.

- Interest groups, individuals, and businesses have specific limits on election contributions to candidates or officeholders. The limit for legislative candidates is $3,200; for all state offices except the governor, $5,300; and for governor, $21,300.

Some public interest groups, such as Common Cause, Clean Money Campaign, and the League of Women Voters, have called for further restrictions on lobbying expenditures and campaign contributions by both individuals and interest groups. Such measures, they argued, would constrain the power of special interests and allow public policy decisions to reflect the overall interest of society.

Recommendations to restrict the power of special interest groups fall into three categories: clean-money elections, contribution restrictions, and conflict-of-interest laws. The first category, clean-money elections, provides public funding to candidates who demonstrate a base of public support by getting a qualifying number of voter signatures and a certain number of small contributions and who agree to forgo any other private donations. Such measures would cover all state legislative and statewide offices and have recently been adopted in Maine and Arizona. In California, it would be difficult to get the political parties and most legislators, who are tied to the current funding system, to support the idea. It would also be difficult to convince the public that it should subsidize campaigns for elective office. Over the years, only 35 to 40 percent of California voters have supported public financing of election campaigns.

The second category, contribution limits, has been a focal point of campaign reform for some time. Most of the effort has come from citizens' groups disgruntled with the current system. Together they have established stricter reporting requirements and limits on campaign contributions and loans to state candidates and political parties. The changes have been accomplished almost wholly through initiatives sponsored by these groups over the past decade—Propositions 63 and 78 in 1993, Proposition 208 in 1996, Proposition 34 in 2000. These efforts will continue in the future as various groups attempt to rein in the free flow of money into political campaigns.

The last category, conflict-of-interest laws, covers a multitude of situations. Sometimes simultaneous activity falls into this category. For example, the California Senate offers lobbyists who contribute to its charity the opportunity to travel with the lawmakers to various foreign counties.[21]

The charity, the Senate's California International Relations Foundation, helps fund entertaining foreign delegations that visit the state capitol and a high school students' exchange between California and Japan. The idea is new in lobbyist-legislator relations.

Each donor contributes $2,000–$3,000 beginning in 2008, which gives the donor a seat on the foundation's board of directors and the invitation to travel with legislators on trade and cultural trips to foreign counties. Since 2004, there have been 18 trips to Tokyo, Jerusalem, Rio de Janeiro, and other foreign cities.

The foundation operates out in the open, and it does not underwrite the expenses of either the traveling legislators or supporters. Critics, however, contend that it provides a unique opportunity for supporters. They gain the goodwill of and access to legislators. This is especially convenient when the supporter's interest group has a bill pending in the legislature.

Interest-Group Politics outside the Legislature

Up until now, we have focused on the influence of interest groups on the state legislature. Interest groups, however, flex their muscles in other ways in the electoral process: through get-out-the-vote campaigns and initiatives.

GET OUT THE VOTE Many interest groups engage in get-out-the-vote (GOTV) operations among their members to help a candidate or an issue win at the ballot box. This is especially true in a hotly contested election. In such instances, GOTV can be the most important activity undertaken, since there are many examples when an election is won or lost by a handful of votes.

GOTV operations are often considered "outsider strategies"—i.e., they take place outside the legislature, the traditional arena of interest-group activity, and the groups that engage in this action feel they have a vital stake in affecting the outcome of the election, as Hispanics did in 1994 with Proposition 187, making illegal aliens ineligible for public services, and all minorities did in 1996 with Proposition 209 to end affirmative action in California.

Some interest groups, like organized labor, religious denominations, and minorities, have a long history of mobilizing their members to vote—and to vote for or against a candidate or critical issue. Other interest groups, like gays, environmentalists, and gender-based groups, have more recently begun to participate in GOTV activities. They mobilize their supporters at the grassroots level, employing a variety of techniques, including email, direct mail, door-to-door canvassing, telemarketing, poll watching, pickup, phoning, and assistance on Election Day, and other campaign tactics. Months of work go into planning the campaign. While the goal is simple—delivering members' votes—the outcome is unpredictable until the final tally of ballots.

INITIATIVES Chapter 2 explored the history of the initiative and the impact of some of those that passed. What was initially considered a tool for citizens to overcome the influence of interest groups in the legislature has "become an instrument of the same special interests it was originally intended to control."[22]

Clearly, interest groups exploit the initiative process. Spending on initiatives has risen substantially over the past thirty years. Today, many interest groups invest huge sums of money to buy signatures on petitions to qualify their measures for the ballot and then put in motion campaigns cloaked in the guise of some societal benefit. Most initiative measures, however, never reach the ballot. Even when they do reach the ballot, only one in three succeeds. Even so, most Californians (92 percent) have come to see the initiative process as controlled by special interests.[23]

Yet, as Elisabeth Gerber persuasively argues, this isn't necessarily the case. Groups with different resources use the initiative process differently. On the one hand, economic interest groups, whose members join because of their occupation or professional status, rely primarily on the mobilization of vast sums of money for initiative campaigns. They use these monetary resources and, to lesser extent, personnel in two ways: "to block initiatives to protect the status quo or to pressure the legislature." On the other hand, citizen interest groups, whose members join as free individuals committed to some personal belief, rely primarily on the mobilization of personnel who "volunteer their personal time and energy" to achieve the group's goal. In doing so, they use personnel and some monetary resources "to pass new laws by initiative."[24]

Californians don't seem overly disturbed about the role interest groups play in the initiative process, principally because they believe direct legislation raises important policy issues that would otherwise go unaddressed. In fact, most Californians believe that "decisions made through the initiative process are probably better than those made by the governor and the legislature."[25]

Finally, for most Californians the media—news stories, paid political commercials, public debate, direct mail—are the most influential source of information on initiatives.

The Role of the Media in California Politics

The term *media* refers to the dispensers of information, including broadcast media (radio and television), print media (newspapers and magazines), and electronic media (the Internet). When we speak of one of these sources individually, we refer to it as a *medium* (the Latin singular of *media*). Sometimes we speak about the mass media but most often the adjective (*mass*) is assumed.

Television

Television is the medium of choice today for political information for the vast majority of Americans, and Californians are no exception. This medium can spread messages quickly, covering everything, including car chases, earthquakes, and the latest political scandals. It tells us about the weather, freeway conditions, and what all those Hollywood celebrities are up to. Television is particularly important for conducting political campaigns in a large state with a diverse population, such as California. Yet for all its speed and ability to reach large numbers of viewers, television is a medium that provides little information on government.

Two facts account for this lack of information: California is so big and diverse that it is difficult to cover statewide political and governmental news, and Californians in general are not that interested in state government and policy. These dynamics, along with a fragmented political structure, produce a stark reality—the largest state in the nation, with some of the largest media resources and markets in the nation, provides relatively little political and governmental news, particularly on television news programs.[26] There are few media correspondents in Sacramento. More important, since there is no newspaper distributed statewide, there is no incentive to cover news on a statewide basis.

The nightly news stations compete with one another for viewers. But in reality, the news formats provide little in the way of important political information.

The half-hour news format is crammed with commercials, weather reports, entertainment news, sports coverage, and a host of other topics that do little to inform the viewer about the political problems that affect the state and nation. Those topics that are reported with any depth are calculated to achieve ratings and are structured to last over several newscasts.

Each local station has its own version of an "action" news team or consumer protection group bringing audiences the latest artificially hyped crisis. From the nature of the issues covered, it is clear that local television, for the most part, has made a concerted effort to treat political news as a secondary issue. Issues related to political parties, government, or interest groups in California don't have the power to reach and energize large populations on political issues on a day-to-day basis.

Local television stations focus our attention on an issue like crime in a way that government representatives cannot by showing one car chase after another. Broadcast media, using surreptitious means to spy on the inner workings of restaurants in Los Angeles, garner viewers' instant attention by showing all the horrible things that food preparation workers do that ultimately make us ill. Even a former mayor's establishment was exposed for its food handling violations. The stations claim that they are protecting the public's interest, but they also sensationalize the stories in order to gain viewers and ratings. Those watching are told to tune in tonight to get the latest list of restaurant closings. Should the public interest demand that viewers be informed at five o'clock, not at eleven, so that they can avoid having dinner at one of those restaurants that is violating local health codes?

Sensational undercover stories are frequently broadcast, including coverage of corruption at the North Hollywood DMV, the financial deceptions practiced by automobile dealers, and the machinations of dishonest auto repair establishments, just to name a few. These exposés help to identify dishonest practices in our communities, but, more important, they show how the ability to identify significant political issues has passed from the political parties to electronic media. The media place the issue on the agenda, and the next day government representatives tell the public what must be done to fix the problem. They are reacting to the media's promotion of the issue.

In California, where voters have the ability to put statute and constitutional initiatives on the ballot, television plays a major role by getting information to the voters about these issues through extensive advertising campaigns. These messages are drafted and paid for by the interest groups that support the initiatives, and the political parties may or may not play a role in the process. The broadcast media have the power to reach a vast audience, something the parties cannot do on their own.

Newspapers

The number of newspapers across the United States has fallen during the last twenty-five years, and newspaper circulation has declined in every year as well. Newspapers still remain active in identifying political corruption, reporting the workings of state and local government, covering political campaigns, and helping to keep the public focused on important political issues. But newspapers in the final analysis are businesses and must be able to generate revenues and profits. To adequately cover state government, reporters and news staff have to be located in Sacramento. At the same time, on-the-spot coverage of county and local government requires a second set of reporters and news staff. The expense is prohibitive, and, over time, newspaper coverage at the state and local levels has noticeably declined. The public is not as fully informed about the activities of its various levels of government as it needs to be. The *Los Angeles Times* and the *Sacramento Bee* cover developments in Sacramento more extensively than other newspapers, but both became victims to cost pressures and the need to reduce news reporting staffs in the 1990s and 2000s.

The drive for profits reduced the news reporting capabilities of broadcast and print media, which now cover only the big stories at the state government level. Ultimately, the public receives little information about the political activities of state and local government. This lack of information leads to a public that constantly finds itself surprised by political crises that seem to develop suddenly, such as rising state deficits, electricity shortages, declining state bond ratings, school facilities that are falling apart, and an overwhelmed freeway system. But for all their failings, broadcast and print media still play an important role in the election process and in formulating the political agenda. The media continue to identify the major political issues, report on the political progress of candidates at all levels, question the candidates and officeholders, and edit the replies that the public gets to hear and read. These powers continue to undermine the role of political parties in California.

One bright spot is the increased coverage of the state capital and its news since the election of Arnold Schwarzenegger in October 2003. Stations that had closed their Sacramento news bureaus have in some cases reopened them. Coverage of state politics and of the governor's activities has increased in general because of the governor's celebrity status. There was more coverage of Governors Edmund G. Brown, Ronald Reagan, and Jerry Brown, who were presidential contenders, than of Governors Deukmejian, Wilson, and Davis, who were not.[27] Since the election of Schwarzenegger, even though he was born abroad and is not eligible to be president of the United States, the same kind of media interest that existed for both Brown and Reagan seems to have returned. Whether this increased activity and coverage will continue is not known, but any signs of increased activity are welcome for those interested in California government and politics.

The Internet

Today, the Internet offers instant access to political information and the opportunity to rapidly communicate one's views to political leaders, news outlets, interest groups, and other individuals in electronic chat rooms. Many experts see the Internet as a catalyst for enhancing the democratic process. It offers candidates the opportunity to communicate rapidly with supporters and to recruit campaign workers. In the recent presidential election season, it proved to be an excellent tool to raise campaign funds. The Internet offers political parties the opportunity to disseminate their issue positions to millions of potential voters in a quick and inexpensive fashion. Whether it will restore some of the power political parties have lost remains to be seen. The Internet is open to all users, and in that environment, political parties will still have lots of competition to control the political agenda.

With the growth of the Internet, access to California political and news sources has expanded exponentially. The major newspapers provide daily e-mails that focus on topics of the reader's interest, and research organizations, libraries, and blogs provide political information, background, and research beyond what any individual can absorb.

Among the major daily news sources are the newspapers that cover state and local government and politics, the *Sacramento Bee* (www.sacbee.com), the *Los Angeles*

Times (www.latimes.com), and the *San Francisco Chronicle*, (www.sfgate.com). Beyond these, several organizations provide daily news summaries that focus specifically on politics and public policy. These include Rough & Tumble (www.rtumble. com); Frank D. Russo's California Progress Report (www.californiaprogressreport. com/); the Flashreport (www.flashreport.org/) with links to newspapers, editorials, columnists, and bloggers; and Calitics for a "progressive" approach (http://calitics. com/). AroundtheCapitol.com categorizes news and opinions as "left," "center," "right," and "news" (www.aroundthecapitol.com/).

Public policy sites abound, including the widely respected Public Policy Institute of California (www.ppic.org), the California HealthCare Foundation (www. chcf.org), and the University of California at Berkeley's Institute of Governmental Studies, whose "inbox" feature contains a paragraph or two on major new studies issued in the state (http://inbox.berkeley.edu/). The institute also has a series of "Hot Topics," which brings together links from the Web in a coherent discussion of the pros and cons of major public policy issues (http://igs.berkeley.edu/library/policy_desk/ index.html) and links to major state and local government sources of information (http://igs.berkeley.edu/library/gallery-ca.html). Many university libraries have one or more pages devoted to state-government sources (see, for example, California State University Bakersfield's www.csub.edu/library/gov/california.shtml). There are several major columnists on California politics, including Dan Walters, Daniel Weintraub, and Peter Schrag of the *Sacramento Bee* and George Skelton of the *Los Angeles Times*. Some of the columnists have blogs as well for shorter items.

Media and Political Campaigns

Running for office is a very expensive endeavor, requiring highly focused political messages. Because of this requirement, electronic media are the media of choice to reach large numbers of citizens. The media are also very useful in mobilizing supporters on Election Day, which is essential to winning elections. Without the media, no effective message is conveyed to the electorate, and consequently no money can be raised to fuel the necessary media campaign. The media have the dual role of getting out the message to supporters and energizing them so that they will contribute the money needed to win public office. Candidates cannot depend on local campaign appearances to reach enough people. They must depend on the power of electronic media to reach the mass audience needed to win elections.

In some cases, the media themselves and their coverage can become a central issue in the campaign, with the candidate running against the media as part of the political establishment. During the recall election of 2003, the *Los Angeles Times* ran a story just before the election about inappropriate sexual behavior on the part of Schwarzenegger in his acting days. The reaction of many citizens was that the newspaper was taking incumbent Governor Gray Davis's side, not that it was uncovering important information that citizens might want to consider in their voting decisions.[28]

Interest-Group Politics in California: Where Are We Now?

Interest groups play an important and often dominant role in California politics. The continued growth in the number of groups and their lobbying expenditures attest to this fact. Moreover, if the past decade is any indication, the number of interest groups doing business in Sacramento will continue to grow, and lobbying expenditures will continue to increase over the next decade. The size and continued incremental growth of the state budget, weak political parties, mandated term limits, increase in public interest groups, and continued dependence of local governments on Sacramento for financial assistance are all factors that will continue to promote interest-group politics.

Much of the time, these groups are self-regulating, with one group checking another, and with the forging of broad-based coalitions of interests to achieve important policy decisions. Of course, interest groups will always be able to achieve advantages for narrow issues affecting their groups, and the most powerful will generally be the most successful, as long as they can get a group of legislators to fall in behind them. And that's why interest-group disclosure rules, campaign expenditure limits, and other reporting requirements are necessary. They enable us to keep these groups in check. That's the theory, at least.

Today, however, there is a disjunction between theory and practice. Interest groups have undue influence on politics in the state. The only check on their power seems to be divided government, whereby one party controls the executive and one controls the legislature, so that no one interest or coalition of interests can ride roughshod over government.

That's the state of affairs in California today. While California's politics are not broken, unless these concerns are addressed, California will continue to hobble along, and interest groups will continue to flourish and prosper at the expense of the general public.

FOR FURTHER READING

Baldassare, Mark. "The California Initiative Process—How Democratic Is It?" Public Policy Institute of California, February 2002.

Gerber, Elisabeth R. "Interest Group Influence in the California Initiative Process." Public Policy Institute of California, 1998. www.ppic.org/content/pubs/R_1198EGR.pdf

McWilliams, Carey. *California: The Great Exception*. Berkeley: University of California Press, 1999.

Michael, Jay and Dan Walters, with Dan Weintraub. *The Third House: Lobbyists, Money, and Power in Sacramento*. Berkeley: Berkeley Public Policy Press, 2000.

Rasky, Susan F. "Covering California: the Press Wrestles with Diversity, Complexity, and Change." In *Governing California: Politics, Government, and Public Policy in the Golden State*, ed. Gerald C. Lubenow and Bruce E. Cain. Berkeley: Institute of Governmental Studies Press, University of California, 1997, 157–88.

Samish, Arthur H., and Bob Thomas. *The Secret Boss of California: The Life and High Times of Art Samish*. New York: Crown, 1971.

ON THE WEB

Around the Capitol: www.aroundthecapitol.com/

California Lobbying Firms: www.aroundthecapitol.com/lobbyists.html
Around the Capitol.com's list of California Lobbyists, ranked by income.

California Advocates, Inc.: www.caladvocates.com/

Lobbying Activity: http://cal-access.ss.ca.gov/Lobbying/
The Secretary of State's office reports on lobbying in California politics.

Sacramento Bee: Capitol & California: www.sacbee.com/capitolandcalifornia/

SUMMARY

Interest groups are at the center of California's campaign and lobbying activities. Some observers believe they play a necessary role in our democratic society. Others see them as detrimental to our political system.

Interest groups exhibit the following characteristics.

1. They are associations of individuals who join together for the purpose of influencing governmental or legislative policy.
2. They can be businesses, trade and professional associations, or labor unions.
3. They have proliferated over the past three decades for four reasons: growth in government, weak political parties, public interest groups, and term limits.

Lobbyists do the work of interest groups, an activity referred to as lobbying. Lobbyists can be citizen lobbyists, contract lobbyists, or in-house lobbyists.

1. Citizen lobbyists are individuals who have an interest in an issue and want to make their views known to their public officials.
2. Contract lobbyists and in-house lobbyists are professionals who must register with the secretary of state and submit a variety of disclosure statements yearly regarding their activities.

Lobbyists perform a variety of activities to accomplish their goals. Here are a few of the most obvious:

1. Preparation for the campaign
   - set goal
   - know the demographics of the interest group
   - establish a grassroots network

2. The campaign (lobbying basics)
   - draft language, amendments, etc.
   - prepare a fact sheet, position papers, etc.
   - contact committee members before the committee hearing

3. Legislative activities
   - testify in person
   - bring expert witnesses from legislator's district
   - always tell the truth

Interest groups contribute to candidates' and officeholders' campaigns in order to leverage their influence. The Political Reform Act of 1974 was passed to regulate lobbying practices and requires the disclosure of lobbying financial activity. Proposition 34, the most recent initiative amendment to the act, includes new restrictions whereby lobbyists cannot contribute to the campaigns of anyone they are lobbying and the amount of money they can contribute during any election cycle is limited.

The media, particularly television and newspapers, and increasingly the Internet (through political Web sites and blogs), are important vehicles in mobilizing and informing voters and candidates' supporters. Little of this mobilization, however, comes from news programs, which generally provide little political information. However, the ability of television news programs to cover scandals and dishonest practices of politicians and to focus viewers' attention on the latest special investigation demonstrates how the power to set the political agenda has passed from the political parties to the media.

PRACTICE QUIZ

1. The term "third house" refers to which of the following entities?
   a) the judicial branch
   b) the executive branch
   c) interest groups
   d) the media
2. Over the past two decades, interest-group expenditures in California have
   a) declined.
   b) increased.
   c) remained relatively the same.
   d) fluctuated from year to year.
3. An individual who offers his lobbying services to multiple clients at the same time is called a(n)
   a) contract lobbyist.
   b) "hired gun."
   c) citizen lobbyist.
   d) in-house lobbyist.
4. The principal function of an interest group is to
   a) provide its members with educational and social opportunities.
   b) contribute money to candidates for public office who favor its programs.
   c) attain favorable decisions from government on issues that it supports.
   d) inform the public on the role of interest in the economy.

5. Political action committees (PACs)
   a) have declined in popularity in recent years.
   b) must disclose campaign contributions and expenditures in connection with state and local elections.
   c) may make unlimited contributions to political candidates.
   d) provide candidates with public funding for their campaign.
6. According to the text, all of the following factors are involved in the media's decisions not to cover more political and governmental news except
   a) Californians are not that interested in political and governmental news.
   b) the ratings for political and governmental news are lower than other kinds of news, such as the weather, consumer news, sports coverage, etc.
   c) so many news programs cover California political and governmental news that there is little for each station to report.
   d) political and governmental news, except during election campaigns, does not lend itself to sensational coverage.
7. One reason the election of Governor Schwarzenegger might signal a new and higher level of coverage of California government and politics is that
   a) there is much more happening in Sacramento with Governor Schwarzenegger than there was with his predecessor, Gray Davis.
   b) Schwarzenegger is a celebrity; thus, television news can cover both him and state government news at the same time.
   c) Schwarzenegger is more similar to other governors who were covered closely, such as Pat Brown, Jerry Brown, and Ronald Reagan, than he is to George Deukmejian, Pete Wilson, and Gray Davis, who weren't.
   d) Schwarzenegger is more telegenic than past California governors.

8. Over the past two decades, the number of newspapers across the United States has _____, and newspaper circulations have _____ in every recent year as well.
   a) risen, increased
   b) remained the same, increased
   c) risen, declined
   d) fallen, declined
9. One reason the election of Governor Schwarzenegger might signal a new and higher level of coverage of California government and politics is that
   a) there is much more happening in Sacramento with Governor Schwarzenegger than there was with his predecessor, Gray Davis.
   b) Schwarzenegger is a celebrity; thus, television news can cover both him and state government news at the same time.
   c) Schwarzenegger is more similar to other governors who were covered closely, such as Pat Brown, Jerry Brown, and Ronald Reagan, than he is to George Deukmejian, Pete Wilson, and Gray Davis, who weren't.
   d) Schwarzenegger is more telegenic than past California governors.
10. Many experts see the Internet as a catalyst for _____ the democratic process.
   a) threatening
   b) enhancing
   c) having little effect on
   d) undermining

CRITICAL-THINKING QUESTIONS

1. Over the past several decades, interest groups have grown and expanded their influence over public policy decisions in the legislature and at administrative agencies. Identify the reasons for this phenomenon.
2. Interest groups use a variety of techniques to accomplish their goals. Suppose you worked for an interest group that opposed stricter requirements for the recycling of plastic bottles. Outline a campaign to achieve your goal. Explain why you would take the action you propose.
3. Some people argue that interest groups provide citizens with another way to become involved in the political process. Others argue that interest groups undermine the political process. Discuss the arguments for both positions. Give your opinion on this question.
4. Interest groups play a significant role in the funding of political campaigns. Should more restrictions be put on their activity? You decide that interest groups should be limited or altogether prohibited from contributing to political campaigns. How would this policy affect political campaigns? What would be the outcome of this reform?
6. What are the factors that have led to relatively low levels of coverage of politics and government in California?

KEY TERMS

At this point you should have a general understanding of the following concepts and terms:

California Political Reform Act (43)
citizen lobbyist (40)
contract lobbyist (40)
in-house lobbyist (40)

interest group (34)
lobbying (34)
media (46)
political action committee (PAC) (41)

public interest group (38)
third house (34)
trade association (33)

4 Parties and Elections in California

WHAT CALIFORNIA GOVERNMENT DOES, AND WHY IT MATTERS

Consider the following about political parties, elections, campaigning, and voting in California:

★ California was the first state in the country to encourage absentee voting by making it convenient and easy. Absentee voters now make up approximately 42 percent of the California electorate.

★ Six political parties qualify for the ballot in California. In addition to the Democratic and Republican parties, four minor political parties are legally permitted to put forward candidates for elective office and have their names appear automatically on the ballot. This number of parties gives voters more choices in deciding whom to elect to public office.

★ Women won the right to vote under California law in 1911, making California the sixth state to give women this right. Women did not win the right to vote in national elections until 1920.

★ California has set the trend for ballot initiatives in other states. After California passed Proposition 13 limiting property taxes, nearly one-half of the states passed similar legislation. After ballot initiatives on bilingual education, term limits, and use of medical marijuana passed in California, similar measures were placed on the ballots in other states.

Political Parties

A political party is an organization of people with roughly similar political or ideological positions who work to win elections in order to take control of the government and change public policy. Political parties perform many valuable functions in a democratic society. One of their most important roles is to mobilize voters at election time, helping to get out the vote. They also function as opposition points to the policies pursued by government at all levels, thereby promoting discussion of important political issues. Parties help to recruit candidates for office and play a major role in the selection process. They are directly involved in political campaigns, providing workers, raising money, and identifying important political issues. Parties help to bring about consensus on important political issues and serve as two-way communication channels between government and the people. Consequently, most political scientists consider them vital to the health of a democratic state.

California has a *winner-take-all* system of voting in which the candidate receiving the highest vote wins the election. Political scientists have long known that such a system promotes two dominant political parties. As a result, two major political parties dominate the political process in California: the Republicans and the Democrats. *Third parties*, which are defined as any party other than the Republicans and Democrats, play only a limited role in California politics, although several third parties are considered qualified and are entitled to appear on the California ballot. They are the American Independent Party, the Peace and Freedom Party, the Green Party, and the Libertarian Party.

The Progressive Impact on Political Parties

The Progressive movement viewed political parties as corrupt organizations operating in concert with big corporations with the intent of controlling and manipulating the political system for their own benefit. Spencer Olin describes the attitude that Progressives had toward political parties:

> Accompanying their democratic faith in the wisdom of the individual voter was a distrust of formal party organizations, which were viewed as the media of special-interest power. . . . Furthermore, it was argued by progressives that science and efficient management would solve the problems of government; parties were irrelevant and unnecessary.[1]

The Progressives attacked the power of the political parties with reforms such as *presidential primaries* and *partisan primaries*. These reforms were designed to take the power to select candidates to run for office away from the parties and put it into the hands of the people. The primary system also opened up the opportunity to run for office to anyone capable of meeting the basic qualifications, such as age and residency requirements. Instead of the party leadership and their corporate allies having the power to select candidates and subsequently manipulate them while they held office, the people now participated in a whole new class of elections, forcing candidates to direct their political messages and loyalty to the average voter.

Nonpartisan elections further weakened parties by preventing party designations from appearing on the ballot. Voters were no longer able to use their party loyalties to make voting decisions on Election Day at the county and city level. The Progressives wanted the electorate to do its homework and find out about the candidates. Instead of a party label on the ballot, voters were to be given only the current occupational status of the candidate. This meant that voters had to inform themselves by reading up on the candidates or even attending a candidate's forum.

The Progressives also installed a new ballot, the *office block ballot*. This type of ballot made it difficult to vote the straight party ticket, which was easy in many other states. Ballots that favored voting for one party, or voting the *straight ticket*, listed all the candidates running for each office by party. The use of the office block ballot in California discourages such behavior by listing each office separately and requiring the voter to make his or her choice. In nonpartisan races held at the county and city level, no party designation is shown on the ballot.

The Progressives continued their assault on the political parties in California through the use of *cross-filing*. Candidates for public office could run in either party's primary or in the primaries of both parties. This allowed a highly popular candidate to be the candidate of more than one political party. Cross-filing had a major impact on political parties in California. The cross-filing law not only helped wreck California parties but contributed to the development of a candidate-oriented system of state electoral politics.[2] Cross-filing was not eliminated until 1959.

Third Parties in California

Voters in California have long had the opportunity to vote for third-party candidates. In the 2006 governor's race, voters could vote for the Republican or Democratic candidates or for the candidates of five other parties: the American Independent Party, Green Party, Libertarian Party, Natural Law Party (which, after 2006, lost its qualified political party status), and the Peace and Freedom Party.

Traditionally, third-party candidates do not win in a political system like that in the United States, which has a *winner-take-all* system. Both major parties make much of the fact that third parties do not win and warn voters against throwing their votes away. However, a significant percentage of voters reject their advice and continue to vote for third-party candidates.

The American political system, which is a *federal system*, delegates power to three levels of government: national, state, and local. One of the powers that states retain is to determine how political parties may organize and gain access to the ballot. Since the legislature in California is dominated by the Republicans and Democrats, they have not made it easy for third parties to qualify to get on the ballot. As a consequence, California politics is almost totally dominated by the Republicans and Democrats.

There are two ways that political parties can qualify to get on the ballot in California. The first method is by *registration*; the second is by *petition*. Both methods are based on a percentage of those persons who voted in the previous general election. In the election held in November 2006, some 8,899,059 persons turned out to vote. In order to qualify a new party by the registration method, the law requires that 88,991 persons or 1 percent of those who voted in the 2006 general election officially register with the new party. The law also requires that the registrations be completed and mailed in by the 154th day preceding the upcoming primary. The second option, the petition method, is even more difficult and tedious. It requires a new political party to collect signatures equal to 10 percent of those who voted in the last general election on petitions asking that the party be included in the upcoming primary. Currently, that number stands at 889,906. Obviously, qualifying as a new political party is not an easy task and requires time, manpower, expertise, and resources.

So what is the role of third parties in politics, particularly in California? One theory is that third parties act as spoilers. They may draw enough votes from one or the other of the two major parties to alter the election outcome. Third parties also help to focus public attention on important political issues. Once an issue attracts enough public attention, it will be taken over by one or both of the two major political parties. Altering election outcomes and raising political issues relegates third parties to a lesser role in politics. Whether that will change over time remains to be seen. Box 4.1 includes the Web sites and e-mail addresses of those parties currently qualified in California.

Party Affiliation of California Voters

A plurality of California voters identify with the Democratic Party. Currently, about 44 percent of voters are registered with the Democratic Party compared to nearly 33 percent affiliated with the Republican Party. A substantial 19 percent of voters decline to state a party affiliation, and the remaining 4 percent identify with one of the minor parties. Party affiliation is fairly easy to determine in the state, because when you register to vote, you are asked to declare your political party. Of the six political parties that have qualified for the ballot in California, two are major parties and four are minor parties. The Democratic and Republican parties receive the lion's share of votes and members.

As Table 4.1 illustrates, during the last sixteen years, registration in the two major parties has declined. The percentage of registered Democrats declined from 48.5 percent in 1992 to 43.8 percent in 2008, a loss of nearly 5 percent. The decline in the Republican Party has been slightly more at 6 percent during the same time period. The minor parties' registration totals increased 1 percent in the same time period. There are two very important trends to note.

TABLE 4.1 ★ Registration by Party for Primary Elections

PRIMARY ELECTION	DEM	REP	OTHER	DECLINE TO STATE	COUNTIES WITH MAJORITY OF DEMS.	OF REPS.
2008 Direct (June)	43.8%	32.5%	4.3%	19.4%	26	32
2008 Presidential (Feb)	43.0%	33.3%	4.3%	19.4%	23	35
2004 Presidential	43.2%	35.6%	4.8%	16.4%	21	37
2000 Presidential	45.7%	35.1%	5.3%	13.9%	29	29
1996 Presidential	47.1%	37.0%	5.2%	10.7%	35	23
1992 Presidential	48.5%	38.6%	3.2%	9.7%	43	15

SOURCE: California Secretary of State's Office. www.ss.ca.gov

First, the number of voters who have declined to state a party affiliation when they register to vote, those whom we refer to as independent voters, has steadily increased, doubling from 9.7 percent to 19.4 percent in sixteen years. Second, notice the change in the number of Democratic and Republican counties. In sixteen years, the number of counties having majorities of Democratic voters decreased by nearly 50 percent. In 1992 there were 43 Democratic counties in the state, and in 2008 this has been reduced to only 26 counties. The Democrats' loss has been the Republicans' gain. The number of counties with majorities of Republican voters has risen sharply during this time period, growing from only 15 counties in 1992, to a robust 32 counties in 2008 (although it is interesting to note the recent slight upsurge of Democratic counties and the accompanying decline in Republican counties).

THE RED AND THE BLUE IN CALIFORNIA Thinking back to the presidential election of 2004, you may recall that most television programs focusing on the election outcome had maps of the United States color-coded to represent the states that voted Republican (red) and those states that voted Democratic (blue). The map was very interesting—the West Coast and most of the Northeast as well as major urban areas of the United States were blue (Democratic) and the South, agricultural regions, and the Great Plains states were red (Republican). The map nicely illustrated the national split between urban areas, predominantly Democratic, and rural, agricultural, and suburban areas, mostly Republican.

The same geographic split appears within the state of California—a split between the coastal counties and the inland counties. Table 4.2 lists the top ten Democratic, Republican, and independent counties in terms of party registration. Most of the Democratic counties encompass major urban areas, whereas most of

TABLE 4.2 ★ Political Party Registration by County

The top ten Democratic Party, Republican Party, and Declined to State counties in terms of party registration as of May 2008.

DEMOCRATIC PARTY		REPUBLICAN PARTY		DECLINE TO STATE	
Alameda	56.90%	Modoc	50.22%	San Francisco	28.98%
San Francisco	55.86%	Placer	49.90%	Santa Clara	24.90%
Imperial	55.12%	Shasta	48.49%	Mono	23.58%
Santa Cruz	54.19%	Sutter	48.38%	San Mateo	22.86%
Marin	53.89%	Lassen	47.75%	San Diego	22.46%
Sonoma	51.78%	Madera	47.22%	Alameda	22.18%
Los Angeles	50.96%	Kings	47.07%	Alpine	22.09%
San Mateo	50.54%	Colusa	46.70%	Marin	20.75%
Solano	50.00%	Glenn	46.55%	Humboldt	20.53%
Monterey	49.69%	Tulare	46.49%	Yolo	20.52%

SOURCE: California Secretary of State's Office. www.ss.ca.gov

the Republican counties are more rural. So, if we color-coded a map of California, most of the coastal counties and those closest to the urban centers of Los Angeles and San Francisco would be blue, and many of the inland, rural, agricultural counties would be red, a pattern not unlike the rest of the country.

As reported by the *Los Angeles Times:*

> Over the last decade, Republican influence has grown more concentrated in conservative inland California—largely the Central Valley and Inland Empire but also the Antelope Valley, the Sierra and rural north. . . . At the same time Democrats have strengthened their domination of counties along California's coastline, building overwhelming advantages in the San Francisco and Los Angeles areas as Latino voters have expanded the party's base. And from San Diego's beachfront suburbs to the Central Coast, Democrats have eroded Republican support among moderates, especially women.[3]

Overall, the Democratic Party has an electoral advantage in California, largely due to the fact that nearly two-thirds of the state's population resides in Democratic-leaning coastal regions. Republicans have an uphill battle winning statewide elections and are more likely to succeed if they nominate ideologically moderate candidates who are able to win the support of Democratic voters.

Party Organizations

All political parties in California have *State Central Committees*, which are made up of partisan officeholders and other party officials. The average political party member or supporter is not represented by this organization. The State Central Committee helps to build support for the party's campaign efforts. Members of *County Central Committees* are elected by the voters in each assembly district. They generally function to help in campaigns. Because of the Progressive reforms, state and county committees are weak and play a diminished role in the party's affairs.

Elections in California

The Battle over the Primary

A political party primary is an election in which those voters identified with the party choose the candidates who will run in the November general election. Prior to 1998 and since 2002, California operated under what is known as a *closed* primary system. In a closed primary system, only voters who declared a party affiliation when they registered to vote are permitted to vote in their political party's primary election. Each political party has its own ballot listing the names of the candidates from that party competing for the party's nomination for various elective offices. Registered Democrats receive the Democratic Party's ballot, registered Republicans receive the Republican ballot, Peace and Freedom Party members receive their party's ballot. Those registered voters who decline to state an affiliation when they register are not permitted to vote in a party's primary under this type of *fully* closed primary system. However, they are permitted to vote on whatever measures and nonpartisan candidates are on the ballot.

In 1996, voters passed Proposition 198, the "Open Primary" Proposition. This changed the state's primary system and went into effect for the 1998 election. Proposition 198 was misnamed because the primary system described in the ballot measure was not an *open* primary but rather a *blanket* primary. Twenty states operate as open-primary states, in which citizens can vote in the party primary of their choice. On primary Election Day, voters request the ballot from the party of their choice, and there usually is no permanent record indicating which party's primary ballot they selected. That primary system is quite different from a blanket primary. In a blanket primary system, there is only one ballot, listing all candidates from all of the parties. All registered voters, including those not affiliated with any party, are permitted to vote, and all receive the same ballot. For instance, a voter who is not affiliated with a party may vote for a Democrat to run as the Democratic Party's presidential nominee and a Republican candidate to run for a U.S. Senate seat. Under this system, voters who are not registered with a party help choose that party's nominees.

In 1996, nearly 60 percent of California voters approved of this new blanket primary system. California joined three other states using the blanket primary system: Alaska, Louisiana, and Washington. Proponents of the blanket primary argue that it is a more inclusive system, since unaffiliated voters are permitted to vote. They also argue that a blanket primary would result in more moderate candidates running in primary races, thus producing more competitive elections. The logic is that if independent, ideologically moderate voters participate in the primary election, they will bring a counterbalance to the more extreme and ideological views of traditional primary voters, the party loyalists. Primary candidates would, therefore, need to moderate their positions in order to attract the votes of moderate, independent voters. Opponents of the blanket primary argue that loyal party members should have the right to choose their own party's candidates. If one is an unaffiliated voter, then one should not have the right to determine a party's nominee for public office.

The Democratic, Republican, Libertarian, and Peace and Freedom parties challenged Proposition 198 on the grounds that it violated the First Amendment's guarantee of freedom of association (see Box 4.2). The U.S. Supreme Court ruled in June 2000 that California's Proposition 198 was unconstitutional, since it allowed members of an opposing political party to choose a party's nominee. After the Court's ruling, California adopted a *modified closed* primary system. About fifteen states operate under some variation of the modified closed primary system. Beginning with the March 2002 primary election, Californians who are registered with a political party are given their party's ballot. Prior to each election, qualified political parties may file a statement notifying the secretary of state that they will allow unaffiliated voters to request their party ballot in the primary election. In the February 2008 presidential primary, only the Democratic and American Independent parties permitted unaffiliated voters to request their election ballots. If an unaffiliated voter does not specifically request such a ballot, he or she is given a ballot containing only the names of candidates for nonpartisan races and measures to be voted upon.

| BOX 4.2 | A Wet Blanket for the Blanket Primary |

California voters approved an initiative in 1996 that would let them vote for candidates of more than one party in the primary election. Called a "blanket primary," this plan puts all candidates from all parties on the same primary ballot, just as in the general election. Thus, it permits voters who are not affiliated with a party to help choose that party's candidates. Proponents said it would boost voter participation in the primary—and it did—and encourage the choice of more moderate candidates. Party leaders saw it differently; the state's Democratic and Republican parties and two minor parties sued to overturn the law. They claimed that by opening up the primary, the plan prevented the party's loyal supporters from choosing the candidates who best represented their views. That, they said, would keep the party from offering a clear and consistent message to the voters. The result was to violate the First Amendment's guarantee of freedom of association.

The state's lawyers countered that a primary belongs to the voters, not to the parties. A U.S. Circuit Court of Appeals agreed. But in June 2000, the U.S. Supreme Court (in the case of *California Democratic Party v. Jones*) sided with the parties. That gave the right to decide who votes in a primary, at least in California, back to the party organization. The future of the blanket primary is in doubt as a result.

SOURCE: Marjorie Randon Hershey and Paul Allen Beck, *Party Politics in America*, 10th ed. (New York: Longman, 2003).

Presidential Primaries: Maximizing California's Clout?

Until 2000, California held its presidential primaries in June of election years, one of the last states to cast its votes for the parties' nominees. It was often the case that states holding earlier primaries and caucuses determined who the presidential nominees were before Californians had a chance to go to the polls. In order to have more influence in the nomination process, California changed its presidential primary election date to early March. Many believed it was only fitting that the most populous state should have an early primary date. Sadly, this earlier primary date did not result in California voters' having more clout in the presidential nomination process, as other states moved their primaries to even earlier dates. So California changed its primary date back to June, effective 2006. In 2007, California changed its presidential state primary date once again, from June 3 to early February 5, the earliest permissible date under national party rules. California's state primaries, however, are still held in June, with only the presidential primary date moved to early February.

Many political analysts and journalists heralded the early February presidential primary date. But did this move really have the intended impact, as hopefully reflected in a 2007 *Los Angeles Times'* article entitled, "Earlier Primary Gives California a Major Voice"? The answer is "yes" and "no," with some interesting and ironic twists. As with most changes in policy, there usually are unanticipated and unintended consequences.

Many who had argued for the early February presidential primary believed candidates would have to campaign early and hard in the Golden State and would have to win support from a very racially and ethnically diverse population, especially the growing number of Latino voters. To win voters' support, issues important to Californians would need to be addressed, and all this would result in California's greater prominence in presidential campaign politics, or so the theory went.

The February 5, 2008, presidential primary proved to be very interesting for a number of reasons. Candidates did, in fact, campaign early and hard in California. And candidates courted the Latino voter. In fact, figures on the Latino vote showed an increase in the number of Latinos in the Democratic Party, with nearly 3 out of 10 Democrats identifying themselves as Latino. This is almost double the number in the 2004 Democratic primary. Hillary Clinton carried the Latino vote on February 5, with a whopping 69 percent of the vote, compared to Obama's 29 percent (as a comparison point, Latino voters' preference for Clinton nationwide was 63 percent and for Obama 35 percent). Los Angeles's very popular Latino mayor Antonio Villariagosa campaigned aggressively for Clinton and was an invaluable member of her team, coordinating outreach to Latino voters. The Latino vote also increased in the Republican Party, with Latinos comprising 13 percent of the GOP voters, an increase of 5 percent since 2000.

One of the unanticipated consequences of California's adoption of an early primary date was that a number of states with long-standing early primaries now set their election dates prior to California's, not wanting to be overshadowed by the most populous state in the nation. And, twenty-three other states moved their primaries to February 5, resulting in something akin to a national primary. California's dream of being in the electoral limelight quickly faded.

California's early primary date did have an impact on the Republican contest, in which Senator John McCain won the state with just over 42 percent of the vote and 90 percent of the state's Republican delegates, essentially winning the Republican Party nomination, thanks to the voters of the Golden State. Hillary Clinton won the Democratic primary, and her California victory kept her campaign alive. Political scholar Sherry Bebitch Jeffe believes that Clinton might have dropped out of the race earlier if she had not won the California primary. Furthermore, if the California primary had taken place in June, as originally planned, California voters might have had some real clout. As Jeffe explains, "With the Democratic race not yet wrapped up, it's now clear that a late-deciding California, with its trove of 440 delegates, coulda been a contender." And, she points out, recent Field Polls show that Californians now prefer Obama over Clinton by a 13 percent margin![14] This shift toward Obama occurred shortly after the February 5 contest. Ironically, if Californians had cast their votes in June, most likely it would have been California, and not Michigan, Florida, and Puerto Rico, giving the nomination to Obama.

Another consequence of the early February primary was that the June 2008 primary election for statewide offices cost the state and counties $100 million and resulted in a historically low voting turnout rate of less than 25 percent of the registered voters. With the November general election, California voters will have been asked to vote in three elections in less than ten months.

Initiative Campaigns: Direct Democracy or Tool of Special Interests?

One legacy of California's early twentieth-century reform movement is the initiative process. Californians can completely bypass the state legislature, their elected representatives, and place proposed policies on the ballot for direct vote by the people. As the name suggests, the electorate *initiates* initiatives. Most people think of the initiative process as direct democracy in action—concerned citizens circulate petitions to qualify their issue for the ballot and then hold an election allowing the public to state its preference for or against the proposed policy. In reality, only a small number of ballot initiatives emerge as a result of grassroots efforts. Initiatives are largely a political tool used by special interest groups to achieve their policy goals. Depending on the issue, interest groups sometimes find it politically expedient to bypass the legislature altogether, believing they have a better chance of achieving their policy goals if they take the issue directly to the voters. One thing is certain—it is usually the more controversial issues that find their way onto the ballot as propositions, issues that the state legislature has been unwilling to address or never had the chance to address.

From 1912, the first year initiatives were permitted, through 2008, nearly 340 statewide initiatives have appeared on the California ballot. These ballot initiatives have dealt with a wide range of issues, such as legalization of marijuana for medical purposes, campaign finance reform, same-sex marriage, taxation policy, legalization of gambling casinos, the establishment of a state lottery, environmental regulations, affirmative action policy, the criminal justice system, and labor issues. Of these hundreds of initiatives, only about one-third have been approved by the voters. In the past three decades, there has been a dramatic surge in the number of initiatives that have been proposed and that have qualified for the ballot. Many surmise that the reason for this increase is that special interests have become more sophisticated in their use of the initiative process to achieve their policy goals.

To qualify for the ballot, the state requires approximately 435,000 signatures of registered voters for initiatives creating new laws (statutes) and nearly 700,000 signatures for propositions that aim to amend the state constitution. Signatures are gathered on petitions, which are then submitted to the secretary of state's office for verification. Collecting hundreds of thousands of signatures of registered voters is a daunting task. Rarely is this a grassroots movement in which ordinary citizens fan out across the state, knock on doors, and stand in front of supermarkets, asking strangers to support their initiative by signing a petition. More common is the hiring of professional signature gatherers. There are political consulting firms who specialize in this very activity. They hire individuals to go to college campuses, supermarkets, malls, and other places where voters congregate, and they are paid an average of $1.50 per signature for every signature they acquire. This means that it costs over $600,000 just to collect the signatures to qualify a proposition for the ballot.

For the more controversial initiatives, in order to wage a successful campaign either in support of or in opposition to an initiative, one needs to have ample political resources. Money is probably the most important of these resources. Not only must a statewide initiative campaign hire political consultants, but it must also plan and implement a sustainable media campaign. Such campaigns are very costly because of California's size and expensive media markets. Therefore, it is not surprising to find the more high-profile and controversial initiative campaigns costing tens of millions of dollars. In 2008 slightly over $60 million was spent on the highly controversial initiative, Proposition 8, a constitutional amendment that would eliminate same-sex marriage in California. Proposition 8 was put on the ballot in response to the State Supreme Court's May 2008 ruling (4–3) declaring that the state Constitution protects a fundamental "right to marry" that extends equally to same-sex couples. Both sides of the issue collected near equal sums of contributions totaling $74 million dollars, with the majority of the contributions in support of Proposition 8 coming from members of the Mormon Church throughout the United States.[5] As expensive as Proposition 8 was, it did not break the record for the most expensive initiative campaign. In 2006 both sides spent more than $150 million on Proposition 87, the alternative energy initiative, which was soundly defeated by a 55 percent vote. This was, by far, the most expensive proposition campaign not only in California history, but in the entire United States.

Political savvy is another important resource. The chances of winning an initiative campaign increase if one understands how the game is played. For example, the naming of the proposition can increase its chance of passage. In the November 1996 election, Proposition 209, officially entitled the Prohibition against Discrimination or Preferential Treatment by State and Other Public Entities, appeared on the ballot. Its supporters referred to the proposition as the "California Civil Rights Initiative." Considering these titles alone, it would be difficult to imagine this proposition failing; in these progressive times, it is fair to say that most voters are opposed to discrimination and are supportive of civil rights. However, in reality, Proposition 209 was not what most would consider to be a civil rights statute. The proposition proposed to eliminate affirmative action programs in California for women and minorities in public employment, education (college admissions, tutoring, and outreach programs), and contracting. Proposition 209 passed and is now state law.

Critics of the initiative process believe that too many complicated issues are presented to the voters as ballot propositions. In some recent elections, voters have had to vote for candidates for federal, state, county, and city elective offices as well as cast their votes for over a dozen important state propositions and numerous county and city measures. In November 2004, California voters faced sixteen ballot initiatives; in 2006, the number was thirteen; and in November 2008, voters were asked to vote on twelve statewide initiatives. Some counties have considered limiting the time a voter could spend in the polling booth, nervous that voters unfamiliar with these propositions and measures will take too long to read the ballot and cast their votes. Voters are encouraged to study their sample ballots beforehand and to bring their marked sample ballots with them to the voting booth to use as their guide in order to expedite the process.

Some argue that many of the issues that appear as ballot initiatives are best suited for debate and deliberation by our elected representatives and should not be decided by misleading television ads aimed at the public. Sometimes the propositions are very confusing in name and in substance, and some question whether we are asking too much of the electorate to wade through all this information. As an example, in the March 2004 election, voters were presented with four different measures (Propositions 55, 56, 57, and 58) dealing with overlapping budgetary issues. To further confuse the electorate, these propositions not only had similar numbers but similar titles as well. Some political observers are concerned that in such situations voter confusion is inevitable. Another problem with the initiative process is that the constitutionality of many propositions approved by the voters is later challenged. It takes years for the courts to render a decision, and it is not uncommon for the courts to declare the law based on the passage of the proposition to be unconstitutional, null, and void. Not only does this complicate the process; it also frustrates the public who voted for a new policy only to see the courts invalidate the public's will.

The legislature understands some of the problems associated with the initiative process and has created state commissions to investigate and reform the process. Some suggested reforms have been to prohibit the use of paid signature gathers whom only the well-funded interest groups are able to afford; to increase the number of signatures required, in an effort to reduce the number of initiatives; to restrict the types of issues that can appear as ballot initiatives; and to review the constitutionality of initiatives prior to placing them on the ballot. Although there have been a couple of these commissions, none of these reforms has been adopted.

The 2003 Gubernatorial Recall Election: A Perfect Political Storm

On October 7, 2003, Governor Gray Davis made history. Only eleven months after he successfully won his re-election bid, he was recalled from office. He was the first and only governor in the state of California and the second governor in the nation's history to be recalled. The recall movement and election of Arnold Schwarzenegger was in every sense dramatic, historic, and stunning. What began as a quiet, small-scale, grassroots movement, sponsored largely by a small cadre of conservative Republicans still smarting over their party's loss in the November 2002 gubernatorial race, evolved into a well-funded, headline-grabbing, sophisticated political campaign.

THE MAJOR PLAYERS

Governor Gray Davis Re-elected to his second term as governor in November 2002, Davis beat his challenger, Bill Simon, by a 47 percent to 42 percent vote. Simon was a neophyte conservative candidate. Although he ran a lackluster, sloppy campaign, he came within five points of unseating an incumbent governor who was an experienced campaigner and consummate fundraiser. Right up until the

November 2002 election, Governor Davis had low job-approval ratings, with a majority of voters disapproving of his overall performance as governor. A statewide survey in November 2002 found that 62 percent of likely voters were not satisfied with the choices of candidates for governor and 56 percent of voters were planning to cast votes for their candidate not because they liked him and his policies but because "he is the best of a bad lot."[6]

The People's Advocate This antitax group was created by Paul Gann, co-author of Proposition 13, which revolutionized taxation policy in California, and Ted Costa. With a cadre of like-minded antitax conservatives and a meager budget of $200,000, this group began working on a plan to recall Davis within two weeks of Davis's re-election. They depended on volunteers and conservative talk radio to obtain the required 900,000 signatures (12 percent of the voters in the previous gubernatorial election) to place the recall on the ballot. By the end of April 2003, they had gathered only 65,000 signatures and were running out of funds.[7]

Darrell Issa Issa, a millionaire and two-term Republican member of Congress (R-San Diego), had ambitions of running for governor. The son of immigrants, Issa made his fortune in the car alarm business. His injection of nearly $2 million into the recall effort allowed for the training and deployment of signature gatherers and the collection of nearly 1.4 million valid signatures. Darrell Issa initially entered the race as a candidate, but a day after Schwarzenegger announced his candidacy, Issa dropped out.

Arnold Schwarzenegger A name and face familiar to all is priceless capital in a political campaign. An Austrian-born actor who married into the staunchly Democratic Kennedy family, Schwarzenegger was the embodiment of the "anti-politician, antiestablishment" candidate. On August 6, with much anticipation and fanfare, he announced his candidacy on Jay Leno's *The Tonight Show*. He immediately became the front-runner among Republican candidates and made national and international headlines with his decision to run. Contrary to his public image, Schwarzenegger was not a neophyte politician. A couple of years prior to the recall, he had assembled a noteworthy team of political consultants and operatives, and was preparing for a possible bid for the governorship in 2006.[8]

Cruz Bustamante As lieutenant governor, Bustamante, a fellow Democrat and ally of Davis, was legally required to schedule the recall election. At first, Democrats thought their best strategy was to oppose the recall, and all resources were directed toward defeating the recall. However, public opinion polls showed that it was likely the recall would succeed and the Democrats would be left without a candidate in the running to replace Davis. Bustamante announced his candidacy on August 6, the same day as Schwarzenegger's announcement.

The Voters Public opinion polls indicated that voters were extremely dissatisfied with the status quo. At the time of the recall election, Davis had sinking job-approval ratings. As Gary South, a Davis adviser, asked, "How do you get 50 percent plus one of the voters to vote for somebody with a 26 percent job-approval rating?"[9] California was in an economic recession and had a deficit of over $30 billion. The state legislature could not produce a budget on time, and voters were becoming increasingly uneasy about the economic future of the state. Add to this a governor who was perceived as distant, too beholden to special interests, and ineffectual. Then, appearing on the scene was a well-known, highly likable, charismatic, moderate Republican antipolitician, antiestablishment actor/businessman: Arnold Schwarzenegger. Politically, it was the making of a perfect storm.

As Bruce Cain, an expert on California politics, explained in a Brookings Institution symposium on the California recall:

> The reality is there was this big structural problem that the economy [was] on people's minds and people were unhappy with the way the legislature was dealing with the stalemate. They were looking for change. Arnold didn't give them much in the way of specifics, but he kept focusing the critique on the existing government and seemed to offer some hope that there might be change.
>
> Now, the other part of the equation is what happened to Cruz Bustamante because I think everybody believed all along that it was going to be very, very hard for Gray Davis to beat the recall and the laws were just basically stacked against him. He had to get 50% plus one and he only got 47% of the vote last time and he was more unpopular than before. So it's not a big surprise that Gray Davis was recalled, but why didn't Cruz Bustamante do better? Why did he get only 32% of the vote when 44% of the electorate are registered Democrats?
>
> Part of it is the tactical confusion that the party never could figure out whether the strategy was no/no or no/yes. Nine percent of the voters ended up voting no on the recall and then not voting on the second part of the ballot. That certainly didn't help.[10]

The 2005 and 2006 Elections

THE 2005 SPECIAL STATEWIDE ELECTION Governor Schwarzenegger called a special election in November 2005 for the voters to decide on four reform measures he endorsed as well as four others. All eight propositions were placed on the ballot by the signatures of voters. Calling a special election in the middle of a gubernatorial term was unprecedented. Governor Schwarzenegger campaigned actively around the state to encourage voters to support his four reform initiatives:

- *Teacher Tenure (Proposition 74)* would have increased the probationary period for public school teachers from two to five years. It would also make it easier to dismiss teachers who receive two consecutive unsatisfactory performance evaluations.

- *Public Union Dues (Proposition 75)* would have restricted the political uses of public union dues.

- *State Spending and Funding Limits (Proposition 76)* would have amended the California state constitution to limit state spending to the previous year's level plus the average revenue growth of the three previous years. The minimum school funding requirements established in Proposition 98 would be reduced. If the state legislature does not pass the budget, then the previous year's budgeted spending levels would continue.

- *Redistricting (Proposition 77)* would have amended the state constitution to take the power to reapportion legislative districts from the legislature and grant it to a three-member panel of retired judges selected by legislative leaders.

The other propositions include one to re-regulate the electric utilities (Proposition 80), another to require parental notification before an abortion can be performed on a minor (Proposition 73), and competing proposals to lower drug prices, one sponsored by the drug companies and the other by consumer groups and labor unions (Proposition 78 and Proposition 79, respectively). Public opinion on three of the four propositions supported by the governor was consistently negative from midsummer to the election; Proposition 75, however, had favorable prospects in the polls, at least initially. Nonetheless, the voters consistently said in opinion polls that they thought the whole idea of a special election for these particular reforms was a poor idea. On Election Day, voters expressed their dissatisfaction by defeating all eight propositions.

THE 2006 ELECTION The November 2006 elections saw a very dissatisfied electorate vote the majority party out of office in both the U.S. House and Senate, handing control of Congress to the Democratic Party. An unpopular war, a series of corruption and sex scandals implicating prominent Republican office-holders, and a president experiencing sliding job-approval ratings were all factors contributing to the electoral trouncing of the Republican Party. In this political climate, one would think, it would be difficult for a Republican to win the governorship in a "blue" state where Democrats outnumber Republicans by 9 percent. (This translates into a 1.3-million-vote edge!) Add to this scenario the incumbent Republican governor's declining popularity. In the summer of 2005, the California Field Poll reported Schwarzenegger's job approval ratings had plummeted to an all-time low of only 36 percent, with a majority (52 percent) disapproving of his performance in office. When asked if they would be inclined to re-elect the governor, only 39 percent gave a positive response. The level of dissatisfaction among the population was close to the levels reported in 2003 prior to the recall election and the ousting of Gray Davis.

All of this did not portend well for Schwarzenegger's re-election. Yet, in a stunning victory over Democratic state treasurer Phil Angelides, Schwarzenegger not only was re-elected governor, but won by a whopping 17 percent margin! (See Table 4.3 for a breakdown of the votes.) What explains Schwarzenegger's victory?

- *Weak challenger:* Phil Angelides, endorsed by the state Democratic Party and its two Democratic U.S. senators, ran a lackluster campaign. Additionally, he had taken a beating in the Democratic Party primary and had barely eked out a victory against his main opponent, State Controller Steve Westly.

- *Move to the middle:* Schwarzenegger adopted more moderate positions, placing him more in sync with the voters. He is pro-choice on abortion, takes moderate positions on the environment, and decided to cooperate with the Democratically controlled state legislature.

- *"Let Arnold Be Arnold":* Susan Kennedy signed on as Schwarzenegger's chief of staff in November 2005 and realized they had to "restore trust and confidence," set a new agenda, and quickly end countless battles with teachers, law enforcement, firefighters, nurses, and other "stakeholders" angry at the governor from 2005.

- *Independent voters and Democrats:* Angelides failed to win the support of independent voters and lost a quarter of his own party's votes. Even union households nearly split their votes between the two candidates, a surprising result considering unions were major opponents of Schwarzenegger in the 2005 special election.

The 2008 Election

The 2008 election was somewhat unusual, even by California standards. A very popular, young, charismatic candidate, Barack Obama, topped the ticket as the Democratic candidate for the presidency, winning 61 percent of the popular vote, the biggest margin in the state of California since 1964. Yet not a single Republican member of Congress was defeated. Likewise, Californians cast votes on twelve ballot initiatives, passing some, defeating others, with no discernible pattern (see Table 4.3). For

TABLE 4.3 ★ State Ballot Measures, 2008

PROPOSED LAWS APPROVED BY VOTERS:

STATE BALLOT MEASURE NUMBER	BALLOT TITLE
1A	Safe, Reliable High-Speed Passenger Train Bond Act
2	Standards for Confining Farm Animals. Initiative Statute
3	Children's Hospital Bond Act. Grant Program. Initiative Statute
8	Eliminates Right of Same-Sex Couples to Marry. Initiative Constitutional Amendment
9	Criminal Justice System. Victims' Rights. Parole. Initiative Constitutional Amendment and Statute
11	Redistricting. Initiative Constitutional Amendment and Statute
12	Veterans' Bond Act of 2008

PROPOSED LAWS DEFEATED BY VOTERS:

STATE BALLOT MEASURE NUMBER	BALLOT TITLE
4	Waiting Period and Parental Notification Before Termination of Minor's Pregnancy. Initiative Constitutional Amendment
5	Nonviolent Drug Offenses. Sentencing, Parole, and Rehabilitation. Initiative Statute
6	Police and Law Enforcement Funding. Criminal Penalties and Laws. Initiative Statute
7	Renewable Energy Generation. Initiative Statute
10	Alternative Fuel Vehicles and Renewable Energy. Bonds. Initiative Statute

example, in this time of economic crisis, voters approved a very expensive high-speed passenger train bond, they approved the animal-rights-sponsored initiative regulating standards for confining farm animals, they passed the redistricting measure backed by the Republican governor, and they narrowly passed Proposition 8, eliminating the right of same-sex couples to marry.

The *Los Angeles Times*, in an article aptly titled "State's Shifting Political Landscape," described the election results:

> Those unpredictable decisions by voters, however, were accompaniments to the election's main theme: the demographic and ideological shifts that have delivered the state into Democratic hands and demonstrated anew the tough road ahead for the Republican minority.[11]

The Democratic Party is hopeful that it can continue to win the support and allegiance of the overwhelming number of voters who cast their votes for Obama, especially 83 percent of first-time voters (see Table 4.4). Seventy-six percent of those 18–29 years of age voted for Obama compared to only 48 percent of those 65 and older. Young voters and older voters also split on two of the more controversial ballot initiatives: Proposition 4 and Proposition 8. Younger voters strongly opposed the measures requiring parental notification prior to an abortion and the ban on same-sex marriage, while older voters strongly favored those two measures. Some believe we have experienced an electoral generational shift where young voters will continue to be active in electoral politics and will continue to support the Democratic Party and liberal policies.

Others, however, believe the gains made by the Democratic Party in 2008 are situational and do not represent a long-term substantial shift to the Democratic Party. They argue that an unpopular war, an economic recession, a very unpopular Republican president accompanied by Republican control of Congress for six of the eight past years, and a highly popular presidential candidate all are temporary factors favoring the Democratic Party. Only future elections will tell us if the voting patterns and pronounced shift to the Democratic Party, as evidenced in the 2008 election, are of a permanent nature.

Campaigning in California

California politics presents many challenges to those seeking elective office or the passage of a ballot measure. First, the immense size of the state means that statewide propositions, candidates running for statewide office, and those running for federal offices, such as the U.S. Congress and the presidency, must plan campaigns that reach voters throughout the entire state. In fact, California has thirteen distinct media markets, making it very expensive to communicate to its 34 million residents about politics. Second, California's population is very diverse, with many ethnicities, races, cultures, professions, occupations, and interests represented. Successful campaigns must find ways to effectively communicate their platform and messages to all of the 15 million registered voters in the state. And third, California has passed a number of political campaign reform acts in an attempt to regulate campaign spending and to provide public information on contributions and expenditures. These laws have proved beneficial to some and not as helpful to others.

TABLE 4.4 ★ How Californians Voted in the Presidential Election, 2008

	OBAMA	McCAIN
Male	58%	40%
Female	64%	35%
White	52%	46%
African-American	94%	5%
Latino	74%	23%
Asian	64%	35%
Aged 18-29	76%	23%
Aged 30-44	59%	39%
Aged 45-64	60%	38%
65 and older	48%	50%
No college education	61%	37%
College-educated	60%	38%
Democrat	92%	8%
Republican	14%	85%
Independent	64%	31%
L.A. County	67%	31%
Southern California	57%	41%
Bay Area	75%	22%
Coastal California	67%	31%
Inland/Valley	47%	52%
Union household	58%	40%
Nonunion household	64%	34%

SOURCE: MSNBC.msn.com. Data based on 2,309 California exit-poll interviews.

Whatever the challenges of campaigning in California, one thing is certain: California's campaign politics are watched by the nation. California is a campaign trendsetter. The title of a recent *Los Angeles Times* article on the California gubernatorial recall speaks to this phenomenon: "Recall Bid Could Launch Another National Trend," questioning whether other states will follow California's lead again.

Money and Politics: California Style

Jesse Unruh, Speaker of the California Assembly from 1961 to 1968, once said, "Money is the mother's milk of politics." This is especially true in California. Campaigning in California requires money, and lots of it. In fact, California is one of the most expensive states in which to conduct a political campaign. Table 4.5 examines campaign spending in governors' races (primary and general election expenditures) across the United States in 2006. Looking at the table, one can see that California's sixteen primary and general election candidates far outspent candidates in the other states by spending nearly $130 million in the 2006 governor's race. The next most expensive gubernatorial race was in Michigan, where six candidates spent close to $59 million. However, it is important to note the "Cost per Vote" column in the table. Although California hugely outspent all other states, its cost per voter is not the highest. Over 8.6 million Californians voted in the 2006 election—the cost per vote was only $14.87. Compare this number to that of Nevada, whose ten candidates spent just under $15 million on the election but had the highest spending per vote. Because only 500,000 voters went to the polls on Election Day, the cost per vote in Nevada was a whopping $25.52. New York, however, holds the record, spending close to $147 million in the 2002 governor's race at a cost of $31.28 per vote.

Running for governor is not the only campaign that is costly. Running for the California legislature is also very expensive. Incumbents far outspend challengers, and that incumbents' spending has increased over time while spending by challengers has not. On average, challengers spent only a fraction of what incumbents spend. This discrepancy helps to explain the high re-election rates of those elected to the California legislature. By 2008 some competitive races for the California legislature cost in excess of $1 million.

The following are some reasons that California campaigns are so expensive:

MEDIA-DOMINATED CAMPAIGNS Because of the size of the state and its thirteen different media markets, candidates must spend enormous amounts of money producing political ads and buying the broadcast time to air them. During the gubernatorial recall election, it cost approximately $2 million a week to run political ads statewide.[12] And in the 1998 governor's race, the one Republican and three Democratic primary candidates were buying 527 television ads every day in the state's five major media markets—that's nearly 16,000 ads a month. It was estimated that it cost nearly $250,000 to run sixty daily TV ads in Los Angeles, the second most expensive media market in the country; New York is the largest and most expensive media market. In the 2006 governor's race, Schwarzenegger's campaign alone spent 9 million on TV ads in the short time span between July 1 and September 30. As one media consultant described it, "There's a lot to be said for traditional politicking, kissing babies and shaking hands, but you have to get on TV to reach voters."[13]

TABLE 4.5 ★ 2006 Gubernatorial Election Spending for all States*

STATE	# CANDIDATES	TOTAL SPENT	TOTAL VOTE	COST PER VOTE
AL	9	18,542,577	1,250,401	14.83
AK	14	5,070,682	238,307	21.28
AZ	7	3,709,599	1,553,645	2.42
AR	4	9,953,116	749,991	13.27
CA	**16**	**129,026,425**	**8,679,416**	**14.87**
CO	5	7,776,977	1,558,405	4.99
CT	5	14,267,105	1,123,466	12.70
FL	13	41,947,768	4,829,270	8.69
GA	7	29,068,945	2,122,185	13.70
HI	12	6,962,704	344,315	20.22
ID	8	3,614,694	450,832	8.02
IL	11	48,460,979	3,486,671	13.9
IA	8	16,653,062	1,048,033	15.89
KS	10	6,414,413	849,700	7.55
ME	8	4,987,665	550,865	9.05
MD	4	28,939,498	1,788,316	16.18
MA	6	42,313,712	2,243,835	18.86
MI	6	52,816,237	3,801,256	13.89
MN	11	8,670,020	2,202,937	3.94
NE	7	5,206,169	593,357	8.77
NV	10	14,857,797	582,158	25.52
NH	3	2,226,874	404,003	5.51
NM	5	8,428,134	559,170	15.07
NY	8	46,107,945	4,437,220	10.39
OH	8	29,353,950	4,022,754	7.3
OK	6	7,325,496	926,462	7.91

STATE	# CANDIDATES	TOTAL SPENT	TOTAL VOTE	COST PER VOTE
OR	14	14,169,367	1,379,475	10.27
PA	2	40,993,556	4,092,652	10.02
RI	2	4,468,747	386,809	11.55
SC	5	12,574,177	1,091,952	11.52
SD	5	1,295,714	335,508	3.86
TN	17	7,040,983	1,810,140	3.89
TX	11	34,547,895	4,399,068	7.85
VT	6	1,747,404	262,524	6.66
WI	3	16,627,424	2,161,700	7.69
WY	4	1,384,696	193,892	7.14
Total Spent, 36 States		727,552,506		
Average Spending Per State		20,209,792		
Total Vote, 36 States		66,490,690		
Cost Per Vote, All States		10.40		

*Total spent in that state's gubernatorial election cycle by all candidates, divided by the number of voters in the general election.
SOURCE: Gubernatorial Campaign Expenditure Database, compiled by Beyle and Jansen, 2007.

POLITICAL CONSULTANTS Professional campaign managers and various consultants—media consultants, pollsters, fund-raisers, direct mail experts, and voter mobilization professionals—all cost money. Because of California's love of direct democracy, especially the initiative process, many well-known political consultants have established offices in California. There is money to be made in California politics, and candidates and supporters of ballot initiatives know that to win elections you must hire the costly services of top-notch political consultants.

WEAK POLITICAL PARTIES California has a comparatively weak political party system. The reform movement of Governor Hiram Johnson implemented many rules that reduced the organizational strength and clout of political parties within the state. Because of the weak party system in California, the party organizations are minimally involved in organizing and conducting the campaigns of candidates running for office. Additionally, California has a relatively large number of registered voters who decline to affiliate with any political party and consider themselves politically independent. These unaffiliated, independent voters compose about 19 percent of all registered voters. The combination of weak party structure and less party attachment means that candidates themselves have to work harder—spend more money—to reach these voters.

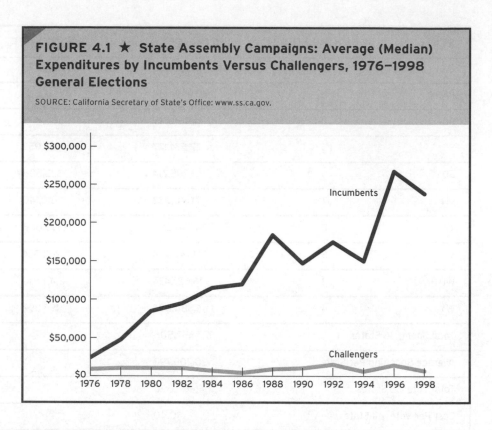

FIGURE 4.1 ★ State Assembly Campaigns: Average (Median) Expenditures by Incumbents Versus Challengers, 1976–1998 General Elections

SOURCE: California Secretary of State's Office: www.ss.ca.gov.

Campaign Finance Reform in California

In order to create more transparency in the electoral process and make public the flow of money in political campaigns, several campaign finance laws have been enacted in California over the past 100 years. Below is a brief description of the various laws.

1893: PURITY OF ELECTIONS LAW This law required that candidates and their committees disclose campaign receipts and expenditures. It covered various illegal activities associated with electioneering: bribery, coercion, fraud, and the secret financing of campaigns. In 1921 legislation was enacted to include the newly added initiative, recall, and referendum campaigns under the Purity of Elections Law. Organizations supporting or opposing statewide propositions would need to disclose their receipts and expenditures.

1949: REGULATION OF LOBBYING One of the most powerful lobbyists ever to walk the halls in Sacramento, Arthur Samish, inadvertently brought about legislation that regulated the practices of lobbyists. Samish posed in *Colliers Magazine*, a very popular magazine, with a ventriloquist's dummy. Samish said to the dummy, "This is my legislature. How are you, Mr. Legislature?" An outraged public and embarrassed legislature passed legislation to curb the influence of lobbyists. A number of amendments were added to the legislation, but little changed until 1974.

1974: POLITICAL REFORM ACT In 1974 a group of reform-minded Californians crafted a statewide proposition that would require the most detailed campaign finance reporting in the nation. Proposition 9 appeared on the ballot during the Watergate scandal, and voters were ready for these reforms. Proposition 9 passed with an overwhelming majority of votes. This act created the Political Reform Division within the office of the secretary of state in order to administer and oversee key provisions of the law. A new independent state agency, the Fair Political Practices Commission, also was created for the purposes of interpreting and enforcing the act.

1988: PROPOSITION 73 In 1988 California voters overwhelmingly passed Proposition 73, which limited contributions to legislative and statewide candidates to $1,000 per donor, including individuals, labor unions, and corporations. A federal judge struck it down in 1990.

1996: PROPOSITION 208 Voters approved this Proposition by a 61 percent vote in 1996. Contributions to candidates from individuals, political parties, committees, corporations, unions, and political action committees (PACS) were limited. Spending limits also were imposed on candidates, although these were voluntary. Candidates who abide by the spending limits are allowed to collect larger contributions, whereas candidates who decide not to comply with the spending limits have lower contribution limits. Proposition 208 was being challenged in the courts when Proposition 34, below, was proposed and passed.

2000: PROPOSITION 34 This proposition was placed on the ballot by the legislature. Spending limits were substantially increased, as were contribution limits. For example, under Proposition 208, individuals were permitted to contribute $1,000 to gubernatorial candidates—$500 if the candidate decided not to abide by the voluntary spending limits. Proposition 34 increased individual contributions to $21,200, more than ten times the contribution limit for presidential contests. Many reform-minded organizations that had supported Proposition 208, such as the League of Women Voters and Common Cause, were opposed to Proposition 34. They saw Proposition 34 as an attempt by the legislature to replace the more stringent Proposition 208 that was under review in the courts. Nevertheless, in November 2000, Proposition 34 passed with close to 60 percent of the popular vote and has replaced the provisions of Proposition 208.

Although it could be argued that Proposition 34 has resulted in less control of campaign financing, California does receive high marks when it comes to laws requiring public disclosure of campaign contributions and expenditures. The Campaign Disclosure Project done at UCLA in 2003 studied the campaign disclosure laws in all fifty states and ranked the states according to their campaign finance disclosure laws. California received a grade of A for its disclosure laws and ranked second in the nation; Washington State ranked first.

Candidates running for federal office must abide by federal campaign laws. For federal office seekers as well, it is important to solicit contributions for their expensive California campaigns. Table 4.6 summarizes the total amount of money collected in the period 2007–2008 by California candidates running for seats in the U.S. House and Senate. Over $300 million was collected during that single year, with Democratic candidates receiving nearly two-thirds of the total. In fact, California's congressional candidates and political parties ranked first in the nation in amount of money collected.

TABLE 4.6 ★ Contributions to Federal Candidates and Political Parties, 2007-2008

CATEGORY	TOTAL	RANK
Total itemized contributions †	$320,107,242	1
Total to Democrats	$210,475,547	1
Percent to Democrats	65.8%	8
Total to Republicans	$108,711,607	1
Percent to Republicans	34.0%	43
Individual donations ($200+)*	$335,070,895	1
Soft money donations	$605,363	1
PAC donations	$18,417,025	2

The "rank" column to the right shows how California compares to all fifty states.
† Includes PAC contributions to candidates, individual contributions ($200+) to candidates and parties, and soft money contributions to parties. To avoid double counting, it does not include individual contributions to PACs.
*Includes contributions to candidates, PACs, and party committees.
SOURCE: The Center for Responsive Politics, www.opensecrets.org.

Voting in California

Of California's 34 million residents, approximately 17 million are registered to vote. In order to register to vote in the state of California you must meet the following criteria:

- You will be eighteen years of age on or before Election Day.

- You are a citizen of the United States.

- You are a resident of California.

- You are not in prison or on parole for a felony conviction.

- You have not been judged by a court to be mentally incompetent to register and vote.

How You Can Register to Vote

Registering to vote is a simple process. Here are the various options:

- Obtain a Voter Registration form from any U.S. post office. Forms are usually set out on counters. Fill out the pre-addressed, stamped form and mail it in.

- Visit a California Department of Motor Vehicles office. The National Voter Registration Act of 1993 (also known as "Motor Voter") permits persons conducting business at a DMV office to register to vote or update their voter registration information. In fact, since 1995 nearly 12.5 million people have registered or reregistered in conformance with this law.

- Go to the secretary of state's Web site and either register online or download a registration form. The Web site address is: www.ss.ca.gov/elections. If you register online, the office will mail you a typed registration form that you will need to sign and mail in. If you download the registration form, you fill it out and mail it in.

You will need to reregister to vote when

- you move;
- you change your name;
- you change your political party affiliation.

You must register at least fifteen days before an election.

Who Votes in California?

Anglo adults constituted 59 percent of the California population in the 2000 Census, but they constituted 72 percent of those who voted in the 2003 recall election. Latinos were 34 percent of the population but only 11 percent of voters. The figures for Asians are similar: 11 percent of the population but only 6 percent of voters. Among minority groups, only African Americans are roughly the same proportion of the two populations: 7 percent of the population and 6 percent of the voting population.[14] The figures on the voting population had been consistent for the last decade.

Why this discrepancy? Research shows that Latino and Asian Californians have a lower probability of registering and voting because of three factors:

- eligibility—a significant proportion of the Latino and Asian populations are not eligible to vote because they are not citizens

- youth—the Latino and Asian populations are both younger, and younger people are much less likely to vote than older people are

- education—the probability of voting increases significantly with a receipt of a college or advanced degree.

Research shows that if you control for these three factors, Latinos vote at rates comparable to Anglos.[15] A fourth factor should be considered in understanding voting rates. In analyzing voting statistics over the decades, political scientists have found that an exciting political race with charismatic candidates has the potential of encouraging more citizens to vote. Apparently, the 2008 presidential election was an example of this. California saw more minority voters registering and voting on Election Day.

TABLE 4.7 ★ 2000 Census data, compared to Turnout Rates for 2003 Recall Election and 2008 Presidential Election

	PERCENT OF POPULATION	PERCENT OF THE VOTE	
RACE	2000 CENSUS	2003 RECALL	2008 PRESIDENTIAL
Anglo	59%	72%	63%
Latino	34%	11%	18%
African American	7%	6%	10%
Asian	11%	6%	6%

THE EVER-EXPANDING GROUP OF VOTERS: THE ABSENTEE VOTER

California now has very liberal absentee voting laws. Prior to 1978, a voter had to have a valid excuse for not voting at his or her designated polling place. You were eligible to receive an absentee ballot if you signed a sworn statement that you were going to be away from your home precinct on Election Day or that you were infirm or bedridden and physically unable to cast a vote in person. All this changed in 1978 when California eliminated the requirement that voters present a valid excuse in order to vote absentee. Now, absentee ballots are available to any voter who wants one. You are permitted to request an absentee ballot for a particular election, or you may request permanent absentee status, meaning that an absentee ballot automatically will be mailed to your home for each election.

From 1962 to 1978, the percentage of absentee voters in primary and general elections averaged slightly under 4 percent of all votes cast. After the change in the law, absentee voting increased substantially. By 1992, about 17 percent of all votes were cast absentee. Of the nearly 9 million votes cast in November 2006, about 42 percent were cast by absentee ballots. What is the impact of this large contingency of absentee voters on campaigns and elections in California?

- Candidates must spend money earlier in the campaign cycle in order to reach absentee voters before they cast their votes. State Senator. Tom McClintock lost a race for state controller by less than one-half of a percentage point because he did not have enough money to buy television ads until the final days of the campaign. Many absentee voters had already mailed in their ballots and did not see his campaign ads until after they had cast their votes.

- Political parties and individual campaigns are targeting absentee voters. More than 2 million voters have permanent absentee status. They are believed to be the most loyal and partisan voters in the state.

- Voters are being encouraged to vote absentee. It is believed that voters who may not want to expend the energy of voting in person at their polling place on Election Day may find it more convenient to vote absentee. MoveOn.org, a liberal online grassroots organization, believes "if we can get the absentee ballot request forms into people's hands, people will be more likely to vote. When it comes down to election day it's just a fact that a lot of people aren't going to vote."[16]

HOW YOU CAN VOTE ABSENTEE To apply for an absentee ballot you may use the application form contained in the sample ballot mailed to your home prior to the election or you may apply in writing to your county elections official. Ballots can be returned by mail or in person to a polling place or elections office within your county on Election Day.

Modernizing Voting Machines

In the March 2002 election, voters approved Proposition 41, the Voting Modernization Bond Act. This act allocates $200 million to upgrade and modernize voting systems throughout the state. In the October 2003 recall election, three types of voting systems were used in California. Of California's fifty-eight counties, thirty-four used some type of optical-scan ballot, twenty counties used some form of punch-card ballot, and only four counties used touch-screen ballots. After the controversial 2000 presidential election and the problem of punch-card voting in the state of Florida—remember those hanging chads?—the state legislature was concerned that if California did not replace its outmoded voting systems, the same calamity might strike here. Presumably, the remaining punch-card ballots and other outdated equipment will be replaced with more accurate voting machines.

What Reforms Are Needed?

It is fascinating to observe electoral politics in California. We live in a state where ballot initiatives are frequently used to make law, bypassing our duly elected representatives and the deliberative process of the legislature. On the November 2008 ballot, voters weighed in on at least twelve propositions on important matters such as same-sex marriage, abortion and parental notification, treatment of farm animals, and renewable energy. Many question whether the initiative process is the best way to make public policy.

Although the legacy of the Progressives included the recall, referendum, and initiative, during the past few decades these tools of direct democracy have been taken over by special interest groups. Some believe that reforms are needed to make it more difficult to recall an elected official or to bypass the legislative branch through the initiative process. Suggested reforms have included the prohibition of paid signature gatherers, judicial review of the proposed initiative before placement on the ballot and increasing the number of required signatures to qualify a recall or initiative for the ballot; for a recall to qualify for the ballot, California law requires the number of signatures to equal 12 percent of the votes cast in the last gubernatorial election, while other states require 25 to 40 percent.

Candidates and initiative campaigns spend enormous amounts of money in hopes of electoral victory. Proposition 34, the campaign finance initiative passed in 2000, substantially increased spending and contribution limits. California's limits on contributions to gubernatorial candidates are far more liberal than federal limits on contributions to presidential candidates. In fact, Californians can contribute more than ten times the amount to gubernatorial candidates than they are permitted to contribute to presidential candidates. Many fear that these high limits will lead to spiraling campaign costs in a state where it is already expensive to campaign.

FOR FURTHER READING

Cain, B. "The California Recall." Interview, Brookings Institution, October 8, 2003.

California Fair Political Practices Commission. "Proposition 34." www.fppc.ca.gov

California Secretary of State's History of Political Reform Division, www.ss.ca.gov/elections

Institute of Governmental Studies. "Recall in California." www.igs.berkeley.edu/library

League of Women Voters of California Education Fund. "Nonpartisan In-Depth Analysis of Proposition 34." www.ca.lwv.org

Lubenow, Gerald C., ed. *California Votes: The 2002 Governor's Race and the Recall That Made History*. Berkeley: Berkeley Public Policy Press, 2003.

Rasky, Susan. Introduction to "An Antipolitician, Anti-establishment Groundswell Elected the Candidate of Change." In *California Votes: The 2002 Governor's Race and the Recall that Made History*, ed. G. Lubenow.

UCLA School of Law, Center for Governmental Studies, and the California Voter Foundation. "Grading State Disclosure 2003: A Comprehensive, Comparative Study of Candidate Campaign Finance Disclosure Laws and Practices in the 50 States." 2003.

ON THE WEB

California Elections and Voter Information: www.sos.ca.gov/elections/ The California Secretary of State offers a comprehensive guide to California elections, including information on how to register to vote.

California General Election Results: http://vote.sos.ca.gov/ Detailed breakdowns of California election results.

The California Voter Foundation: http://calvoter.org/

Fair Political Practices Commission: www.fppc.ca.gov/

Join California: www.joincalifornia.com/

SUMMARY

Campaigning in California poses many challenges. The vast size of the state, the diversity of its population, and ever-changing campaign laws are just a few of the issues facing those waging statewide campaigns. Political campaigns in California are media-dominated and expensive. Candidates and groups involved with ballot measures need to spend excessive amounts of money in order to mount competitive campaigns. The cost of a governor's race in California is second only to New York, with recent gubernatorial races costing upward of $100 million. Running for the state legislature is also increasing in cost; the more competitive races now cost over $1 million.

California voters are becoming less partisan as affiliation with the Democratic and Republican parties declines. Over the years, there has been a slight increase in the number of voters identifying with minor parties that have gained ballot access in California. The group experiencing the largest increase, however, has been independent voters, those declining to state a party affiliation at the time of registration. They now compose over 19 percent of all registered voters in the state. Looking at voting rates among various ethnic groups,

we find that Anglos and African Americans have higher voting rates than Latinos and Asian Americans. Age, educational level, and eligibility help explain the lower voting rates of these populations.

The initiative process has been in place since 1912. Initially, this procedure provided ordinary citizens the opportunity to bypass an unresponsive legislature and directly decide policies. More recently, special interest groups have realized that they could successfully use the initiative process to achieve their policy goals. These groups have the resources necessary to wage competitive initiative campaigns. The state legislature often chooses not to deal with controversial policies, and these issues sometimes appear on ballots as propositions.

California currently operates under a modified closed primary system. The Supreme Court invalidated Proposition 198, which had instituted a blanket primary system. Business groups have put forth Proposition 62, which would have California adopt the Louisiana-style blanket primary. Republicans and Democrats have sponsored Proposition 60, a constitutional amendment that would counter Proposition 62.

Since the liberalization of absentee voting laws, more voters are electing to vote absentee. Absentee voters now make up approximately 42 percent of the California electorate. Recently, with the passage of Proposition 41, voting systems throughout all fifty-eight counties are being modernized. The problematic punch-card voting machines have been decertified by the state and will be replaced by more modern equipment.

California remains a trendsetter in political campaigns and elections. Its campaign financial disclosure laws have been rated the second best in the nation, its recall of Governor Davis spurred recalls of elected officials in other states, and many states follow California's lead in adopting similar ballot initiatives—property tax limits, medical marijuana, term limits, and bilingual education. California is still a state to watch.

PRACTICE QUIZ

1. Which of the following is NOT a reason why political campaigns in California present a challenge to candidates:
   a) the size of the state
   b) the blanket primary system
   c) the diversity of the population
   d) campaign finance reform laws
2. In running for the state legislature, winners and losers spend nearly the same amount of money on their political campaigns.
   a) true
   b) false
3. Political campaigns are so expensive in California because
   a) campaigns need to hire political consultants.
   b) campaigns need to spend a substantial amount of money on media advertising.
   c) political parties are not very involved in the planning and running of campaigns.
   d) all of the above
4. Special interest groups often use the initiative process to achieve their policy objectives.
   a) true
   b) false
5. Which of the following is NOT true about Proposition 34, which deals with campaign finance:
   a) The League of Women Voters and Common Cause supported Proposition 34.
   b) Proposition 34 increased individual contributions to candidates to $21,200.

   c) Proposition 34 has resulted in less control on campaign financing.
   d) Proposition 34 replaced the stricter campaign finance law enacted through Proposition 208.
6. Of California's 34 million people, approximately how many are registered to vote?
   a) 30 million
   b) 25 million
   c) 5 million
   d) 16 million
7. Democrats are the plurality party in California.
   a) true
   b) false
8. The number of voters who decline to state a party affiliation at the time they register is declining.
   a) true
   b) false
9. Most of the Democratic counties encompass major urban areas, whereas most of the Republican counties are more rural in nature.
   a) true
   b) false
10. California presently operates under which of the following primary election systems:
   a) open primary
   b) blanket primary
   c) modified closed primary
   d) fully closed primary

CRITICAL-THINKING QUESTIONS

1. How might the cost of campaigning be reduced in California? Since incumbents spend much more money than challengers, what reforms might level the playing field of campaign politics?
2. What do you think have been the successes and failures of campaign finance laws in California? Do you think that additional reforms are needed? Why or why not?

3. How do you think the increase in unaffiliated voters and the increase in absentee voters will affect campaigns and elections in the future?
4. Why do you think so many states follow California's lead in the areas of ballot propositions and recall efforts? Do you think this is a good or bad development? Explain why.

KEY TERMS

At this point you should have a general understanding of the following concepts and terms:

absentee voter (80)
ballot initiative (64)
blanket primary (62)
campaign finance reform (76)
cross-filing (57)
decline to state (61)

fully closed primary (61)
media-dominated campaign (73)
media market (65)
modified closed primary (62)
Motor Voter (79)
office block ballot (57)

political consultant (73)
political party affiliation (58)
State Central Committees (61)
Voting Modernization Bond Act (81)
weak political parties (75)
winner-take-all (57)

5 The California Legislature

WHAT CALIFORNIA GOVERNMENT DOES, AND WHY IT MATTERS

Consider the following activities of the legislature in 2006:

★ Passed legislation that would mandate a 25 percent reduction in greenhouse gases by 2020.

★ Pressed by the governor to pass a package of emergency legislation to ease prison overcrowding, the legislature adjourned in September without passing any bill on the subject.

★ Passed legislation establishing the framework of a "single payer" health insurance bill for all Californians. (The governor vetoed the bill.)

★ Cooperated with the governor in writing the legislation for five bond issues to appear on the November 2006 ballot. The bond issues authorized over $42 billion in bonds, an unprecedented amount in California, to help rebuild the state's highways and transportation systems, housing, levees, educational buildings, and water/flood-control facilities.

Californians give little if any thought to their legislature. We have a general sense that it is made up of a group of elected individuals who write laws. Beyond that, our knowledge fades, although we believe strongly that the legislature does not work well. In fact, when the Field Poll asks whether they approve of the job the state legislature is doing overall, Californians have responded positively above 40 percent (and just barely so) only once since 2002 in twenty different surveys. Quite often, the proportion stating that they disapprove of the legislature's performance is twice the proportion stating that they approve.

Our lack of knowledge is related to the minimal coverage that legislatures receive in the media. The media find it difficult to cover institutions with multiple members who are doing many different things and have no single voice. They find it much easier to focus on a chief executive who has a press office to provide news-ready stories. Additionally, media coverage of state politics is minimal. Although most people get their news from television, prior to the election of Governor Schwarzenegger no Los Angeles television station had a Sacramento bureau. Since his election, the legislature has been depicted mainly as the fall guy for the governor's initiatives.

Our dissatisfaction with the legislative process is related to the dysfunctional condition of our state. While the legislature is not the principal cause of this state of affairs, it is the most public arena where the consequences are felt. Term limits and voting rules make it difficult for the legislature to function well, leading to gridlock and highly partisan disputes. Americans dislike politics in general and tend to believe that we should all be able to work together to achieve our common goals. Bipartisanship has a lot of appeal, but at the same time citizens want their individual interests forcefully represented against competing interests. We have conflicting expectations of legislatures, and the legislature's attempts to balance these expectations often contribute to our dissatisfaction. Bismarck may well have been correct in suggesting that the making of laws, like the making of sausages, should not be observed.

In reality, legislatures, although poorly understood, play a vital role in our government. The framers of the national constitution, fearing a powerful executive, viewed Congress as the first branch of government and gave it the most significant and most explicit powers, including control of money and the writing of all laws. The fact that the president gets the most attention in the media today and that some congressional powers have gravitated to the president does not negate the fact that Congress is a very powerful body.

Most state legislatures have been modeled on the Congress in structure, process, and functions, and this is true in California, although there are some significant differences, explained below. Ours is a bicameral legislature (a two-house legislature) consisting of the forty-member Senate (sometimes called the upper house, but not by members of the Assembly) and eighty-member Assembly. Like Congress, members of both bodies represent geographically based districts and are elected by winner-take-all elections. As in Congress, bills become law by being approved by both houses and signed by the chief executive. The bulk of the work of each house is done in committees. Each house is organized by party and the party leadership determines committee membership. Compared to Congress in Washington, in the legislature seniority is much less important in determining committee memberships and chairs.

The recent history of the California legislature has been remarkable in its extremes. In the 1960s the legislature was changed from an often corrupt, amateur body to a well-paid, well-staffed professional legislature that was the envy of other states. It was regarded by many as the best state legislature in the country. This was accomplished under the leadership of the Assembly Speaker Jesse Unruh. Yet in 1990 the voters of California passed Proposition 140, imposing term limits on the legislature. While this did not change the basic structure of the legislature, it did change the effectiveness and power of the legislature by reducing the time that legislators are permitted to serve and reducing the size of the staff that makes legislative work possible.

Functions

Legislatures have two principal functions: representation and policy making. The tensions between these make it difficult for a legislature to perform as citizens might wish.

Representation

The legislature is the principal representative institution in our society, although the executive branch and interest groups also lay claim to this function. It is the duty of legislators (also called members, representatives, or assemblypersons or senators) to represent the voters and other residents, collectively known as constituents, within their districts, as well as the dominant interests within these districts. This is easier said than done. In the first place the term *representation* has many meanings. Here we will simplify it to mean that our representative is our counterpart in Sacramento, and that he or she will do what we would do were we there, especially when it comes to influencing legislation or voting. Of course, there are many of us, and we all do not see things the same way. Some of us are wealthy and educated, others destitute. Some see government as the means to solve society's problems; others see government as the main problem.

Furthermore, representatives face many different and difficult issues—gay marriages, lower taxes versus improved services, new highways versus preservation of neighborhoods, more spending on prisons versus lower college tuition. We do not communicate with our representatives very well, and our wishes may have to be intuited rather than known. Under the best of circumstances, knowing what you should do for 800,000 constituents is difficult. Beyond that is the question of whether you should give your constituents what they want—maybe lower taxes and less regulation—or what they need—perhaps higher taxes and improved infrastructure. Political scientists talk about two polar forms of representation: the delegate who tries to find out what constituents want and do only that, and the trustee who tries to use his or her own best judgment to do what is right. Delegates would most often try to provide what constituents want, while trustees would be more inclined to provide for the district's needs. Both orientations involve difficulties, since it is often impossible to know what constituents want, and determining district needs is often influenced by ideology or other subjective factors.

Some legislators identify closely with a particular group and view themselves as representatives of that group: women, ethnic minorities, sexual preference groups. There are others who want to get the representatives' ears: party leaders, the governor, campaign contributors, organized special interests. And those groups are better organized and have better access than average constituents. Large campaign contributors do not give their donations without expecting something in return, so the legislator is unable to ignore them. Ultimately it is the constituents who have the vote, but even this principle has been weakened in recent years because of gerrymandered districts and term limits. Rarely do voters have a realistic chance to keep the good representatives and "throw the rascals out."

In addition to representing our policy views, representatives try to look out for us when we have specific problems with government—not getting an entitlement check, being treated unfairly by an inspector, worrying that a new highway will be built through our living room, being opposed to liquor being sold near our

BOX 5.1 | Keep on Top, Keep in Touch

It is easy to stay on top of what is happening in the legislature by using the Internet. Both houses have Web pages. The Senate page is www.sen.ca.gov; the Assembly page is www.assembly.ca.gov. From these sites you can find out about the legislative process and about the status of individual bills. You can also find out how to stay in touch with your legislators. If you type in your address, the site will tell you who your legislators are and how you can contact them. Another useful site is that of the Legislative Counsel: www.leginfo.ca.gov.

State legislators are surprisingly accessible, especially in the district. If you have an issue for which you want to contact your legislator, be informed, call for an appointment, and be brief and forthright. Do not threaten. Information is helpful, and a good anecdote is always useful! Thoughtful letters are also helpful. E-mail is used too much, and staff can recognize form mail as soon as it is opened.

Of course, working through a lobby is also effective, and you may belong to an organization that lobbies; environmental groups, unions, and student organizations are just a few of many that write, track, and try to influence legislation in their area of concern.

kids' school. This ombudsman function is called "constituency service" or "casework," and it involves intervening with the bureaucracy to solve specific problems. Representatives also try to get favorable treatment for economic interests in their districts—a restaurant owner wants a liquor license that he is being unfairly denied, or a construction company wants to build more buildings at the local state university. Representatives will also take stands on issues that are largely symbolic but still important to their constituents, such as marriages of gays or prayer in schools.

Another important part of representation is being available to constituents. Representatives spend much of their time in their districts; they attend many functions, speak to many groups, educating them about the activities of government, and listen to many constituents in their offices. Constituents and representatives of organized groups also visit with them in Sacramento.

Policy Making

The representatives described above come together to make policy, most obviously through the complex process of making laws, which involves writing bills, holding committee hearings, conducting legislative debates, and adding amendments.

Policy making also involves seeing that legislation is carried out as the legislature intended and looking out for potential problems in the implementation of policy. This function, called oversight, is carried out through a variety of means, including legislative hearings, staff follow-up on constituents' concerns, budgetary hearings, and confirmation hearings.

The job of the legislator involves both representing the district and making policy. It also involves fund-raising. Legislators live in two worlds, Sacramento and their districts, and they have offices in both places. Mail and phone messages are answered from both places. In the districts they listen to the concerns of their constituents on the one hand, and on the other they tell these constituents about government activities, policy, and politics. In Sacramento they also interact with those constituents who travel to the capital as well as representatives of interest groups. Additionally, they work on policy, mostly in committee. Fund-raising takes place largely in the state capital, often involving important interest groups. Most often legislators are in Sacramento Monday through midday Thursday and return to the district for the remainder of the week; however, this varies with the time of the year. Special events often bring them back to their districts. It is necessary to keep a high profile in the district to discourage potential election opponents. The worst charge that can be brought against legislators is that they are ignoring their districts.

Members and Districts

Unlike Congress, both houses of the California legislature are apportioned by population. The state is divided into eighty Assembly districts and forty state Senate districts. In each of these districts a single representative is elected. This means that representatives will be paying attention to local interests, since local voters determine who gets to go and stay in Sacramento. As a former speaker of the U.S. House of Representatives once said, "All politics is local." Local interests often take precedence over statewide interests. Our legislative system is designed to favor local interests.

Legislative elections are winner-take-all elections, which means that minor or third parties are generally excluded from the legislature, even though they may have substantial support statewide. If they cannot muster the most votes in any one district, they will not have a representative in Sacramento.

Most members, if they have previous elective experience, have served on school boards, city councils, or, in the smaller counties, county boards of supervisors. Many are self-selected. Others are tapped by party leaders or interests who see them as viable.

Campaigns can easily cost half a million dollars, and fund-raising is one of the big obstacles to winning an election. The nature of California and the size of the districts, make winning elections by old-fashioned precinct work unlikely. Use of electronic media is also impractical in the larger markets because of cost. Most candidates have campaign consultants and engage in polling and targeted distribution of literature.

Because of the relatively small size of the legislature, the districts are among the largest in the country. Senate districts have over 900,000 constituents, Assembly districts, over 450,000. District lines are drawn by the legislature, often leading to charges of gerrymandering, a term that has been around since the early 1800s, when Massachusetts Governor Elbridge Gerry oversaw a redistricting that benefited his party and resulted in district lines that resembled, in a famous cartoon of the day, a salamander. *To gerrymander* means to draw district lines in a manner that favors one party over another, generally by packing most of the opponent's voters into a few districts and spreading the remainder thinly over the remaining districts. The courts have generally accepted this practice, saying only that districts must be equal in population and must not be drawn to diminish the voting strength of any minority.

Redistricting is done following each census and must pass both houses and be signed by the governor, like any other piece of legislation. The Democrats controlled both houses and the governor's office last time around, but chose to preserve the status quo, which maintained a majority with which they were comfortable. Since the incumbent Republicans were not in danger of losing their seats, they did not challenge the scheme in court. The result was that the vast majority of seats in the legislature are now safe seats for one party or the other, and an incumbent is unlikely to be defeated in the general election.

Most action, therefore, takes place in the primaries, but since the advent of term limits, incumbents rarely face a serious challenge. Knowing that an incumbent assemblyperson will be out of office in no more than six years, the astute challenger waits for that vacancy to occur rather than engaging in an expensive, divisive challenge. If one believes that the real power of voters is to throw the rascals out, then term limits have had an unintended consequence of insuring that that is unlikely to happen. The legislature is more immune from direct electoral challenge than ever before.

Organization

Leadership

The leader of the Assembly is the Speaker, and he or she has a remarkable array of powers, although these are now diminished, since no member of the Assembly occupies his or her position for a long period of time. In an attempt to increase the power of the Speaker by increasing his/her time in the position, in 2003 the Democrats elected a first-term legislator to the speakership. The Assembly Speaker's powers are considerably more extensive than the Speaker of the U.S. House of Representatives. Most notable of these powers—which begin with control over parking spaces and offices—is the almost complete control over establishing committees, assigning members to serve on committees, and removing them if the Speaker chooses. Since the bulk of legislative work is done in committee, members are dependent upon the Speaker if they are to have any meaningful role in the legislature. The Speaker is also the presiding officer when the full Assembly meets and in this role controls debate. If the Speaker does not personally preside he or she designates the person who does. The Speaker also appoints the majority floor leader, who assists in running legislative sessions.

It is difficult to overestimate the extent of the power of the Speaker. This power is used to move bills and can be used to help supporters and hurt opponents. It is also used to raise money, which in turn is used to solidify support. Members find it advantageous to cooperate with the Speaker. The Speaker is elected by the entire membership of the Assembly, but in most cases the outcome is determined in advance by the majority party caucus, all of the members of the majority party meeting together. Only when the majority is split does the full Assembly vote become significant.

The minority caucus elects the Assembly minority leader, who is the public voice of the minority party and who works with the Speaker to determine minority party assignments on committees. The Speaker, however, has the final say.

The other important element of the leadership is the Assembly Rules Committee, which is made up of nine members, four elected by each caucus plus a chair appointed by the Speaker. Its responsibilities include hiring staff and assigning bills to committees and reviewing legislative rules. Rarely does this committee operate independently of the Speaker's wishes.

The organization of the Senate is similar, but the leader, the president pro tempore, does not have the absolute power that the Assembly Speaker does. Many of the Speaker's powers in the Assembly rest with the Rules Committee in the Senate. Yet in recent years the president pro tempore—most notably John Burton—has become the most influential legislator, largely because of the impact of term limits, which have created an Assembly that is far less experienced than the Senate. Assembly members have a maximum of six years' experience. Senators have often been in the Assembly first and then have an additional eight years to serve. By the time a senator becomes a Senate leader, he or she may have had ten or twelve years' experience in Sacramento. John Burton, who may be the last of his breed, had far more experience than that, including experience in the U.S. Congress.

Committees

The bulk of legislative work is done in committees. Committees allow for greater specialization, greater expertise of those involved, and greater attention to detail. In 2007–2008 there were twenty-nine standing or permanent committees in the Assembly and twenty-two in the Senate (see Table 5.1). Each member sits on several standing committees. In addition to standing committees, there are select committees that exist to study specific issues, and joint committees to look at issues that concern both houses. Members may serve on a dozen or more of these less important committees.

Committees are at the heart of groups of players often referred to as issue networks. These networks consist of committee members and staff, senior members of the respective executive-branch agency, and interest groups concerned with issues in a committee's jurisdiction. The bulk of policy details are worked out in these networks. Lobbyists and bureaucrats tend to be specialists. They generally spend their careers in a single subject area and are experts in this area. It would be unusual for someone who has spent a career in transportation to move to education. Previously, legislators would spend their careers in specific issue areas as well. Term limits have changed that, or rather have shortened the length of careers. While policy is still worked out in these networks, power has shifted to those with greater experience and expertise—namely, lobbyists and bureaucrats. The less experienced and less knowledgeable legislator is now more dependent than before on these individuals for policy details. Experienced staff can help, but often staff members are no more experienced than legislators.

Staff

Prior to Proposition 140, the staff of the California legislature was the best in the nation. The proposition required a staff cut of 40 percent and resulted in layoffs and the departure of many of the best staffers, especially the experts committees relied on. Staff is still a significant factor in the legislature, and over the years, it has inched back toward its previous size.

Without staff, the legislature could not do its job. Staff is crucial in both the policy-making and representative functions of the legislature. All legislators have staff in both their Sacramento and district offices to help with constituency contacts, including casework, scheduling appearances, and answering mail and phone

TABLE 5.1 ★ STANDING COMMITTEES OF THE CALIFORNIA LEGISLATURE, 2007-2008

STATE SENATE

Agriculture	Judiciary
Appropriations	Labor and Industrial Relations
Banking, Finance and Insurance	Legislative Ethics
Budget and Fiscal Review	Local Government
Business, Professions and Economic Development	Natural Resources and Water
Education	Public Employment and Retirement
Elections, Reapportionment and Constitutional Amendments	Public Safety
Energy, Utilities and Communications	Revenue and Taxation
Environmental Quality	Rules
Governmental Organization	Transportation and Housing
Health	Veterans Affairs
Human Services	

ASSEMBLY

Committee on Aging and Long-Term Care	Committee on Insurance
Committee on Agriculture	Committee on Jobs, Economic Development, and the Economy
Committee on Appropriations	
Committee on Arts, Entertainment, Sports, Tourism, and Internet Media	Committee on Judiciary
	Committee on Labor and Employment
Committee on Banking and Finance	Committee on Local Government
Committee on Budget	Committee on Natural Resources
Committee on Business and Professions	Committee on Public Employees, Retirement and Social Security
Committee on Education	
Committee on Elections and Redistricting	Committee on Public Safety
Committee on Environmental Safety and Toxic Materials	Committee on Revenue and Taxation
Committee on Governmental Organization	Committee on Rules
Committee on Health	Committee on Transportation
Committee on Higher Education	Committee on Utilities and Commerce
Committee on Housing and Community Development	Committee on Veterans Affairs
Committee on Human Services	Committee on Water, Parks, and Wildlife

calls from constituents. In addition, committees have staff, called consultants, to help with the policy work of that committee, and consultants are critical components of the issue networks. Each Assembly member is allotted an office budget of just over $210,000. Additional staffing depends on the generosity of the Speaker. In addition, the house leaders and caucuses have staff. This staff, which numbered 170 for the Democrats in 2004, helps with bill analysis for individual members and public relations for individual members as well as the party.

There are over 2,200 legislative aides. It is not unusual for majority legislators to have thirteen or fourteen staff. Minority members may have only four or five. While most aides are modestly paid, some, especially highly valued committee consultants, make over $140,000. These aides are supplemented with members of the prestigious Assembly and Senate Fellows program and many college interns.

There are three important and well-regarded groups of staff who are nonpartisan and work for the entire legislature. The first is the Legislative Analyst's Office, which analyzes budget proposals and the fiscal impact of ballot propositions. The second is the Legislative Counsel, which helps write bills, analyze ballot propositions, and provide legal advice. Third is the State Auditor's office, which does management and fiscal audits of the executive branch.

The Legislative Process

There are three types of items that may pass the legislature: bills, which if successful become laws; constitutional amendments, which require a two-thirds vote of both houses and a referendum by the voters; and resolutions, which are largely symbolic expressions of opinion. For the remainder of this section we are concerned largely with bills.

Bills are introduced only by legislators, even if the content was originally proposed by someone as politically important as the governor. Indeed, bills are often not written by the person that introduces them. Many bills may be written by, or in conjunction with, lobbyists, and the nonpartisan Legislative Counsel's office may help in drafting language. Senators are limited to introducing sixty-five bills in a two-year session, while Assembly members may introduce only thirty. Bills may be introduced for a variety of reasons, such as impressing constituents or paying off a political favor, and most go nowhere. During the 2005–2006 legislative session, 5,517 bills were introduced in the legislature. About 35 to 40 percent of them became law. Bills must pass both houses with identical language before they are forwarded to the governor for his signature.

Once bills are introduced, the rules committee of the appropriate house assigns the bill to a standing committee or perhaps two committees, depending on their content. The bill is also numbered and printed. Committees cannot act on a bill until it has been in print for thirty days to allow comment from interested parties. Committees hold hearings, scrutinize the language carefully to make sure that it says what members intend, add amendments, and pass or reject bills. An absolute majority of the committee must vote favorably to report a bill out. If a bill is reported out of committee, it goes to the floor for discussion by the entire house. Amendments may be added at this time. Amendments require only a majority vote. Bill passage requires an absolute majority (forty-one in the Assembly, twenty-one in the Senate). Once a bill has passed one house, it goes to the other house for similar consideration. If a bill is successful in both houses and the wording is the same, it goes to the governor for his signature. If he vetoes a bill, then it requires a two-thirds vote in each house to override the veto.

Most likely, a bill passing both houses will have different wording. In this case one house may acquiesce to the wording of the other house, or a conference committee will be established to work out the differences. A conference committee consists of three members from each body. The Assembly members are appointed by the Speaker, and Senate members are appointed by the Senate Rules Committee. They suggest compromise language that must pass both houses. If this attempt fails, two additional attempts may be made before the bill is put to rest.

This is the textbook approach. However, much legislation is able to shortcut some of these steps, especially near the end of a legislative session, when bills tumble over one another and deals are made in back rooms in a rush to adjourn. Many bills reappear as amendments to other bills, with even less public attention than in the normal process. At this time, the party leaders become more important because they are able to grease the skids for compromises and logrolling. (Logrolling is vote trading, the process in which members exchange votes—the classic "You vote for my bill, and I will vote for yours.")

A classic end-of-session legislative tactic is to hijack a bill and then "gut and amend" it. A bill that started out to deal with state courts could suddenly reappear—with no public notice or hearings—as a bill offering in-state tuition to undocumented immigrants. Or take 2001 bill AB 1389 (insiders and insider wannabes always refer to bills by numbers, like AB 1389 or SB 1785). This bill started out dealing with squid fishing and came back as a bill dealing with transferring public lands for development of a cruise ship terminal in San Francisco.[1]

Differences from Congress

While the California legislature is modeled closely on the national legislature, there are important differences, and, collectively, these make the California legislature a weaker body.

Term Limits

Unlike members of Congress, who can serve as long as they are re-elected, California legislators are limited to three two-year terms in the Assembly and two four-year terms in the Senate. Term limits were enacted by the passage of Proposition 140 in 1990. There were numerous reasons for the success of this proposition. In part it was a reaction to the highly effective Assembly Speaker Willie Brown, a flamboyant African American who was immensely unpopular with conservative voters. In part it was a reaction against divided government (a Republican governor and a Democratic legislature) and gridlock. Partly it was a reaction against the large fund-raising efforts of incumbents. Partly it was a reflection of a national trend against entrenched incumbents. Finally, it was a belief among some Republicans that term limits would be a way to get rid of the Democratic majority.

Item Veto

In Washington, the president has to sign or reject bills passed by Congress in their entirety. He cannot approve parts that he likes and reject parts that he dislikes. In California, as in most states, the governor has a line-item veto on appropriations, including those in the budget. This power allows the governor to reduce or eliminate a specific spending item, although he cannot increase items. This means that the legislature cannot force the governor's hand by including an item that he opposes in a larger bill, most of which he supports.

Apportionment and District Size

Both houses of the California legislature are apportioned by population, unlike Congress, in which the Constitution allots two senators to each state, regardless of size. Wyoming, with about the same number of residents as Long Beach, has the same number of senators as California, which is about seventy times larger. Since California is so populous (more than 37 million people) and since its legislature is relatively small, its legislative districts are among the largest in the nation. Senate districts have over 900,000 constituents, while Assembly districts contain over 450,000 residents. New Hampshire, with 400 members in its lower house, has one representative for about every 3,000 residents. While its representatives are very accessible and elections are not expensive, most cannot wield very much influence in their very large chamber. California senators, unlike any other legislative body, represent more constituents than members of Congress and more than the U.S. senators of seven states. This means that they are considerably less accessible than their counterparts in other states and that their elections are considerably more expensive.

The fact that both houses are apportioned by population has led some informed observers to suggest that a unicameral legislature of 120 members would make more sense. This would result in smaller districts and increased accessibility among legislators.

Media Visibility

In Washington the president dominates the news. The media interpret the national government by focusing on the president. Members of Congress are generally used to give more depth to a presidential story. Most often, these are party leaders, committee chairs, or the occasional legislator who has managed to make a name for himself or herself on a given issue.

The same is true in Sacramento, but the difference is that the statewide media rarely cover news in Sacramento. As mentioned earlier, until the election of Governor Schwarzenegger, no Los Angeles television station had a Sacramento bureau. Only the four party leaders receive air time, and since they hold their positions for so few years, the public has difficulty knowing who they are. Consequently, most of what happens in Sacramento occurs out of the spotlight.

Court Appointments

Some of the greatest legislative battles in Congress have been the Senate's hearings to confirm judicial appointments, especially to the Supreme Court. In California many judges are elected. Those that are appointed by the governor are approved by a judicial council. The Senate does get to approve many other gubernatorial appointments to executive positions and regulatory boards and commissions.

Filibusters

In the U.S. Senate—a body that is not apportioned on the basis of one person, one vote—41 percent of the members, potentially representing slightly more than 30 million people (fewer than the 33 million represented by California's two senators), can block the passage of most legislation. California has no such provision. Indeed, in most cases the majority rules. The principal exceptions are the budget and raising taxes, which require a two-thirds vote.

Initiatives

Unlike the U.S. Constitution, the California constitution provides several means of taking issues directly to the voters. Most significant is the initiative. This is important in the legislative context, because those who are thwarted in their attempts to get legislation passed can always threaten to take it, or an even more extreme measure, to the voters. This tactic can persuade the legislators to vote for measures that they would otherwise oppose and significantly weakens the legislature.

Seniority

In the U.S. Congress, seniority is used as an informal rule in appointing members to committees and choosing each committee's majority and minority leaders; once members are appointed to their committee positions, they are almost never removed. In the California legislature, both the appointment and removal power resides with the Assembly Speaker and Senate majority leader, with seniority playing a much smaller role. Both the Speaker and the Senate majority leader in 2007 and 2008 removed members of both parties from committee leadership roles for disagreeing with the leadership over various issues.

Problems, Real and Perceived

When voters pay attention to the legislature, it is most often to complain or criticize its actions. At times these objections are on target, at times not. State government currently is dysfunctional, and the legislature is an easy target. It is easy to be repulsed by the contentious process of arriving at legislative agreements. Moreover, the misbehavior of any one of the 120 legislators is amplified out of proportion and reflects badly upon the whole institution. Individual members often attack the legislature to play up their own importance, or they run for the legislature by running against it.

Among the most common criticisms of the legislature are the following:

Money

In the California legislature, as is the case throughout American politics, money carries a great deal of clout. Elections are expensive, and the money for elections comes from many sources, including the candidate's personal wealth, small contributions from many individual contributors, and larger contributions from business, unions, and other special interests. Large contributions are generally given to insure support for a particular interest. While legislators claim that their vote cannot be bought and that contributors are only buying access, that claim would be difficult to support, as the previous chapter has shown. Moreover, simply having access that the ordinary voter does not have is a significant advantage. We have the best legislature that money can buy, and short of moving to public financing of campaigns, those with money will always have an advantage over those who do not.

Money is usually distributed to those who support the position of a given interest or to those who might be swayed by the offer of monetary support. It also goes to party leaders, who then distribute it to solidify their support both within their party and against the other party. Indeed, it was the amassing of a large war chest that contributed to the distrust and dislike of Speaker Willie Brown and led to the proposing and passing of Proposition 140, setting term limits. However, term-limited legislators, having little background in fund-raising, have become more dependent than their predecessors on large donations from special interests. Jesse Unruh once said, "If you can't take their money, eat their food, drink their booze . . . and then vote against them, you don't belong here." On this basis there are probably more legislators now than before that "don't belong here."

Term Limits/Lack of Experience

It was felt that term limits would remove a remote professional class of legislators and bring in a new breed of legislator with closer ties to their districts. The ballot argument said that term limits "would remove the grip that vested interests have over the legislature" and create a "government of citizens representing their fellow citizens."[2] The expectations for this proposition were overhyped, and the results were unfortunate.

Legislative politics works best as an ongoing game among a relatively stable group of experienced players. Many of the aphorisms about politics, such as "Politics makes strange bedfellows" and "Don't burn your bridges," are based on ongoing relationships played out over a period of years. Over time legislators not only learn the game and how to play it, but also whom they can trust, whom they can work with, and whom they should avoid. This knowledge facilitates cooperation across party lines. Legislators come to learn that not all good is on their side of the aisle and not all evil on the other side. In a short six years, legislators cannot all learn that; the players change too rapidly. The people who can work out effective compromises seldom emerge, and even if they were to emerge, they would not know whom to work with.

Nor can effective leadership emerge in six years. In recent years the legislature has chosen freshmen legislators as committee chairs and as Speaker. But a freshman legislator, no matter how talented, cannot effectively lead a large collegial body. Contrast this with Congress, where members may serve a decade or more before assuming a leadership position, and where Speaker Nancy Pelosi was first elected in 1987. Had she been in Sacramento, she would have been out of the Assembly for more than a decade by now.

Nor in six short years is there time to develop expertise in process or subject matter, the ordinary skills of a legislator. In Congress, by the time they assume leadership positions, members know the subject matter, the history, and the players. By the time ten years have passed in Sacramento, members have been gone for four years. This dilemma was summed up by a lobbyist:

> I feel sorry for the first-term members who faced the energy crisis. They don't know who's smart; they don't know who knows what they're doing; they don't know the policy; they don't know the politics. And they are faced with a crisis.[3]

In Sacramento, effective power has shifted to the Senate, whose members are more experienced. Senators can spend eight years in the Senate, and many have already spent six years in the Assembly. But real power has shifted from the legislature to the permanent establishment—the bureaucracy and interest groups. Members in these institutions may spend a career in Sacramento outlasting five sets of Assembly members. Much as they were dissatisfied with the legislature, it is doubtful that the voters wanted to shift power to either of those two groups.

If there has been a positive aspect to term limits, it is in the increased diversity of the legislature. The percent of Latino legislators rose from 6 percent in 1990 to 23 percent in 2008, the percent of women in the legislature increased from 17.5 percent to 32 percent in the same time period. The new Speaker of the Assembly, Karen Bass, is female, as is the senate majority caucus chair, Jenny Oropeza.[4]

Partisanship

Many believe that partisanship has increased in the legislature in recent years. This trend is often attributed to current districts being safe, electing representatives who cannot lose in a general election and are responsive only to their party's majority, which determines the primary election outcome and which is more extreme than the average voter. Safe districts result in increased partisanship and less willingness to compromise.

As usual, the issue is more complex than this, although more competitive general elections might result in the election of more moderates. The problem is not that there are strong partisans in the legislature. It has always been so. But in recent years, the quality of public discourse has become less civil, and the participants have come to have less regard for their opponents and have become less willing to work with them. Part of this incivility is a reflection of national politics brought on by the fact that the two national parties' leadership has become homogeneous and much more polarized. Part may also be attributed to term limits. Recognizing that they will not have to deal with them for years into the future, legislators make less effort to develop civil working relationships with their opponents.

But legislators should be partisan. We elect representatives on a partisan basis. Parties should stand for something. If we vote for Republicans rather than Democrats, then the Republicans should deliver on their partisan promises. Even those who rail against partisanship still want their interests to be forcefully proposed and protected.

Some of the greatest legislatures in the world, such as the British Parliament, are fiercely partisan and yet manage to govern. The difference is that in those bodies, the majority is permitted to govern. In our system, partisanship can and often does lead to gridlock.

Gridlock, Minority Rule, and Lack of Accountability

Our system has many checks and balances that make it difficult for a majority to rule, for our Founding Fathers distrusted the masses as much as they distrusted a strong executive. They were more comfortable with a system that did not work well than with a system that might do something that they did not like. While California does not have the filibuster that thwarts majority rule in Congress, it does have two major checks on effective majority governance. One is that the legislature and the governor are elected separately and may represent different parties. The second is that a two-thirds majority is required to get budget or appropriation measures passed or taxes raised, requiring, in the absence of an overwhelming one-party majority, that the two parties work together to produce a budget.

Perhaps no other provision of California governance has contributed more to the dysfunctional state of the state than this provision. Californians may elect a majority in the legislature and even a governor of the same party, but unless that party controls two-thirds of each house, it cannot control fiscal policy. Voters blame the majority party for gridlock, when in fact the control rests with the minority party. This provision is even more restrictive than the filibuster that often locks up the U.S. Senate. The filibuster can work only with 40 percent of the Senate actively backing it, while California fiscal policy is held hostage to a one-third minority sitting on its collective hands, insuring gridlock. As Peter Schrag relates it:

More than any other structural flaw, it [the two-thirds rule] diffused accountability and brought on much of the budgetary gridlock that California became notorious for in the 1980s and early 1990s.[5]

It also produced the gridlock that led to Proposition 13 and the frustration that led to Proposition 140.

Initiatives

Initiatives are often used to bypass the legislative process. That this can be done reduces the need to carefully construct legislation that can pass. Moreover, initiatives have passed that have weakened the legislature or weakened the legislature's ability to make responsible policy. Proposition 140, which instituted term limits, greatly weakened the ability of the legislature to function effectively. Propositions 13 and 98 each limited the ability to make responsible fiscal policy, the first by limiting the use of a stable tax tool, the second by locking up a huge chunk of the available funds for a single purpose.

We will probably see many more propositions, since it may be easier to get agreement with a majority of the voters than two-thirds of the legislature. We appear to be in a destructive cycle. The voters feel dissatisfied with the legislature and pass a proposition that makes the legislature work less effectively. That makes voters more dissatisfied, and they vote for another proposition. And so on.

Conclusion

The legislature serves two principal functions: policy making and representation. The different requirements of these two functions create tensions. Legislators are also pressured by the needs versus the wants of the district; state versus local interests; the demands of interest groups, campaign contributors, party leaders, and the governor. California is a large state with diverse needs. Legislative districts are among the largest anywhere. These factors turn the making of policy into a complex and often unseemly process. It is a process moved by imperfect humans that will always be somewhat flawed. Even the highly regarded legislature before term limits passed some bad legislation and left problems unaddressed.

Yet it could work better than it does. The state is dysfunctional, and in many ways the legislative process contributes to this. It is valid to ask if the legislature is the creator or the victim of this dysfunction. In large part, this problem has been created by outside forces. Term limits and the two-thirds vote requirement for passing appropriation and tax legislation are the most notable outside factors. The declining level of civility in the legislature is a reflection of the impact of term limits and of the increasing political polarization in the nation. But it is also caused in part by the safe districts created in the last legislative redistricting, a process carried out for the most part in the legislature. Legislators representing safe districts do not have to pay attention to moderate elements in their party or voters from the opposition party. Finally, individuals are responsible for their own behavior. Regardless of outside forces, individual legislators of good will could make a difference.

As long as we have the current structure and policy limits placed on the legislature, often by initiatives, it is difficult to see how the system can improve. Given the diverse nature of the state and an electorate that tends to elect a legislature that is divided on many important issues, which in a democracy should be a plus, positive change cannot be anticipated. Moreover, the public has little understanding of legislative functions or the legislative process, making positive change through the initiative process even more unlikely. Indeed, more draconian measures, such as a part-time legislature, have been suggested. As the popular cartoonist Walt Kelly's Pogo said, "We have met the enemy and he is us."

FOR FURTHER READING

Cain, Bruce E., and Roger G. Noll, eds. *Constitutional Reform in California: Making State Government More Effective and Responsive.* Berkeley: Institute of Governmental Studies Press, 1995.

California Journal and State Net. *Roster and Government Guide.* Sacramento: California Journal, 2004.

Institute of Governmental Affairs. "IGS Goes to Sacramento to Assess Ten Years of Term Limits." *Public Affairs Reports* 42, no. 3 (Fall 2001).

Muir, William K., Jr. *Legislature: California's School for Politics.* Chicago: University of Chicago Press, 1982.

Schrag, Peter. *California: America's High-Stakes Experiment.* Berkeley: University of California Press, 2006.

———. *Paradise Lost: California's Experience, America's Future.* New York: New Press, 1998.

Wilson, E. Dotson. *California's Legislature.* Sacramento: Office of the Chief Clerk, California State Assembly, 2000.

ON THE WEB

Assembly Democrats: www.democrats.assembly.ca.gov
Assembly Republicans: www.republicans.assembly.ca.gov
California State Senate: www.sen.ca.gov
California State Assembly: www.assembly.ca.gov
Legislative Counsel: www.leginfo.ca.gov
    The Legislative Counsel of California's official site, maintained by law.
Rough & Tumble: rtumble.com
    Daily summary of California news
Senate Democrats: www.democrats.sen.ca.gov
Senate Republicans: www.republicans.sen.ca.gov
University of California, Berkeley, Institute of Governmental Studies, Library: http://igs.berkeley.edu/library/

SUMMARY

Legislatures are not well understood but are critical to a democratic form of government. Indeed, a working legislature is practically a definition of democratic government. The California legislature, like most state legislatures, is modeled on Congress.

- It is bicameral.
- Members are elected from geographically based districts.
- Unlike the U.S. Congress, both houses are based on population.

Legislators must both represent their constituents and make policy. These two items are not always linked. In representing their districts, members must decide whether to follow the wants or the needs of their constituents and whether to follow directions from the district or use their own best judgment. Poor communication from constituents makes these actions difficult. Legislators have offices both in Sacramento and in their districts.

The California legislature was once the envy of most states, the most professional of all state legislatures. Proposition 140, the term-limit proposition, greatly weakened the legislature by limiting members to serving six years in the Assembly and eight in the Senate. As a result, legislators are always inexperienced compared to the bureaucracy and lobbyists.

The California legislature is relatively small and so has some of the largest legislative districts in the world (over 900,000 constituents for the Senate and over 450,000 for the Assembly). These districts are gerrymandered to provide safe seats for both Republicans and Democrats.

The leader of the Assembly, the Speaker, is elected by all of the members, but the majority party caucus usually determines the outcome. The Speaker controls most of the resources and is very powerful, although term-limited like all of his colleagues. In the Senate, the president pro tempore shares powers with the Senate Rules Committee.

The bulk of legislative work is done in committees. Bills are read and amended here. Committees are the heart of a group of individuals—lobbyists, staffers, members, and bureaucrats—that make and control policy in a given area.

Professional staff, which perform the bulk of the work, makes the legislature possible. Some work in districts, some in members' offices, some for committees, and some for the leadership. The best-paid are usually experts working for committees.

Bills are introduced by members and sent to committees. They must pass the floors of both houses with identical wording before they are sent to the governor for his signature. If he vetoes a bill, it takes a two-thirds vote of each house to override it. Budget, appropriation, and tax bills also require a two-thirds vote, giving the minority party immense power in the legislature and making it difficult for the majority party to govern.

The state legislature is different from Congress in that it is term-limited and the governor has a line-item veto—he can cut or eliminate any item in a budget bill without rejecting the entire bill. The legislature does not have a filibuster rule like the U.S. Senate's, which requires an absolute 60 percent majority to cut off debate and pass a bill. However, the two-thirds requirement on money bills has a similar impact in thwarting the majority. California also has the initiative process that allows the legislative process to be bypassed, most often by interests with deep pockets.

The effectiveness of the California legislature is limited by

- term limits;
- lack of experience;
- the two-thirds vote rule in budgetary matters, which
  - ➤ keeps the majority party from governing,
  - ➤ makes accountability difficult,
  - ➤ increases partisanship and the power of big money.

PRACTICE QUIZ

1. An item veto allows
   a) the governor to reject any single item in an appropriations or budget bill.
   b) the Speaker or the president pro tempore to pull any single item from the agenda.
   c) a single member to block a single piece of legislation by signing a written objection.
   d) a petition by a group of ten legislators to block any single piece of legislation.

2. Proposition 140
   a) limits the time that legislators can serve in Sacramento.
   b) limits the legislature from raising property taxes.
   c) sets aside 40 percent of the budget for education purposes.
   d) requires the Speaker to assign staff to the minority party.

3. The legislature is composed of
   a) eighty members in the Senate and forty in the Assembly.
   b) 120 members in a single body.
   c) sixty members in each body.
   d) eighty members in the Assembly and forty in the Senate.

4. A two-thirds vote is needed to pass
   a) appropriation bills.
   b) budget bills.
   c) tax bills.
   d) all of the above.

5. Partisanship in the legislature
   a) has declined because of apportionment.
   b) has declined because of the blanket primary now in effect.
   c) has led to greater ease in getting budgets improved.
   d) has increased in recent years.

6. The power of the Speaker of the California Assembly includes all of the following *except*
   a) the power to assign parking spaces.
   b) the power to assign office space.
   c) the power to assign members to committees but not to remove them during the current term.
   d) the power to assign a member to a committee against both the member's wishes and the wishes and needs of his or her constituency.

7. Proposition 140 resulted in all of the following *except*
   a) an increase in office budgets.
   b) the establishment of term limits.
   c) a reduction of committee staff and personal staff.
   d) laying off some of the most knowledgeable staff experts from committees.

8. The legislative process is biased in favor of
   a) the speaker's legislation, provided he or she can get sufficient minority support for a two-thirds majority.
   b) the status quo.
   c) change that interest groups' favor.
   d) legislation proposed by the governor, who can introduce a limited number of bills directly to both houses, bypassing some of the steps of the legislative process.

9. California has some of the largest legislative districts in the nation. This means that
   a) elections in California tend to be expensive.
   b) citizen access to legislators is unusually good because legislators need to face the voters so often.
   c) staff levels are unusually high to handle the volume of business from constituents.
   d) California has an unusually large number of legislators.

10. Term limits have resulted in the following:
    a) an increase in expertise among legislators, who have only a few years to make a name for themselves;
    b) an increase in citizen legislators, people with little or no political experience who are able to run because seats are open;
    c) an increase in staff members, who are needed to help legislators with little experience;
    d) a decline in the knowledge needed to pass good quality legislation.

CRITICAL-THINKING QUESTIONS

1. Should a legislator vote for what his/her constituents want or what his/her constituents need?
2. Who should apportion the legislature?
3. What criteria should be used to apportion a legislature?
4. Should a legislator take orders from constituents or use his or her own best judgment, even if it is unpopular?
5. How much access should lobbyists have to legislators?
6. When should a legislature have rules that allow a minority to block legislation?

KEY TERMS

At this point you should have a general understanding of the following concepts and terms:

apportionment (94)
Assembly Rules Committee (90)
Assembly Speaker (90)
bicameralism (86)
committees (91)
gerrymander (89)

gridlock (98)
"gut and amend" (94)
lack of accountability (98)
line-item veto (94)
minority rule (98)
representation (87)

Senate president pro tempore (91)
staff (91)
term limits/Proposition 140 (91)
two-thirds vote (95)
veto (93)

6

The Governor and the Executive Branch

WHAT CALIFORNIA GOVERNMENT DOES, AND WHY IT MATTERS

Consider the following activities in the executive branch of our state government:

★ Governor Schwarzenegger holds a fund raiser in New York; it costs $50,000 to attend.

★ Governor Schwarzenegger is asked to pardon a woman convicted of killing a man who raped and beat her.

★ Governor Schwarzenegger proposes that the legislature approve over $30 billion in new infrastructure bonds in 2007, on top of the $42 billion approved on the November 2006 ballot.

★ Governor Schwarzenegger calls for universal health insurance coverage in 2007, including insurance for undocumented residents of the state.

★ Governor Schwarzenegger removes the assertive, consumer-oriented head of the Bureau of Automotive Repair.

When Governor Schwarzenegger gave his first State of the State address in January 2004, the event was covered by several Los Angeles TV stations. This coverage, however, was an anomaly attributable to his movie-star status and the financial morass that the state was in. On most occasions there would have been no television coverage of this entire event in southern California. While he is the most visible political figure in the state, the governor is almost invisible in comparison to the president of the United States.

The Invisible Governor?

There are a number of reasons for this invisibility. We are dependent upon the media for most of what we know about our government, and for the most part the media in the state are not interested in state politics or governance. From the media's perspective, there is little that is newsworthy about Sacramento: it is a long way from the major population centers of the state, and what happens there just does not capture the audience the way a good car chase does. The media work best by focusing on a well-known or riveting personality. But the governor is often perceived as boring—think of governors Davis, Wilson, and Deukmejian, and if you cannot remember them, that may have something to do with the media coverage they received. With the exception of U.S. senators, long-serving, high-visibility politicians are rare in our term-limited government.

The president's job is often divided into two roles: head of government and head of state. So, too, the governor, but, while the head of government role is similar in both cases, the head-of-state role is vastly different; and it is that role that gives the president most of his visibility.

The role of the head of government is to "govern"—that is, to develop policy, get it passed through the legislature, and implement it in the bureaucracy. It is often divisive. Think of the prime minister of Great Britain, who not only develops policy, gets it passed, and implements it, but actually appears on the floor of Parliament to answer questions, often shouted, from his own and the opposition party. In contrast, the queen is the head of state in Great Britain. Her role is highly visible, ceremonial, important for bringing people together. She cuts ribbons, attends public events, greets foreign visitors, participates in parades. In fact, this is her major role. Most of the time when you see the president between campaigns, it is in his role as head of state: welcoming the troops home, attending funerals, dedicating buildings, posing for pictures with foreign dignitaries, making major or minor public announcements. Being head of state is largely a symbolically positive, noncontroversial role offering lots of photo ops for the media. In this role the president represents the entire nation, symbolically speaking and acting for all of us.

The governor does not have this range of opportunities for public visibility, or, if he does, the events are at such a relatively low level that no one cares. Few dignitaries of note visit Sacramento, and the press simply does not warm to filming the governor talking to teachers or highway patrolmen, although pictures of Governor Schwarzenegger congratulating Jet Propulsion Laboratory scientists on a successful Mars landing were in all the papers in 2004. It is hard to imagine similar coverage if Governor Davis had done the same thing. It is not worth the cost for profit-oriented TV stations to keep reporters and camera crews in Sacramento for these largely uninspiring moments—unless the governor has his own star power, as Schwarzenegger does. Nothing else so clearly demonstrates the difference between the chief executive of the United States and the chief executive of one of the most important states in the union than this difference in visibility.

There are important similarities between the two positions as well, and most notable here is that these are offices of limited powers. It is hard for the public to understand that the most powerful political leader of the most powerful nation on earth has strictly limited powers; the same is true of the governor of the largest state in the union. Just as the president does not run the nation, the governor does not run the state. Our Founding Fathers feared a strong executive, having experienced such rule under a king and under capricious colonial governors. Consequently, they created a system in which the powers of the executive were secondary to the legislature and where the powers of all institutions were strictly limited.

The governor does have important powers, in some cases more than the president, but as Richard Neustadt has documented for the president, the governor's power is mostly the power to persuade.[1] His power to command and direct in any way he chooses is seriously limited.

As with the president, people have many incomplete, incorrect, and conflicting views of the governor. Tom Cronin has compiled a list of what he calls the paradoxes of the presidency:

- We want the president to be an effective politician while being above politics.

- We want him to be a common person and an extraordinary person at the same time.

- We want him to be powerful but not too powerful.[2]

In part, we want the president to be all things at all times, and, of course, this is not possible.

The governor is not burdened with as much symbolic baggage as the president, and yet many misperceptions carry over to this office as well. These misperceptions are amplified by the fact that people think that they understand the office. After all, it is an executive office, a position with which all of us who work in organizations have some familiarity. But it is much more than and much different from presidency of a corporation. It is a political executive office, and that is an entirely different position in an entirely different organization, an organization that does not respond well, if at all, to direct orders.

Our greatest misperception is thinking that the governor is more powerful than he in fact is. Our state government is modeled on the weak executive federal government that our Founding Fathers created. The governor does not control the legislature, and it is difficult to make policy without the cooperation, or at least acquiescence, of legislators who may have little reason to support the governor. He can get this cooperation only through persuasion—perhaps hardball persuasion, but persuasion nonetheless. Within the executive branch, it is possible to be more direct. But the executive branch is large and in many cases very remote from the governor. How does the governor get a highway patrolman in San Diego or a park ranger in Marin County to do what he wants?

Moreover, much of the executive branch is insulated from direct gubernatorial influence. The executive branch comprises many independently elected executives, as discussed above, often from the opposing party. And some organizations, such as the University of California, are governed by boards that can be influenced only by appointments, budgetary threats, or strongly voiced public opinion.

Besides, we often elect governors who are not especially knowledgeable about government agencies, Sacramento politics, or the many interests in our very large and diverse state. Now you begin to sense the limits on the governor being a strong executive. More important than formal powers are political skills, political resources, a favorable environment, and luck. Ability to bargain, friends in important positions, a good economy, and an absence of natural disasters, collectively and individually, are sometimes more important than formal powers.

Schwarzenegger is nearly unique in California politics, exceeding the popularity of even Ronald Reagan and demonstrating a level of immunity to criticism that President Ronald Reagan, known as "the Teflon president," could only dream about. As a governor, Schwarzenegger is even more of a phenomenon than he was as a movie star. By sheer dint of personality and the threat to go to the public with initiatives, he managed to score a series of impressive victories in the early days of his governorship. His formal powers were no greater than those of Gray Davis—and his political positions may not have been that different—but his personality and the political climate made all the difference in the world.

Formal Powers of the Governor

The formal powers of the governor, while limited, are still formidable. The governor has powers—most important, the line-item veto—that are denied to the president. Yet impressive as this list of powers is, these powers are most important as vantage points upon which the governor bases his informal powers or powers to persuade. A governor who expects to use only his formal powers to govern will not accomplish much. He must use those powers as a basis to persuade other political actors to support his goals. For instance, he can use his appointment power to try to persuade an important legislator to support his budget by promising to appoint one of the legislator's supporters to an important state commission.

The state constitution vests supreme executive power in the governor. What those words mean is not clear, but it probably is both more and less than meets the eye. Less, because the governor's office is an office of limited powers in which nothing is supreme. More, because executives often reach beyond what was constitutionally

BOX 6.1	Powers of the Governor

The governor has important formal and informal powers, among which are

FORMAL POWERS

organizing and managing the executive branch, including appointing many top executives

independent executive actions

commander in chief of the National Guard

appointing people to head executive agencies, to independent boards and commissions, and to the judiciary

drawing up the budget

making legislative recommendations

vetoing legislation

line-item vetoes of budget and appropriation items

granting of clemency, including pardons and reprieves

INFORMAL POWERS

bargaining with legislators and other independent power sources

access to the public to make his case

developing a vision or agenda for the state

raising money for political campaigns

intended. When a governor overreaches, recourse through the legislature or the judiciary takes time, and the results are often unclear.

Organizing and Managing the Executive Branch

The governor is empowered to organize and manage the executive branch. "Organize" means that he can make a number of administrative appointments. "Manage" means that many of these appointees must report to the governor, at least indirectly, and he can remove them from office. Again, this power can be overstated. First, the state government does not do as much as one might think. Much of the money that it collects is passed on to local government and school districts to spend. Second, the rest of the elected executive branch, most notably the attorney general, limits his actions, and some state employees report to these elected officials—5,000 to the attorney general alone. Third, some of the appointments that the governor makes are to boards that can, and do, act independently of the governor; these appointments may be for fixed terms. The best-known of these independent boards is the Regents of the University of California. This twenty-six-member board consists of seven ex officio members, who sit on the board because they occupy another office, including the governor himself; one student; and eighteen members appointed by the governor for twelve-year terms—terms that are longer than his. Control over this board, if he wishes to exert it, is possible only through new appointments, through the loyalty of previously appointed members, and through persuasion. Fourth, the governor must make appointments to agencies about which he knows little, often appointing individuals about whom he knows little. Information coming out of these agencies is limited, so the governor often is in the dark about what is happening until something goes terribly wrong and appears in the press.

Independent Executive Actions

The governor's powers are constitutionally restricted by the legislature, but he is able to act independently of the legislature in some cases. These are actions permitted by the constitution or under laws passed by the legislature. They are most significant in times of an emergency.

Few laws passed by the legislature are self-implementing. Most require positive action on the part of the administration. This process of implementation involves clarification of the law and the assembling of finances and an administrative structure to allow action to take place. All of this requires prioritization and the finding of funds, decisions that will have to be made by the governor's appointees or the governor himself. This is a process that allows for far more influence by the governor than might be apparent on the surface.

Commander in Chief

The governor is the commander in chief of the California National Guard. This role is of little significance until times of civil disorder or natural disaster; and then the significance is in the calling out of the guard rather than actually directing their actions.

Appointments

Making appointments is one of the governor's most significant powers. The governor appoints four distinct groups of individuals: his personal staff, heads of major administrative divisions, some judges, and members of a variety of boards and commissions. Some of these appointments require confirmation by other bodies, some do not; some appointees work at his pleasure, while others serve for fixed terms; some are answerable directly to the governor, and others are several steps removed or protected from his intervention. Over the course of his administration, a governor can make more than 2,500 appointments. At the start of his term there will be about 500 positions to be filled.

The governor appoints his personal staff, which consists of about 100 individuals who make the governor's life possible—the individuals who structure the life of the governor, package him, and present him to the public. Governors hire, fire, and move these individuals about at will. No confirmation is required.

Next closest to the governor are the members of his cabinet. The governor determines who will serve in the cabinet and what role, if any, the cabinet plays in policy development. The heads of the superagencies of state government are in the cabinet, as well as the director of finance and others whom the governor finds useful and appropriate. These positions require confirmation by the Senate, but the governor can fire them as he wishes.

The governor also appoints the heads of major departments, most of whom are in the superagencies. These individuals have the responsibility of overseeing more than 200,000 state employees.

Additionally, the governor appoints members to more than 325 boards and commissions, important and unimportant, visible and invisible. Once appointed, individuals do not have to answer to the governor, although political pressure, including budget pressure, can be brought to bear in many ways.

Legislative Powers

Much of the success of the governor depends on his ability to persuade the legislature to go along with his programs. This is a difficult task, since the legislature owes him little. He does not help elect them. They represent smaller and different constituencies, with legislators looking out for local rather than statewide issues. And they are on different career paths with different time constraints. His ability to persuade legislators depends on his political skills as well as many factors beyond his control, including the partisan makeup of the legislature and the political and economic environment. While much of this influence depends upon the governor's informal powers and the use of his other formal powers, he has several powers that are directed primarily toward the legislature.

Budget

Perhaps the governor's most significant power is that of preparing the budget, along with the line-item veto of budget provisions. At the federal level, the president presents Congress with a budget proposal, but it is just that, a proposal; the House of Representatives has constitutional authority over fiscal matters. The California constitution gives the power of preparing the budget to the governor. This means that all budget requests from executive branch agencies must pass through the governor. The actual work on this process is done by the Department of Finance.

The budget is prepared and sent to the legislature by January 10, with revisions following later in the spring as the financial picture becomes clearer. The governor then has the problem of getting the budget approved by the legislature, where a two-thirds majority of each house is required. To reach this two-thirds majority, the governor must gain support not only from the majority party, but from the minority party as well. This may require some expensive trade-offs for some recalcitrant legislators who withhold their support until they receive an offer they cannot refuse. There are in effect five major players in the budget game—the governor and the leaders of both parties in both houses of the legislature. The need for one or two marginal votes may create even more key players. Because of his role at both ends of the budgetary process and because one person needs to broker the deal, the governor is usually the key player, but even he can be held hostage by recalcitrant legislators. Republican legislators have become very recalcitrant about tax increases in recent years.

Veto and Line-Item Veto

The second most significant power of the governor is the veto. Simply put, just as in Congress, all bills passed by the legislature can be vetoed by the governor. The veto can be overridden only by a two-thirds majority of each house of the legislature. Equally important, and unlike the national government, the governor has a line-item veto, which permits him to reduce or delete any appropriation in a spending bill. That means that legislators cannot force the governor to accept funding for programs that he does not like by burying them inside a large spending bill that he must sign. The governor cannot add items, but the ability to reduce or eliminate the favorite programs of legislators is a powerful tool. It is a key item in the governor's box of bargaining tools, one that no other player has.

Legislative Recommendations

At the beginning of a legislative session, as required by the constitution, the governor presents a State of the State speech to the legislature. This speech may be short or long, general or specific. It is normally not covered in detail by the media, unlike the president's State of the Union speech; but as noted at the beginning, the first State of the State speech by Governor Schwarzenegger was covered in its entirety by a multitude of media outlets. This speech may contain the governor's legislative program, but whether or not it is spelled out here, most governors have a program that addresses the problems of the state as he sees them and that he hopes to get passed through the legislature.

The governor cannot introduce legislation but can readily get allies to introduce his specific proposals. As the most visible political figure in the state, he is in a position to press for action on these proposals. His success once again depends on a variety of factors, including his political skills. Because of his star power, Governor Schwarzenegger has greater access to the public through the media and can bring more outside pressure to bear on the legislature than most governors. He can also use this power to support initiatives that bypass the legislature, another source of pressure on the legislature to respond to his wishes.

Judicial Powers

The governor has the power to grant pardons and commute or shorten sentences. He can also reverse parole decisions or delay a death sentence. These are significant powers, but they are used relatively rarely and with extreme caution, since these decisions can have serious political consequences. Among other judicial powers of the governor is that of nominating justices to the supreme court and appellate courts and appointing other judges if positions are opened by retirement or resignation.

Public Roles of the Governor

While the governor's role as head of state does not provide as much access to the public as the president has, he still is occasionally seen cutting a ribbon, bestowing an honor upon some citizen, attending a funeral, or observing a natural disaster. These and other ceremonial and symbolic appearances may have little policy content, but they keep the governor in the public eye and give the impression that he is on top of things and that the state is in good hands. While far less visible than the president, governors do not underestimate these appearances. They remind people that the governor is on the job, that he does care about their concerns, and that, in the case of a disaster, the governor and the resources of the state will be available.

Occasionally there is some issue of such overwhelming importance—the energy crisis is a prime example—that the media are willing to give the governor lots of air time. On other occasions he can stage policy-related events, such as showing up at a school to emphasize his education policies, or to mask his actual opposition to certain policies.

The governor also moves into the public spotlight during elections, and not only when he is campaigning for reelection. California governors often think they have a chance to become president—and why not, since governors of far less significant states have been elected. When governors sense a chance for the presidency, they try to get in the national media as much as possible. They also campaign for political allies—perhaps a candidate for president or a loyal endangered assemblyperson. Finally, governors may take an active role in an initiative or referendum campaign, either to bolster the chances of an initiative that they support or to gain more public attention.

The governor's extensive fund-raising appearances also may gain significant public attention. This attention is useful, since it shows the opposition that the governor has a formidable war chest and shows the party faithful that the governor is out there stumping on their behalf.

Arnold Schwarzenegger in Office

Elected as governor in the recall election of October 2003, Arnold Schwarzenegger took office the next month. His first and biggest challenge was to deal with the budget crisis, and to do that he needed help from the state legislature and the support of the voters. He proposed two key financial initiatives for the March 2004 ballot, both of which the legislature endorsed and the voters approved. One refinanced a portion of the "inherited debt" with a $15 billion bond issue; the other established a set of rules to reduce spending. In April 2004, the legislature passed and the governor signed a comprehensive workers' compensation insurance reform. He also negotiated a compact with local governments to stop the shift of local property taxes to the state except in a fiscal emergency and also to cease the practice of unfunded state mandates. Endorsed by the legislature, this agreement was placed as a constitutional amendment (Proposition 1A) on the November

2004 ballot, and the voters approved it overwhelmingly by an 84 percent to 16 percent vote (see Chapter 9). The governor also negotiated new contracts with two of the state's labor unions and an agreement with the Indian tribes to produce more state income from their casinos. He balanced the state budget through a combination of cuts, borrowing, moving funds from one fiscal year to another, and the other traditional means that many governors use to balance the budget without raising taxes.

The challenge of balancing the budget was eased somewhat in 2004 and 2005 by an improving economy that produced more funds than expected. Housing prices remained high, with the state's median home price around $500,000. Bond rating companies raised California's general obligation bond rating from the levels attained around the time of the recall election in 2003, when they lowered the ratings to just above "junk" status.

If 2004 was a year in which the new governor cooperated with the legislature in attempting to solve California's problems, 2005 was the year in which he attacked the political establishment. He called for a special election in November 2005, asking voters to approve several propositions that came from the conservative part of the political spectrum. Following the advice of key advisers to avoid further compromise with Democratic state legislators and to take his proposed reforms directly to the people, Governor Schwarzenegger campaigned actively around the state to persuade voters to support the four reform initiatives discussed in Chapter 5's section on the special 2005 election. The result of the special election was a stunning defeat for the governor and his supporters. Not only did all four propositions that the governor supported fail, but the governor's approval ratings fell from over 50 percent in January 2005 to figures in the 30 percent–40 percent range by August and September of that year. Table 6.1 shows the statewide election results for the governor's four initiatives along with voting statistics for San Francisco, Los Angeles, and San Diego counties to illustrate the continuing differences in regional political cultures.

Why did the governor turn so far to the right in 2005? The answer is unclear, but the lack of success in solving the state's problems with the more moderate 2004 measures, his conservative business-oriented advisers, difficulty working with the Democratic legislature, the perception that public employee unions were behind

TABLE 6.1 ★ Support for Governor Schwarzenegger's Initiatives in the 2005 Special Election

	SAN FRANCISCO COUNTY	LOS ANGELES COUNTY	SAN DIEGO COUNTY	STATEWIDE
Prop. 74 Teacher Tenure	23%	38%	55%	45%
Prop. 75 Public Union Dues	24%	38%	58%	46%
Prop. 76 Spending/Funding	16%	32%	48%	38%
Prop. 77 Redistricting	21%	34%	47%	40%

SOURCE: California Secretary of State, Official Statement of Vote, Special Statewide Election, November 8, 2005.

many of Sacramento's problems, and the sense that, as a celebrity, Schwarzenegger could persuade the public to vote for "his" measures in a special election—are probably part of the answer.

Targeting the public employee unions turned out not to resonate with the average voter. The nurses', police, and firefighters' unions developed very effective public campaigns against the governor following an earlier proposition designed to cut back public pensions and a decision to oppose the hospital staffing ratios the nurses had succeeded in writing into law. Turnout also was unexpectedly high in the special election, in part due to the unions' "Get Out the Vote" efforts. Schwarzenegger's put-down of the legislators as "girlie men" certainly didn't encourage a cooperative response. Nor did his condemnation of opponents as "special interests" when he himself was milking corporate lobbyists for campaign funds.

In 2006, the governor discarded his 2005 strategy and began to cooperate with the Democratic legislature. The legislature approved the state budget on time. The legislature and the governor cooperated on the development of five propositions for the November 2006 ballot that totaled over $40 billion in borrowing to rebuild the state's infrastructure. While he vetoed a Democratic proposal for a single-payer health system, he cooperated with the legislature on legislation to cut greenhouse gases in the state. Consequently, his approval ratings returned to the 2004 levels—over 50 percent—and Governor Schwarzenegger easily defeated his Democratic opponent, State Treasurer Phil Angelides, in the November 2006 election. In 2007, his State of the State speech proposed more borrowing to rebuild the state's infrastructure, a health insurance proposal to cover all California citizens, including undocumented residents, and decisions to implement the greenhouse gas cutbacks.

In late 2007, the governor proposed a health reform plan with both an individual mandate (everyone in California would have to purchase health insurance) and an employer mandate (all employers would have to offer health insurance or, in lieu, pay the state a special fee). But the legislature did not pass the proposal, faced with one bloc that wanted only a single-payer system and was generally reluctant to approve such a substantial reform when state revenues seemed so uncertain. Indeed, state revenues were forecast to be short of expenditures for the 2008–2009 fiscal year by some $15 billion (on a $140 billion budget). Faced with such a substantial deficit, Schwarzenegger proposed borrowing against the California lottery to make up one-third or more of the difference, but neither the public nor the legislature found the alternative appealing. As a backup, he proposed a 1 percent increase, for three years, in the state sales tax. In both 2007 and 2008, the legislature passed the budget long after the June 15 deadline, as it proved difficult to obtain the required two-thirds vote, and both the legislature and the governor struggled to find the funds to bridge the gap between revenues and expenditures.

As of 2008, California's bond ratings were up with the passage of three successful state budgets, but the 2008 standoff and the economic downturn—California's unemployment rate increased to more than 8 percent by the end of 2008—caused state revenues to decline precipitously, and the state budget was later than it had ever been and then had to be revised midway through the fiscal year. The result was a slight lowering of the short-term bonds at the end of 2008, and an unprecedented deficit of more than $40 billion spread over a two fiscal-year period. The standoff at the end of 2008 produced two groups: the governor and the Democrats, both willing to close a good portion of the gap with budget cuts and revenue increases of approximately equal size, and the Republicans, unwilling to raise taxes and revenues under any circumstances and demanding that budget cuts close at least half the gap before negotiations could begin.

At the end of 2008, two tentative steps had been taken, with the governor's support, toward tackling the biggest long-term problems facing the state. Although some doubted it would have any real impact, Proposition 11, approved in November 2008, will take the power to draw the state legislative districts from the legislature and give it to a citizens' commission; and the voters approved Proposition 1A, a large first step of $9.9 billion borrowed to construct a high-speed rail connection between Anaheim, Los Angeles, the central valley, San Francisco, and Sacramento. However, no firm steps have been taken toward fixing the distortions caused by both Proposition 13, the 1978 proposition that limited property tax increases, and the series of initiatives that have "locked in" certain parts of the budget and made passing the annual budget close to impossible in the best of circumstances. California's revenues are far more volatile than other states, and Californians' willingness to govern by initiative remains undaunted.

The boldness of Governor Schwarzenegger's approaches and his ability to change course indicate a willingness to tackle the state's problems. But the budget process will remain dysfunctional until the two-thirds vote requirement to pass budgets or raise taxes is changed—or until Republican legislators become more flexible on tax issues.

Structure of the Executive Branch

The executive branch of California has several significant divisions: the governor's personal staff, the appointed cabinet and other department heads, the other elected officials of the executive branch, appointed boards and commissions, and the more than 300,000 state employees, divided into more than eighty-five agencies and thirty educational institutions. Not all of these agencies and employees are under the control of the governor. Figure 6.1 provides a graphic representation of the executive branch.

Personal Staff

Closest to the governor is his personal staff. The members of this staff include schedulers, speechwriters, and press officers. In addition there are individuals who oversee the appointments process, the general development of policy, and liaison with the legislature. They structure his day, develop statements for the press and the public, arrange relations with various groups, and set up his appearances throughout the state. Members of this staff are expendable, and they tend to be young and transient. Their positions are totally dependent on staying in the governor's good graces.

The Cabinet and Agency Heads

The governor uses his cabinet as he determines. It has no official policy function but can be used to help formulate policy. The cabinet is often more a symbolic body than an integral structure of governing. The executive branch is divided into seven superagencies, and the heads of these agencies, called secretaries, are generally in

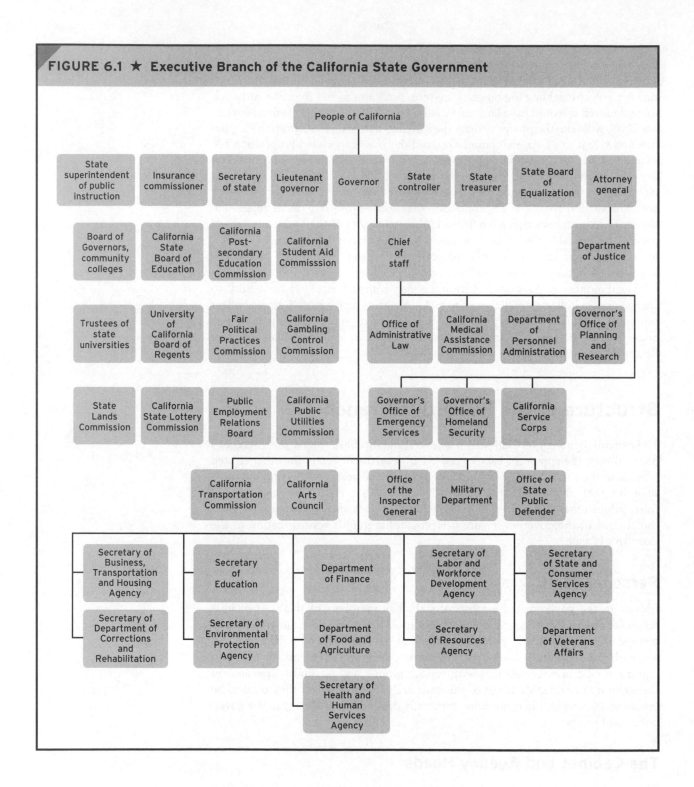

FIGURE 6.1 ★ Executive Branch of the California State Government

In addition to the selected duties listed below, all sit ex officio on various state boards.

Governor: Organizes the executive branch, prepares the budget and legislation, signs or vetoes bills

Lieutenant Governor: Replaces the governor if he is out of the state or incapacitated, or if he leaves office for any reason

Attorney General: Enforces laws, oversees and assists district attorneys

Secretary of State: Holds elections and oversees the records and archives of the state

Treasurer: Manages state money

Insurance Commissioner: Regulates insurance companies

Controller: Monitors collection of taxes, provides fiscal controls for receipts and payments

Superintendent of Public Instruction: Administers the state role in public education, sits on the state Board of Education

Board of Equalization: Oversees the assessment and administration of property taxes and the collection and distribution of sales taxes and the collection of excise taxes. The controller is a member of this body.

the cabinet. These include State and Consumer Services; Youth and Adult Corrections; Environmental Protection; Health and Human Services; Labor and Workforce Development; Business, Transportation and Housing; and Resources. These superagencies contain most of the agencies of the state. It is the agencies that actually carry out functions, and they may act independently of the superagency secretaries. The governor appoints these agency heads, although he often does not have a free choice. He needs to appoint someone with expertise in the area, and sometimes the qualifications are spelled out in law. These agencies and superagencies are called line agencies, the term used to describe organizations with their own statutory authority to carry out functions and provide services.

In addition, the governor has several staff advisory agencies, including the Department of Finance, the Office of Planning and Research, and the Department of Personnel Administration. Perhaps the most important of these is the Department of Finance, which prepares the governor's budget.

The Plural Elected Executive

One of the most notable features of California government is the number of statewide elected administrative offices. It has seven of these positions, plus the Board of Equalization, which oversees the administration of property, sales, and excise taxes. These offices, especially that of attorney general, substantially limit the power of the governor.

How many people are employed by the state of California? We actually don't know. The national ratings of how well the state is managed are "C" at best and in the lower half of the states nationally, symbolic of the fact that one reason we don't know how many employees there are is because the state is not well managed and its computer systems are out of date. The figures range from 176,000 to almost 500,000.

First, when most people speak of "state employees," they mean those who report to the governor. But in fact because of the plural executive branch, UC/CSU, the legislative and judicial branches, and other independent boards, only half to two-thirds of state employees report to the governor.

The state also lacks a consistent definition of an employee. Some employees are full-time and have civil service protection. Others are full-time and temporary. Others are part-time with long-term contracts. Still others are part-time and temporary—although some of them work for years. (And some are nonstate employees who are employed under state contracts, just to complicate the situation.) Many, definitely not counted as state employees, actually work for local government but with state funding.

The bottom line is that without modern management practices and a consistent definition of who is who over time, we are left with estimates. The Legislative Analyst's Office estimates the total personnel-years for state employment as 335,384 in 2006–2007, but part-time employees here would be included only as a proportion of full-time, so the total number of people employed by the state is even higher.

Compared with other states, California has relatively few employees. The U.S. Census Bureau comparison tables show that in 2005, the latest figures available, California is fourth from the bottom, with 107 state employees per 10,000 population, compared with the national average of 142 and the highest state, Hawaii, with 426. The average for the top ten states was 271. Most of the states that are most "efficient" are larger states, suggesting that economies of scale for larger states will yield fewer employees to do similar amounts of work. For total state and local employees, California is seventh from the bottom in 2005, with 490 total employees per 10,000 population, compared with the national average of 537 and the average for the top ten states of 699.[3]

THE LIEUTENANT GOVERNOR The lieutenant governor exists to replace the governor if he becomes incapacitated. He also acts in the governor's absence from the state, providing occasions for great mischief. He can also preside over the Senate, breaking tie votes. He is often of a different party than the governor. Perhaps more than others, this position captures the imagination of those who would restructure government, who would either eliminate the office or link the election of the lieutenant governor to that of the governor.

THE ATTORNEY GENERAL The attorney general oversees the department of justice, which employs more than 5,000 persons and has responsibility to see that the laws are enforced. He has the freedom to set priorities for which areas get the most attention and resources. He has oversight responsibilities for local district attorneys and county sheriffs. He is legal counsel to the state and defends the state in lawsuits. He has no obligation to cooperate with the governor and is often viewed as a rival. In 2004 the governor ordered the attorney general to intercede with the state supreme court to stop gay marriages in San Francisco. The governor had no statutory basis for giving such an order, and although the attorney general ulti-mately did just that, he did it on his own authority. This office is very powerful, and incumbents often see themselves as leading candidates for governor, although few have successfully made this transition. The attorney general is able to set his own agenda, and it may run counter to the governor's agenda. He can use his substantial powers to counter or even embarrass the governor.

THE SECRETARY OF STATE This office oversees the records and archives of the state. It also has the responsibility for holding elections, including publishing election pamphlets, certifying initiative petitions, keeping records, and publishing the results of elections.

THE CONTROLLER The controller is the fiscal officer for the state and oversees the state's money and the collection of taxes. The controller sits on a large number of boards, including the very important Board of Equalization and Franchise Tax Board, discussed below.

THE TREASURER This is a relatively unimportant office that manages the money after it comes in and before it is spent. It manages the investment of this money and the sale of bonds.

THE SUPERINTENDENT OF PUBLIC INSTRUCTION The superintendent is the chief administrator of the Department of Education. Unlike the other elected statewide officers, the superintendent is elected on a nonpartisan basis. Education is a confusing policy area; the superintendent shares power with an appointed Board of Education and a secretary of education appointed by the governor. This arrangement insures controversy and battles over turf and policy.

THE INSURANCE COMMISSIONER This office was made elective by Proposi-tion 103 in 1988, the only position of the plural executive created by an initiative. The commissioner regulates the insurance industry, and Proposition 103 passed because the public felt that the appointed commissioner was not doing his job. It is not clear that making this an elective post has improved matters, since most of the contributions to the campaigns for this position come from the insurance industry.

In addition to these positions, voters elect by district four members to the Board of Equalization, which oversees the assessment and administration of prop-erty taxes, although much of the work is done at the county level; collection and distribution of sales taxes; and the collection of excise taxes. Income taxes are handled by a different nonelected body, the Franchise Tax Board.

Agencies and the Bureaucracy

Most of the work of California state government is carried out by more than 200,000 state employees housed in over eighty-five agencies. Most of these agen-cies are located within the seven superagencies, and most are invisible to the gen-eral public, leading to the idea that state government runs by itself. A few agencies, such as the DMV and Caltrans, are well known if not well understood. Others, such as the Office of Small Business Development or the Department of Aging, rarely make it into the news or the public consciousness. Few Californians could name anyone in the executive branch up to and including department heads; few governors could do that either. Many of these individuals are permanent experts on policy subjects who quietly go about doing their jobs.

Most California employees have civil service protection. Many are also represented by unions. A few of these unions, notably the prison guards' union, are very powerful and politically well connected to the point where the wishes and desires of the union are more likely to become state policy than the wishes and desires of the governor, the head of the Department of Corrections, or the administration of the department.

There are more than 325 state boards and commissions. Positions on these boards are filled by the governor subject to approval of another body, most often a legislative body. These boards and commissions include important ones, such as the Air Resources Board, the Public Utilities Commission, and the Gambling Control Commission. Again, probably the most visible are the Board of Regents of the University of California and the Trustees of the California State University, which together are responsible for more than 100,000 employees. On the other hand, boards such as the Board of Chiropractic Examiners or the Apprenticeship Council are probably known only to those with a direct interest in that area. Most members serve for fixed terms, some as long as twelve years, and, once appointed, do not have to respond to the governor's wishes.

Conclusion

It is critical to understand that the office of the governor is one of greatly limited powers. He does not run the state or even state government or even the executive branch. In the public sphere, state government is hemmed in by the actions of the federal government and local governments. Within state government, the governor is limited in his actions by the judicial branch, the independently elected legislature, and the independently elected statewide executives, including the attorney general.

Although the governor has some important formal powers, including preparing the budget and the line-item veto, his real power is the power to persuade. As the single most powerful political figure in a system of divided powers, he is the chief persuader and has the most resources to do that. Yet, given the vast diversity of issues in the state and the complexity of issues, persuasion is time-consuming and limited in effectiveness. The result is that, short of an obvious emergency that everyone can see, it is rare that we have strong leadership from the governor. Governor Schwarzenegger, because of his star quality and because of the fiscal crisis the state faces, may provide one of those rare examples when the governor can use his office as a bully pulpit to persuade the public, and thus the legislature, that action needs to be taken. But, in general, we do not have strong leadership, and it is not the fault of any individual. It is rather the result of the system that exists in California and the United States. Interestingly, while many agree that our state is dysfunctional, there is relatively little that reformers would change in the governor's office. Most prefer a weak governor to an autocratic one.

FOR FURTHER READING

Cain, Bruce E., and Roger G. Noll, eds. *Constitutional Reform in California: Making State Government More Effective and Responsive*. Berkeley: Institute of Governmental Studies Press, 1995.

California Performance Review. *Prescription for Change, Report of the California Performance Review*. Vols. I–IV. Sacramento: California Performance Review, 2004. http://cpr.ca.gov/#cpr

Gerston, Larry N., and Terry Christensen. *Recall!: California's Political Earthquake*. Armonk, NY: M. E. Sharpe, 2004.

Lubenow, Gerald C., ed. *Governing California: Politics, Government, and Public Policy in the Golden State*, 2nd ed. Berkeley: Institute of Governmental Studies Press, University of California, 2006.

Mathews, Joe. *The People's Machine: Arnold Schwarzenegger and the Rise of Blockbuster Democracy*. New York: Public Affairs Press, 2006.

Schrag, Peter. *California: America's High-Stakes Experiment*. Berkeley: University of California Press, 2006.

———. *Paradise Lost: California's Experience, America's Future*. New York: New Press, 1998.

ON THE WEB

California Department of Finance: www.dof.ca.gov/

Center for Governmental Studies, Los Angeles: www.cgs.org/

Governor of California: www.gov.ca.gov/ The official site of the Office of the Governor, where you can find background information and up-to-date news, and even e-mail the Governor.

Public Policy Institute of California: www.ppic.org/

Rough & Tumble: rtumble.com
    Daily summary of California news

University of California, Berkeley, Institute of Governmental Studies, Library, Hot Topics: http://igs.berkeley.edu/library/hot_topics/HotTopicsMainPage.html

---

SUMMARY

While the governor's position is modeled on that of the president, there are significant differences, mostly having to do with the visibility of the office. Both positions can be divided into two roles: head of state and head of government. The latter role involves making policy and trying to get it passed by the legislature and implemented by the executive branch. That role is partisan and divisive. It is also an almost invisible role. The head of state role is largely ceremonial, symbolizing the unity of the state or country. In this role the governor makes public appearances in activities that bring people together. The president in this role is on TV almost every evening. The governor has fewer opportunities to play this role, and even when he does, television stations in the state seem uninterested.

The formal powers of the office seem to favor the governor. He has most of the powers of the president in domestic policy, as well as a line-item veto, which gives him much more control over the political process of the budget. In addition, California requires a two-thirds vote of the legislature to pass a budget, which may hamper the governor. On the other hand, it has an initiative process that a popular governor can use to attempt to bludgeon a legislature into action.

Still, the office of governor is one of limited powers. His powers are restricted by the legislature, the judiciary, the other elected officers of the executive, and the permanent executive branch. His formal powers include making appointments and organizing the executive branch, instigating independent executive actions permitted by law, being commander in chief, proposing the budget, making legislative recommendations, and exercising the veto, including the line-item veto. His public roles include cutting ribbons, signing bills, dealing with natural disasters, campaigning and fund-raising, and advocating initiatives.

The structure of the state government includes the governor's personal staff; his cabinet, which includes the heads of major departments; the eighty-five or more agencies that comprise these departments; and more than 300 boards and commissions, including such important ones as the Public Utilities Commission and the Regents of the University of California. In all, California employs the equivalent of more than 300,000 full-time employees to staff the government.

In addition to the governor, the state is headed by other elected executive officers, who compose the plural executive, including the lieutenant governor, the attorney general, the secretary of state, the controller, the treasurer, the superintendent of public education, the insurance commissioner, and the state Board of Equalization.

PRACTICE QUIZ

1. Which of the following is not part of the plural executive?
   a) the chancellor of the California State University
   b) the secretary of state
   c) the superintendent of public instruction
   d) the controller
2. Which power does the governor have that the president does not have?
   a) legislative veto
   b) line-item veto
   c) power to declare war
   d) power to appoint judges
3. Which of the following activities of the governor would be considered part of his role as head of government?
   a) proposing a budget
   b) vetoing legislation
   c) proposing new air quality standards
   d) all of the above
4. Which of the following group of employees are under administrative control and report ultimately to the governor?
   a) legislative aides
   b) supreme court clerks
   c) highway patrol
   d) professors at California State University, Fullerton
5. How many state boards and commissions are there?
   a) fewer than 50
   b) between 50 and 150
   c) between 150 and 250
   d) between 250 and 350
6. The California governor is "invisible" under normal conditions for all of the following reasons except:
   a) California's governors appear in events where they are visible to the public, but for the most part, there is little interest in them.
   b) for almost every recent governor, there has been little media interest in Sacramento.
   c) the governor splits his power with other state executives, who are also trying to attract the media.
   d) the governor's "star power" is only of interest to those who like "superhero movies."

7. The governor manages the executive branch, but this power is limited by all of the following except:
   a) the governor appoints so many people that many of those he appoints will be appointed to agencies the governor doesn't know much about.
   b) some of California government is outside the power of the governor to supervise, like the University of California and the California State University.
   c) the boards and commissions that the governor makes appointments to are mostly, except in extreme cases, outside of his power.
   d) the attorney general must approve appointments to many boards and commissions, and that appointment power is difficult to obtain.
8. The line-item veto allows the governor to adjust any appropriations item up or down, including reducing it to zero.
   a) true
   b) false
9. All of the following are true of the governor's appointments to the cabinet except:
   a) most cabinet appointments are routine, given to the governor's political supporters and campaign contributors.
   b) the cabinet as a whole has no official policy function, unless the governor wants to give it a role.
   c) some cabinet and subcabinet positions require an appointment of someone with qualifications that are spelled out in law.
   d) the superagency heads are usually considered part of the governor's cabinet.
10. The job of the lieutenant governor, one columnist wrote not entirely in jest, consists of getting up in the morning, checking that the governor is still alive, and making arrangements for lunch!
    a) likely to be true.
    b) likely to be false.

CRITICAL-THINKING QUESTIONS

1. Is the state government too large?
2. Does the plural elected executive contribute to effective or efficient government?
3. What is the value of having independent boards such as the Regents of the University of California that employ large numbers of people?

4. Which is more important for governing, the formal or informal powers of the governor? Think about this question in terms of "necessary" versus "sufficient" powers.

KEY TERMS

At this point you should have a general understanding of the following concepts and terms:

boards and commissions (118)
cabinet (113)
formal powers (106)

head of government (104)
head of state (104)
informal powers (106)

line-item veto (109)
personal staff (113)
superagencies (113)

7 The California Judiciary

WHAT CALIFORNIA GOVERNMENT DOES, AND WHY IT MATTERS

Consider the following:

★ An indigent criminal defendant sits in jail, awaiting his trial.

★ A worker is disabled on the job and sues her employer for compensatory and punitive damages.

★ A university applicant is refused admission, believes he has been discriminated against based upon his race, and sues the university and the state.

In each of the scenarios above, courts play a role in resolving the dispute. In this respect, judges who serve on courts behave a lot like referees in competitive sports. For example, one of the duties of a judge is to make certain that the lawyers in a case follow the rules of the game. Judges are required to ensure procedural fairness in their courtrooms. Judges must also make choices regarding penalties such as jail time, prison terms, or fines for breaking the law in criminal cases. The same applies to judicial behavior in civil cases. Judges enforce the rules while presiding over hearings and trials, determining fault in accident claims, dissolving marriages in divorce cases, and imposing penalties on the losing party. Even though judges have legal training, volumes of procedure, and the law to guide them in coming to their decisions, a judge's job is not an easy one. This is especially true in states like California that have a sizable, diverse geography and sizable, diverse populations.

Judges and State Government

State courts are an integral and necessary component of state government. They exist and function to ensure that a state's citizenry is guaranteed due process of law and that the other branches and levels of government within the state uphold the state's statutes and code as well as the provisions in the state constitution. Therefore, judges play a much larger role than simply punishing criminals or imposing fines on a polluting company. Courts make decisions that are often political and affect many of us on a daily basis.

For example, the courts in California will decide whether or not the mayor of San Francisco violated state law when he permitted gays to wed in his city. When citizens or groups of citizens believe that government has trampled on their civil rights and civil liberties, they turn to the courts. The judges serving on California's courts decide if the law does or doesn't violate the rights of Californians.

Many legal scholars argue that a number of factors make the life of a typical California judge very different from judges serving in other states. California, as noted in Chapter 2, has a lengthy constitution with many provisions in its declaration of rights, especially when compared to the Bill of Rights in the United States Constitution. California also has a professional, full-time legislature, and the initiative and referendum. The quantity of existing law, the presence of institutions and structures that can create more law, and the abundance of attorneys in this state mean that there is always opportunity for litigation. Although some rules restrict access to the courts for civil claims, for the most part, California courts are very accessible to citizens and noncitizens alike.

There is also a recent trend to criminalize more behavior and increase the penalties for offenders. For example, California, like many other states, has modified its laws to allow juveniles to be tried as adults in some criminal cases. While the intent of this law may have been to let juveniles know that California has little tolerance for certain types of crime, regardless of the defendant's age, the effect has been to shift cases from the courts of judges who deal exclusively with juveniles to the already overburdened courts handling crimes involving adults. Additionally, victims' rights legislation, which has elevated some misdemeanors (nonserious crimes) to felonies (serious crimes), increases not only the severity of the penalties for the accused, but also the workload for the courts. California's three-strikes law, which was enacted to punish repeat offenders, has had a similar impact. Keep in mind that these are just a few examples.

To be sure, most of the civil cases filed in California's civil courts will be resolved through negotiation between the parties and their attorneys. The courts are still involved, however, in processing the paperwork and dealing with the other administrative issues each civil case may involve.

It is also true that in reality, most of the criminal cases in the state's criminal courts will be resolved through plea bargaining, in spite of what we see in film or on television. Full court trials for the prosecution of high-profile crimes, like that of Scott Peterson, charged with murdering his wife, Laci Peterson, and their unborn son Connor, are rare. A plea bargain is the norm. Even so, the courts are still involved in the process. Even if a criminal case never goes beyond the formal filing of charges against a defendant, judges are part of a plea bargain. As a referee, the judge's job is to determine if the plea bargain is appropriate and if the defendant entered into the plea bargain knowingly. The judge asks defendants if they understand the terms of the plea bargain and if they agreed to the terms voluntarily. If the judge decides that the terms of the plea bargain are inappropriate, it may be thrown out. The same applies to the defendant's ability to comprehend the terms of the plea and whether or not it was truly entered into voluntarily. If the judge concludes that any of these elements are problematic, then a new plea may have to be negotiated or the case may actually go to trial. Regardless, this single case involves many people in the criminal courts, from clerks to administrators and, of course, a judge.

To understand the role courts play in California government and politics, consider the following: In 2006 through 2007, almost 9,500,000 cases were filed in California Superior Courts (trial courts of general jurisdiction).[1] Of these, over 80 percent were criminal in nature. And each one of these approximately 9,500,000 cases had to be handled individually by the appropriate state court in one way or another until it was resolved. To put this into context, let's consider the number of people living in this state. According to the U.S. Census Bureau, California's population was estimated at 36,756,666 as of July 1, 2008. This number includes all persons who could be counted from newborns to the very old, people who are incarcerated and institutionalized, small children, and people with challenges that may inhibit them from participating in a range of activities.[2] Age, health, disabilities, and other factors exclude a number of Californians from committing crimes. Even if we grant that some individuals may be involved in more than one of 9.5 million lawsuits, 9.5 million cases filed in one state's courts in a single year is phenomenal. What is more, despite the incredible workload, California's criminal courts typically resolve cases involving felonies within twelve months. Civil cases are also resolved fairly quickly; on average, 65 percent of civil cases filed in a given year are resolved within a year.

It is easier for an individual to go to criminal court—just drive over the speed limit and get caught—than to civil court. Civil courts have rules about the types of cases they can hear. In civil disputes, parties must also have what is known as "standing to sue." In order to bring a case to court, an individual must suffer personal and real injury. Typically, one cannot sue on the behalf of another. As well as standing, California courts, like the federal courts, will not handle collusive suits. Collusive suits are lawsuits in which both parties want a similar or the same outcome. Our legal system is an adversarial one, in which it is presumed that parties want opposite outcomes, and when one party wins, the other loses.

Both criminal and civil courts in California are limited as to the cases and controversies they handle because of jurisdiction. Jurisdiction refers to the kind of law the court handles. For example, there are criminal courts that deal with violations of state and local laws, and there are civil courts that hear cases involving disputes between individuals or classes of individuals. Civil courts may rule on cases involving breach of contract, tort liability, and wrongful-death suits, to name a few. Jurisdiction also refers to geographic boundaries. There are fifty-eight superior court divisions in California, with at least one branch in each county. Cases are assigned to these courts depending upon where the parties in civil suits reside or where alleged crimes have been committed in criminal cases.

Some Historical Background on California Courts

California's judiciary began back in 1849. Since then, the size of the judiciary and the method by which judges have been chosen have changed a great deal. The list below includes a number of significant state statutes and constitutional amendments that have affected California's judiciary. Many of these changes reflect reforms that have attempted to insulate the state's courts from politics as much as possible, while still allowing for some electoral accountability. For example, the 1928 constitutional amendment making judicial elections nonpartisan removed party labels and the perception of partisanship from judicial campaigns, the ballot, and the bench. It also contributed to other reforms of this era, such as primary elections and the civil service system, that weakened California's political parties.

- 1849. The judges of the California Supreme Court and district court are elected by the people for six-year terms.

- 1862. The length of terms for supreme court justices is changed to ten years.

- 1879. The length of terms for supreme court justices is changed to twelve years.

- 1904. The California Court of Appeals is created.

- 1911. The state legislature establishes nonpartisan elections for judges.

- 1928. The state constitution is amended to provide for nonpartisan judicial elections.

- 1934. Selection of appellate judges for the supreme court and courts of appeals is changed from nonpartisan election to appointment by the governor and confirmation by the Commission on Judicial Appointments. This change was made through the statewide initiative.

- 1960. The Commission on Judicial Performance is created through a statewide initiative.

- 1979. The state legislature requires the State Bar of California's Commission on Judicial Nominees Evaluation to evaluate all potential nominees.

- 1986. A constitutional amendment enacted through the initiative (Proposition 49) bars political parties from endorsing, supporting, or opposing candidates in nonpartisan offices. This amendment was invalidated in the federal courts in 1990.

- 1998. Ballots for elections concerning judicial retention (California Supreme Court judicial elections) are changed. These ballots no longer include the length of the term of office a justice is seeking or the name of the governor who appointed the candidate.

California's judiciary is a political branch of the state government, just like the legislature and the plural executive. As you read through the remainder of this chapter, keep in mind that because it is a political creation, the judiciary often engages in politics. California's judges come to their courts through a political process, either appointment or election. Judges have their own opinions about politics and can be influenced by their ideologies when they are confronted with political issues in the cases they review. California's judges can overturn the laws of the state legislature, enjoin the executive from enforcing laws or implementing orders, and rule on cases that affect our daily lives.

How Are the California Courts Structured?

California courts have three levels: superior courts (trial courts), courts of appeals, and the California Supreme Court.

Superior courts adjudicate cases that involve violations of state and local criminal and civil law. These are the trial courts of California. When cases come before the superior courts, a jury or judge reviews the facts of the case and determines guilt or innocence in a criminal proceeding. If it is a civil case, the jury or judge determines which side presents the best case and awards damages accordingly. There are 400 courts located in the state, with approximately 1,500 judges presiding. The superior courts are also staffed with commissioners and referees. The superior courts are also the busiest courts of the state court system.

The California Courts of Appeals are intermediate appellate courts; those who lose their cases at the superior court can appeal first to the California Courts of Appeals. The purpose of this intermediate appellate court is to review the trial or the superior court records for error. California courts of appeals are divided into six districts across the state. One hundred and five justices preside over these courts. These judges sit in three-judge panels to review cases.

The California Supreme Court is the highest court in the state. Like the California Courts of Appeals, it is an appellate court that reviews appeals from losing parties in the lower courts. When a party to a case is unhappy with the ruling of the California courts of appeals, the next step would be to appeal to the California Supreme Court. In California, the supreme court has what is known as discretion. Discretion allows the justices on the state supreme court to decide which cases they wish to review. Therefore, there is no guarantee that an appeal filed with the California Supreme Court will automatically get reviewed. This is the only court in California that has discretionary authority that provides the high court with a tool to moderate its workload. Justices on the supreme court cannot exercise discretion regarding death-penalty sentences or disciplinary cases involving judges or attorneys. All death-penalty sentences are automatically appealed and go directly to the California Supreme Court for review. Four out of the seven justices must agree in order for a party to win the case. The supreme court includes one chief

Current members of the California State Supreme Court. (Sirlin Photographers)

justice and seven associate justices. (Table 7.1 provides a list of current Supreme Court members.)

The court is diverse with regard to gender and race/ethnicity: three of the justices are women and three are nonwhite. However, the court is not as diverse ideologically. Six of the seven justices seated on the court were appointed by Republican governors—only one justice, Carlos Moreno, was appointed by a Democrat. Why should this matter? Generally, Republicans are more conservative than Democrats on issues of ideological preference, such as civil rights or civil liberties. For example, a liberal judge is more likely to uphold laws that involve regulating business than a conservative judge. This expectation, that ideology or party identification translates into differences in judicial decision making, is even more important when we consider issues such as affirmative action, voting rights, freedom of expression, and capital punishment. Because the decisions of the California Supreme Court are binding on all persons residing in the state, the composition of the state's high court and the judges' political ideology can be very important.

Governors who have the opportunity to appoint judges to the courts take advantage of this possibility and put qualified jurists on the bench whose political beliefs most closely resemble their own. From time to time, a governor may be very open about who should be serving on the state supreme court. In the 1980s, former governor George Deukmajian spoke out to the press and public about his desire to put more conservatives on the state supreme court, because the liberals serving on the bench at the time were making decisions he vehemently disagreed with. Additionally, governors may have other political goals for the bench. They may, for example, seek to place more women and minorities on the state supreme court so that it is more representative of the state's diverse population.

From time to time, judges who have served on the California Supreme Court have had success at being promoted to the federal bench. The most recent promotion from the state high court to the federal courts of appeals met with significant political opposition. Janice Rogers Brown's appointment to the U.S. Court of Appeals for the District of Columbia Circuit was nonetheless confirmed in June 2005. Her confirmation was a result of a political compromise after a two-year bipartisan battle between Democrats and Republicans in the Senate over several of President Bush's judicial nominees. Janice Brown, a Republican and conservative, was appointed to the California Supreme Court in 1996 by Governor Pete Wilson. President George Bush attempted to nominate Judge Brown to the D.C. Circuit Court of Appeals in 2003, but he was unable to get her nomination confirmed by the United States Senate. The reason that her nomination was initially unsuccessful was political. Justice Brown's detractors argued that her voting record as an appellate judge on California's Supreme Court reflected a much too conservative bias. Additionally, organized interests such as the National Organization for Women (NOW) noted that Justice Janice Brown received an "unqualified" rating from the California State Bar Association. She is the only member of the state supreme court to receive such a rating since the state bar has been evaluating judicial nominees.

Justice Brown's confirmation struggle also illustrates the debate regarding judicial independence versus judicial accountability that we will address later in this chapter. Federal court judges are appointed by the president and confirmed by the Senate for terms of life with good behavior. This selection method was designed to protect the federal judiciary from political influences, including public opinion. Because their appointments are for life terms, many interest groups and other interested members of the Senate pay close attention to judicial appointments and the nominee's positions on important issues and voting records. Appointments to the federal bench, unlike elections to state courts, are often the topic of heated partisan debate. Once a judge is appointed to a federal court, the only way to remove him or her is through impeachment. Thus, it isn't possible to hold federal judges to the same level of accountability as most state judges. Therefore, partisans and interest groups act as gatekeepers, blocking nominations of those jurists whose political preferences differ from their own.

Judicial Selection

California's court system is the largest in the nation. Serving on the bench involves two things: (1) a person must be qualified, and (2) the qualified person must be selected to serve. The qualifications for judge are the same for the three court levels. Potential jurists in California must have at least ten years of practice of law in the state of California or service as a judge of a court of record.

Judges serving on the California Supreme Court and California Courts of Appeals are initially nominated to serve on the appellate bench by the governor. The Commission on Judicial Appointments must approve the governor's nominations. The Commission on Judicial Appointments consists of the chief justice of the supreme court, the attorney general, and a presiding judge on the California Courts of Appeals. In addition, all nominees for California's appellate courts are reviewed by the State Bar of California's Commission on Judicial Nominees Evaluation. This body evaluates the nominees by conducting thorough background checks on their qualifications as judges and as citizens. The governor may use the commission's decision as a source of information when making his selections, but he is not bound by the commission's findings. After a judge's appointment is confirmed, the judge holds office until the next retention election. To remain on the appellate courts in California, judges must face a retention election. These elections are noncompetitive; the voters are asked whether or not the judge should remain on the appellate bench.

Judges serving on California's superior courts are elected to the bench through nonpartisan elections. However, in most cases, judges initially come to the superior court bench by gubernatorial nomination. Vacancies on the superior court occur because a judge retires, leaves due to poor health, or dies. Although judges are elected to the trial courts of California, the reality is that these elections typically draw very little attention. California voters are not highly aware of the judicial candidates for these positions, nor are they as concerned about judicial offices as they are about other political offices, such as state representatives or executive officials. From time to time, however, voter awareness about a judge's performance on a particular case or rulings in a specific issue area may lead voters to remove a judge from the bench.

Removing Judges from the Bench

As we have already discussed in this chapter, voters may remove judges from the bench during an election. There are other means for removing judges if there are concerns regarding judicial misconduct or judicial competency.

- Impeachment: California's judges may be impeached by the assembly and convicted by a two-thirds majority of the State Senate.

- Recall election: Like the governor, California judges are subject to recall election if the voters petition a recall.

- Regulatory Commission investigation: The Commission on Judicial Performance may, after investigation of complaints regarding misconduct or incapacity, punish, censure, or remove a judge from office.

Who Has Access to the Court?

The California constitution and its statutes provide rights to the people of California regarding access to the courts. Recently, Chief Justice Ronald M. George has become engaged in overseeing the pursuit of reforms to statewide court access. According to "California Courts, Reference—How to Use: Guide to California Courts" Californians have

- the right to sue for money owed and for other relief;
- the right to defend oneself against a lawsuit;
- the right to be presumed innocent if charged with a crime;
- the right to defend oneself against all criminal charges;
- the right to a public and speedy trial by jury if charged with a misdemeanor or a felony;
- the right to an attorney at public expense if one is charged with a felony or misdemeanor and cannot afford an attorney.

These rights listed above apply to citizens of the state and noncitizens alike. These rights do not mitigate against concerns about quality of legal representation for indigent persons. The lack of resources in some local court jurisdictions, especially in smaller localities, and the impact of the current budget crisis on the state's judiciary as a whole will affect the access to the courts.

Judicial Independence versus Judicial Accountability

Unlike the federal judiciary, which consists of appointed judges who serve life terms with good behavior, many states have some form of election system for selecting their judges. The reason that federal judges are appointed is to allow for an independent judiciary. Theoretically, appointed judges are less likely to be influenced by politics in their decision making, because they do not have to rely on the electorate to maintain their jobs on the bench. Most of the states, however, adopted some kind of election system for selecting their judges or retaining their judges, because states wanted judicial accountability. Elections allow for accountability by giving the voters the opportunity to select members of their courts and also to remove them through the election process if the jurists make decisions that are contrary to the public's preferences.

Although the voters rarely pay much attention to competitive judicial races or judicial retention elections, there have been instances when judges have lost their seats on the bench because of voters' perceptions about judicial rulings. In the November 1986 election, six of the seven justices serving on the California Supreme Court were seeking retention. Of these six, Governor George Deukmejian targeted three and spoke out publicly against their retention on the state supreme court. Deukmejian criticized these judges for their rulings in death-penalty cases. The governor was especially critical of Rose Bird, who was the chief justice of the California Supreme Court at that time. He warned Bird and two associate justices, Cruz Reynoso and Joseph Grodin, that if they didn't change their rulings in death-penalty appeals and uphold the death-penalty sentences, he would oppose their retention elections. Numerous interest groups and political action committees joined the governor's campaign against Rose Bird and her two colleagues. Political advertisements against the retention of Bird, Grodin, and Reynoso aired on radio and television. In response, Chief Justice Rose Bird produced a television ad explaining her decision-making record to the voters. Her explanations did not satisfy the electorate, however, and on November 4, 1996, Bird, Grodin, and Reynoso lost their seats on the California Supreme Court. Shortly thereafter, Governor Deukmejian appointed three justices to replace them, including Malcolm Lucas, who was nicknamed "Maximum Malcolm" because of his rulings sentencing convicted criminals to maximum penalties, including death.

Despite the low visibility of judicial elections, these elections have many political scientists and jurists concerned, particularly over the amount of money being spent by candidates in judicial elections.

A 1995 study of contested elections in Los Angeles County Superior Court reported that campaign spending by trial court judges had risen a great deal in the years between 1976 and 1994. In 1976, the median cost of a judicial campaign for an L.A. County Superior Court seat was approximately $3,000. By 1994, the median skyrocketed to $70,000. Incumbents running for re-election spent, on average, $20,000 more than the median challenger, or $95,000 in 1994. Compare that to the $1,000 median campaign expenditure of an incumbent in 1976.

The Civil Justice Association of California (CJAC), a group of citizens, taxpayers, and professionals, reviewed campaign contributions to the California judiciary from 1997 to 2000 and found the following:

- from 1997 to 2000, contributions to candidates in contested superior court elections totaled over $3 million for four counties;

- in a single race in Sacramento County, over $1 million was raised;

- attorneys are the largest contributors to most judicial races;

- two supreme court justices seeking retention in 1998—remember, these are uncontested elections—received contributions of $887,000 and $710,000.

The escalation of campaign spending in judicial elections is controversial, because it usually requires judicial candidates to seek funding support from outside sources. Like candidates seeking election to state legislative or executive offices, judges are now receiving and even soliciting financial support from organized interests. This phenomenon has even spilled over into retention elections for the state supreme court, even though they are noncompetitive. Judges must solicit campaign contributions in order to retain their seats on the bench. Contributors often include trial lawyers' associations and other special interests. This connection has raised concern, because when interest groups contribute financially to a judge's campaign, the potential for influence over judicial decision making arises. While elections allow for accountability, the notion is that accountability is to the citizens or voters, not to the more narrow preferences of an organized interest group.

Most people consider the judiciary the least political of all of the branches of government, yet the increased spending in competitive and noncompetitive elections for judgeships compromises this assumption. Even judges are expressing concern. In 2001, an opinion survey, "Justice at Stake Campaign," revealed that 53 percent of California judges are dissatisfied with the current climate of judicial campaigning in the state. Over 80 percent of the judges surveyed believed that voters knew little about candidates for the bench and were electing judges based on criteria other than qualifications for office. The majority of judges polled agreed that reform of campaign financing of judicial elections is necessary and that public financing of these elections would be an appropriate alternative.

In response to stories in the media, including a series of articles published in the *Los Angeles Times*, and the concerns of the public, judges, public officials, and others, a task force has been created to examine judicial campaigns in California. The Judicial Campaign Task Force for Impartial Courts was established in 2007. It consists of 14 members appointed by California Supreme Court Chief Justice, Ronald M. George, and it is investigating several issues, including the structure of California judicial elections as well as filing, reporting, and accessibility of judicial campaign contributions and spending. The findings of this commission are due later this year (2009).[3] It is worthwhile to note that reforms and current state policies include the following:

- Judicial candidates are prohibited from making statements that commit or appear to commit them with respect to cases, controversies, or issues that could come before the courts.

- Judicial candidates may not knowingly misrepresent the identity, qualifications, present position, or other facts concerning themselves or an opponent.

- Judicial candidates are not prohibited from soliciting campaign contributions.

- Like all other state political candidates, judicial candidates are required to report all campaign contributions and expenditures.

- Any contributions to or expenditures of judicial candidates of $100 or more must be itemized. Judicial candidates for superior court may file a candidate statement to be included in the voter's pamphlet. These statements are very expensive, however, and the cost is prohibitive for most candidates.

There is one further caveat that should be mentioned. Whenever limits or rules are placed on campaign spending, the rights of freedom of expression and freedom of association guaranteed by both the California and United States constitutions may be abridged. Campaigning for political office is guaranteed by the right to speak freely, and in today's political contests, it is becoming increasingly expensive. Therefore, it is almost impossible to impose limits on campaign spending. So judges running for retention on the California Supreme Court or running to serve on the state's trial courts must exercise their own restraint—not an easy thing to do if your opponent or opposing forces are spending a lot of money to keep you off the bench.

The Politicization of the Judiciary

While the judiciary is ostensibly the least political of all of the branches of government, state courts are often called upon to mediate important political issues. For example, on May 15, 2008, the California Supreme Court ruled in the case *In re Marriage Cases* that the state of California does not have a compelling state interest to limit marriage to the traditional definition—one man and one woman—and that prohibiting same-sex couples from marrying is a violation of the equal protection clause. The repercussions from this ruling have been significant. Mobilization of interest in opposition to the ruling was swift. The repercussions from this ruling have been significant. Mobilization of interest in opposition to the ruling was swift, and as a result Proposition 8, which sought to eliminate same sex marriage in California, appeared on the November 2008 ballot. This ballot measure was written specifically to overturn the California Supreme Court's ruling. The 2008 California *Official Voter Information Guide*, which provides arguments for and against ballot propositions, quotes Proposition 8 advocates Ron Prentice of the California Family Council and Rosemarie Avila, Governing Board member of the Santa Ana Unified School District, "It overturns the outrageous decision of four activist Supreme Court judges who ignored the will of the people." Over 52 percent of the electorate agreed and Proposition 8 passed. Politics are dynamic, however, and there are currently a number of legal challenges to the validity of this measure. Therefore, the status of this new state constitutional amendment is in question and, ironically, it will be judges once again who will determine the outcome.[4]

As mentioned earlier in this chapter, judges, even justices of state supreme courts, have their own political beliefs. We are most likely to witness these beliefs when judges are confronted with issues that tap into their ideological preferences in cases that come before them. These issues are often controversial. For example, one issue that California State Supreme Court justices must deal with is the death penalty. The case of former Chief Justice Rose Bird illustrates this well. In 1977, Rose Bird was appointed chief justice to the California Supreme Court by Governor Jerry Brown. Her appointment was important politically because she was not only the first woman to serve as chief justice, she was the first woman to be appointed to the state high court. Rose Bird was staunchly against the death penalty. During her tenure as chief justice, she ruled in sixty-one death-penalty cases. In each of these cases she voted against the imposition of the death penalty. As with the recent gay marriage ruling, many citizens mobilized prior to Bird's retention election in 1986 and campaigned vigorously to have her removed from the court. Citizens and special interests who were pro–death penalty argued that she was ruling contrary to what the law and the citizens preferred. In addition, voters were urged by these same groups to not retain Associate Justices Cruz Reynoso and

Joseph Grodin, who served with Chief Justice Bird and often voted similarly to her in death-penalty cases. This opposition movement was successful, and in 1986 Chief Justice Bird and Associate Justices Reynoso and Grodin were removed from the bench by the voters.

These are just two illustrations of the politicization of the courts. Every term, judges serving on the California bench across all court levels (trial, intermediate appellate, and supreme) are confronted with cases that require them to make political decisions or decisions that have political effects. One final example of this is political redistricting. The redrawing of electoral districts is always a political process. Political parties seek to either maintain or increase their odds of getting candidates re-elected through the redrawing of district lines. It is very common for redistricting plans to end up contested in the courts by political parties, elected officials, candidates seeking political office, and/or organized special interests. Since the 1980s, the California courts have been involved in many cases and controversies regarding redistricting. Perhaps the most controversial was in 2005, when Governor Schwarzenegger and others proposed an initiative, Proposition 77, that would reform redistricting procedures in the state. Rather than having legislators redraw district lines after each census, the responsibility would be given to a panel of three retired judges (selected by legislative officials). This ballot measure was contested in the California Courts of Appeals before it even appeared on the ballot. Those opposed to the measure argued that judges should not be put in the role of redrawing or creating new political districts. Although there was some success with procedural challenges to the initiative at the Courts of Appeals, attempts to block the initiative from the ballot finally failed, and the voters had the opportunity to decide in November 2005 whether or not retired judges should be redrawing the state's electoral district lines. The voters vetoed the measure by a margin of approximately 19 percent.

All of the issues mentioned here point to the many political dimensions of the judiciary. While it is most common for us to consider the "political branches" such as the legislature and the executive first when we think about politics, it is important to remember that courts play a significant role in political processes and that this is especially true in California. The presence of the initiative, referendum, and recall facilitate this role further. The increased spending on judicial campaigns at the trial and appellate levels adds another dimension that may call some of these other political actions into question.

Judicial Review and the Statewide Initiative

Another issue of concern regarding the judiciary in California is the relationship between direct democracy and judicial review. It is vitally important to keep in mind that, regardless of the method of selection of judges, judicial decisions or rulings may have far-reaching consequences for all of us. California is one of twenty-six states in the United States that allows for citizens to propose and enact their own legislation through the initiative. Moreover, the California state constitution permits citizens to use the initiative to enact statutes and constitutional amendments.

The popular initiative was implemented in this state during the early twentieth century by Progressives such as the Lincoln-Roosevelt League, along with other like-minded groups seeking political reform in California government. As an alternative policy-making tool, the initiative allows citizens to circumvent the legislature and write and enact policies reflecting their own political preferences. Theoretically, the initiative performs as another check against unresponsive government. Therefore, when citizens believe that the legislature is not responding to their demands—that is, when the legislature is not enacting laws that they would like them to—the people may propose their own laws and, if they are successful at getting them on the ballot, persuade the voters to enact them.

The initiative, however, is also subject to judicial interpretation and judicial review, just like a piece of legislation coming out of the state legislature. Since the success of Proposition 13, the property tax reform initiative, in 1978, the use of the initiative in California has increased greatly. Organized interests and citizen-based movements have attempted to use the initiative to enact policies in California in nearly every conceivable issue area. Victim's rights and penalty enhancements for criminals, such as the three-strikes law, have been enacted through the initiative. The decriminalization of marijuana for medicinal purposes was adopted via the initiative. Term limits for many of California's elected officials were also ballot initiatives. Voters in California have also enacted policies for insurance reform, registration of sex offenders, anti-immigration policies, and anti-affirmative action laws in the past thirty years. While it is erroneous to argue that all initiatives in California reflect controversial issues such as those listed above, it is clear that the initiative has been used increasingly over the past twenty years to enact a wide array of policies that reflect citizen dissatisfaction with elected state government.

When the initiative is used to enact controversial policies, it is usually debated in the press, and if that controversial initiative is successful at getting voter approval, there is a very strong likelihood that it will be contested in the courts. In fact, the constitutional validity of each of the initiatives described in the preceding paragraph has been challenged in at least one court of law. The outcomes of these court cases have varied. But what is important is this: just like judges on federal courts, state court judges have the power of judicial review. When state judges have the power to overturn laws enacted by the people as well as laws composed by state legislators, the tension between lawmaking and law reviewing is heightened.

Is this tension all that important? Many scholars and many voters would argue that it is. In fact, the common opinion among the electorate in California is that the initiative as an alternative policy-making tool has become an exercise in futility, precisely because of legal intervention. The consensus among California voters is that once an initiative passes at the ballot box, it ends up in a court of law. In truth, courts are reactive bodies. Judges must wait until a case comes to their courtrooms in order to make a legal decision. So why do so many initiatives end up in the California courts? The answer is simply politics. California is a very diverse state, and our diversity can be measured in a number of ways. We are diverse in race and ethnicity, we are diverse in culture, we are diverse economically, we are even diverse in terrain and climate. Given so many dimensions of diversity, there is no dearth of conflict in our state regarding which political problems are important and which solutions to these problems should be adopted. Hence, California courts also function as another arena for the continuation of political debate. Hence, California courts also function as another arena for the continuation of political debate. The response to the State Supreme Court's 4–3 ruling in *In re marriage cases* and the subsequent proposal and adoption of Proposition 8 illustrate this well.[5]

California Courts: Where Are We Now?

A number of issues currently confront California's courts. Although there was a slight decrease in the total number of cases filed between 2001–2002 and 2002–2003, this trend has changed and the number of filings have been increasing since 2003–2004 and through the 2006–2007 fiscal years. The most recent data indicate that overall caseload has increased for all court levels. Despite the increase in filings, California superior courts have continued to dispose of slightly over 90 percent of criminal cases within twelve months. At the appellate court level, the California Supreme Court's caseload has fluctuated somewhat in recent years, but the percentage of petitions granted review has remained relatively stable. In 2006–2007, for example, the court granted review to only 8 percent of the petitioners who filed during that term. The judiciary's ability to effectively dispose of its workload may be compromised by the status of the state budget and the allocation of resources. The concern about adequate resources is felt most strongly at the superior court level.

Reforming judicial campaigns in the state is also a critical agenda item. Some attempts at reform, such as campaign finance reporting, have been implemented and have not been found unconstitutional. However, when voters amended the state constitution in 1986 to prohibit political parties from endorsing judges, who run in nonpartisan elections, the California Supreme Court found the initiative unconstitutional because it violated our rights to freedom of expression and freedom of association. Obviously, judges have a lot of say when it comes to these reforms, and it is up to the individual judge to decide how much is too much when it comes to campaign spending.

FOR FURTHER READING

American Judicature Society (AJS). *Judicial Selection in the States*. www.judicialselection.us/

Bonneau, Christopher W., and Melinda Gann Hall. *In Defense of Judicial Elections*. New York: Routledge Press. Forthcoming May 2009. This forthcoming book is a critique of previous empirical studies of judicial elections. Bonneau and Hall argue that elections as a selection method for judges is actually beneficial to democratic society.

California Courts, Guide to California Courts. www.courtinfo.ca.gov/courts

Civil Justice Association of California. "Campaign Contributions to the California Judiciary 1997–2000." www.cjac.org/

Judicial Council of California Strategic Plan, March 2000. www.courtinfo.ca.gov/reference/documents/stplanzk.pdf

The National Organization for Women. "NOW Opposes Extremist Judicial Nominees—Regardless of Gender." www.now.org/issues/legislat/nommees/brown.html

Streb, Matthew J., ed. *Running for Judge: The Rising Political, Financial and Legal Stakes of Judicial Elections*. New York: New York University Press. 2007. This edited book is a collection of contemporary research conducted by professors who study state courts and judicial elections. Each chapter examines current issues and controversies that are confronted by state courts and state court judges.

ON THE WEB

The California Supreme Court Historical Society (CSCHS): http://cschs.org
CSCHS catalogs and archives information about the California Supreme Court's history.

The National Center for State Courts (NCSC): http://ncsconline.org
NCSC is an organization that provides services for court administrators, practitioners, and others interested in state courts. The Web site includes information, datasets, and articles about state courts and court related topics.

SUMMARY

The California judiciary includes the courts, branch agencies, branch administration, and the State Bar of California. California is a highly litigious state, and the courts must accommodate a tremendous workload. In recent years, California courts have adjudicated more than 9,000,000 cases in a year.

The California judiciary consists of three levels:

1. Superior courts. These are the trial courts of the state court system. These courts handle cases involving criminal and civil violations of state and local laws. Judges on superior courts determine sentencing for convicted persons and have some discretion when giving punishments.
2. The Courts of Appeals of California. This is an intermediate appellate court. These courts review the majority of criminal and civil matters appealed from the superior courts.
3. California Supreme Court. This is the highest court of the state. It has discretion over the cases it reviews on appeal from the lower state courts. However, all death-penalty judgments are automatically appealed to the California Supreme Court.

Judges are initially appointed to the California Supreme Court by the governor with the advice of the Commission on Judicial Appointments. The governor may choose to ignore this advice and does not need the approval of the commission to make an appointment. Judges on the state supreme court serve twelve-year terms. To retain their seats on the bench, they must be approved by the electorate in retention elections. Retention elections are uncontested elections in which the voters vote either "yes" to retain a judge on the California Supreme Court or "no" to remove the judge from the bench. This same method of selection is used for judges on the California Courts of Appeals.

Superior court judges are selected to their courts by non-partisan election. These trial court judges serve six-year terms.

Students of law, courts, and journalists have become increasingly concerned about judicial elections. On the one hand, judicial elections provide for some level of accountability. For example, if judges are not following statutory sentencing guidelines in criminal cases or making huge monetary awards for punitive damages in civil suits, there should be some mechanism in place to keep their rulings in line with public preferences. On the other hand, judicial elections have become increasingly expensive. Special interests with deep pockets may be able to influence not only the outcome of judicial elections, but also how judges decide in some situations. Even judges are becoming concerned about the influence of money in judicial elections and the effects that money may have as a constraint on who runs for judge and who ends up on the bench. Finally, of greatest concern is the public's perception of courts and their legitimacy, as campaign contributions from organized interests play an increasing role in these electoral contests.

The qualifications for judge are the same for the three court levels. Potential jurists in California must have at least ten years of practice of law in the state of California or service as a judge of a court of record.

There are three ways to remove California judges from office. They may be impeached by the Assembly and convicted by a two-thirds majority of the State Senate, they may be recalled from the bench, or the Commission on Judicial Performance may after investigation of complaints regarding misconduct or incapacity punish, censure, or remove a judge from office.

Judges who have served on the California Supreme Court have had success at being promoted to the federal bench. The most recent attempt at promoting a state supreme court judge to the federal courts of appeals however, was very controversial and initially unsuccessful. Janice Brown, a Republican and conservative judge, was appointed to the California Supreme Court in 1996 by Governor Pete Wilson. President George Bush attempted to nominate Judge Brown to the D.C. Circuit Court of Appeals in 2003, but he was unable to get her nomination confirmed by the United States Senate until June 2005.

PRACTICE QUIZ

1. The method of selection for California State Supreme Court judges is
   a) gubernatorial appointment.
   b) popular election.
   c) gubernatorial appointment with confirmation by the Commission on Judicial Appointments.
   d) legislative selection.

2. Trial courts in California are known as
   a) municipal courts.
   b) appellate courts.
   c) superior courts.
   d) inferior courts.

3. State judicial elections are controversial because
   a) they are too competitive.
   b) they are becoming increasingly expensive.
   c) judges may be influenced in their decision making by special interests.
   d) both b and c

4. The California Supreme Court has discretion over most appellate cases.
   a) True
   b) False

5. The two types of jurisdiction California courts have are known as
   a) limited and geographical.
   b) original and limited.
   c) original and special.
   d) original and appellate.

6. Approximately 9,000,000 cases were processed by California courts in 2000–2001. How many of these were criminal cases?
   a) 20 percent
   b) over 80 percent
   c) 50 percent
   d) less than 60 percent

7. On average, criminal cases are decided within how many months?
   a) six months
   b) twenty-four months
   c) twelve months
   d) ten months

8. Many states have some form of election for their judges because
   a) they desire more accountability.
   b) they value judicial independence.
   c) they believe in free and open elections.
   d) judges prefer election systems over appointment systems.

9. Electoral margins for the approval of justices in retention elections is
   a) approximately 80 percent.
   b) approximately 60 percent.
   c) approximately 90 percent.
   d) approximately 70 percent.

10. Which of the following is *not* a means of removal for California state judges
    a) gubernatorial removal.
    b) recall election.
    c) impeachment.
    d) removal by the Commission on Judicial Performance.

CRITICAL-THINKING QUESTIONS

1. Given the concern over the role of money in judicial elections, what kinds of reforms might be implemented that would still allow for accountability? Is it possible to keep money or special interests out of judicial elections?

2. What factors do you believe are responsible for the tremendous criminal caseload in the California superior courts?

3. Is judicial independence important for state court judges?

4. What kinds of checks are there on the California judiciary? How do the other branches and other political actors hold the state courts accountable?

KEY TERMS

At this point you should have a general understanding of the following concepts and terms:

appellate jurisdiction (129)
civil courts (124)
judicial accountability (130)

judicial discretion (127)
judicial independence (130)

retention election (129)
superior courts (127)

8

The State Budget and Budgetary Limitations

WHAT CALIFORNIA GOVERNMENT DOES, AND WHY IT MATTERS

Consider those who wait for the state budget to be passed:

★ A nonprofit agency that wants to sponsor a low- to moderate-income housing development that depends on state housing construction funds

★ Librarians, waiting to see whether cities and counties will have sufficient funds to keep their branches open during the forthcoming fiscal year

★ Cities, waiting to see if there are sufficient funds to avoid having "no city services" days when staff members would be furloughed

★ Part-time university faculty members, who know that without sufficient funding, they may not be able to obtain sufficient classes to support themselves

★ College students, who need sufficient classes to maintain their work schedules and graduate on time

★ School districts, whose level of funding is dependent in part on whether the state continues its policy of paying for small class sizes in the early grades

★ Park rangers, whose maintenance budgets depend on a combination of the fees users pay to use the parks and the state budget

The range is wide, from parks to schools, and almost everyone in the state is affected in one way or another. The state of California has a budget of over $130 billion, and the total state and local budget is even higher. And what do we get for that money? Almost every governmental service or regulation that can be imagined, from police and fire services and the permit for your house addition to the classes at the University of California, California State University, and the community colleges.

It's hard to imagine anything this large, but consider that the state is the fifth or sixth largest economy among the nations of the world. Its projected deficit in 2008-2009 was larger than the entire budgets of all but the five to ten largest states. Over 2.5 million workers in California—one out of six—work for the federal, state, or local governments, and a significant number of the rest are indirectly funded by the public sector.[1]

For something this large and significant, it is amazing that the process to approve the budget and some of the items in it is so controversial. The public itself is split—most Californians are opposed to spending cuts in public programs as well as increases in taxes or fees. They are also distrustful of the state government and disapprove of the job their politicians are doing. One political party won't increase taxes under any circumstances; the other wants to borrow to fill part of the gap. One group of legislators considers the entire budget so illegitimate that they won't vote for it under any realistic set of circumstances, and, in fact, at least one of them hasn't voted for a budget in over a decade. On the other hand, the legislature came within one vote of increasing the sales tax in 2002, but that one vote couldn't be found under any circumstance.

The amount—and intensity—of political controversy over this budget, a document that embodies the values and decisions of the citizens, its legislature, and its leaders, is truly remarkable.

Passing the budget is at the center, both in difficulty and in scope, of what state government does each year. Since the passage of Proposition 13, state government has received less revenue, which has become more volatile, rising and falling with the economy. The state constitution says that the legislature is to pass the budget by June 15. Since 1990, the legislature has met the deadline only four times, and two of those four were budget surplus years, when it is easier to pass a budget.

How Is the Budget Formed?

The process of forming a budget has four steps. Most governments today follow a similar process—proposal by the executive branch, enactment by the legislature, approval by the governor, and implementation by the executive branch.

Executive Proposal

Each fall, state agencies send their budget proposals to the governor through the State Department of Finance. The governor formulates his budget proposal and sends it to the legislature in January. In late spring, he revises the proposal in what is called "the May revise."

Actually, prior to 1922, agencies proposed their budgets directly to the legislature; there was no unified state budget proposed by the governor or anyone else. "Budgeting was the domain of interest groups, department heads, and ranking committee members." Progressive Governor Hiram Johnson in 1911 asked for justification for the amounts contained in the appropriations bills sent to him. Finding little or no justification, he created a Board of Control to advise him on the fiscal justification for each appropriation.

In 1922, California adopted its own version of new federal legislation (1921) unifying the budget process. The legislation called for a consolidated administration proposal in the form of a governor's budget that must be balanced, contain justifications for the amounts proposed, and be accompanied by bills in each house that legislative leaders are required to introduce, thus providing a starting point for the negotiations and decisions each year. The existence of a governor's budget was an improvement over the situation before 1900, when "government structures . . . hid more than they revealed to the public."[2]

Legislative Adoption

The legislature adopts a budget based on the governor's proposal. Both the Assembly and the State Senate must adopt the budget by a two-thirds majority of the entire membership of the body. The Assembly and Senate budget committees and their subcommittees hold hearings on the budget bills, receiving testimony and input from individuals and groups, including the affected departments and agencies, the Department of Finance, the Legislative Analyst's Office, committee staff, and interest groups.

The **Legislative Analyst's Office** provides nonpartisan and independent review of the entire budget, including alternative ways to accomplish the same goals and objectives. The Legislative Analyst, Elizabeth Hill, has been called "the Budget Nun . . . because her fiscal reports are incorruptible. They're the bible. The one source of truth. . . . She's the most influential non-elected official in the Capitol."[3]

Normally, the Assembly budget and the Senate budget differ, resulting in the appointment of a **Budget Conference Committee** to work out the differences, always with an eye on compromises that will maximize the probability of receiving a two-thirds vote on final passage. If the conference committee cannot resolve an issue, the **Big 5** group, consisting of the governor, Assembly Speaker, Senate president pro tempore, and the Assembly and Senate minority leaders, meet to resolve the issue.

Gubernatorial Action

The governor may use his line-item veto to lower any line-item appropriation in the budget, including lowering it to zero. The legislature may override the governor's veto by a two-thirds majority in each of the two houses and replace the lowered number with its own amount, although this action is rare.

Implementation

Agencies implement the budget as passed. The Department of Finance states explicitly that agencies and departments are expected to operate within their budgets and comply with any provisions enacted by the legislature. "The general expectation is that state agencies comply with the legislative intent."[4] There is some flexibility in implementation, but, compared with other states, the governor's flexibility is limited, as we shall see.

BOX 8.1 | The Constitutional Requirements for California's Budget

1. Within the first ten days of the calendar year, the governor must submit to the legislature a unified budget that is balanced, contains an explanation for each proposed expenditure, and is accompanied by a budget bill itemizing the recommended expenditures.

2. The budget bills must be introduced immediately in each house by the respective appropriations chairs.

3. The legislature must pass the budget by June 15 of each year; however, there is no penalty for not reaching the June 15 deadline.

4. Appropriations from the general fund must be passed in each house by a two-thirds majority of the membership. This is a very strict requirement compared with other states. Note that the requirement is "of the membership," not just those present and voting. Interestingly, education funding (K-12) is exempted from the two-thirds rule, but in practice the entire budget is approved as a whole by a two-thirds vote.

5. When the governor signs the budget bill(s), he is allowed to reduce or eliminate an item of appropriation. This is the line-item veto, a powerful tool.

Other Groups Involved in the Budget Process

In addition to the governor and legislature, who are at the center of the process, the agencies mentioned above—the Department of Finance on the executive side and the Legislative Analyst's Office on the legislative side—are closely involved in the process, as well as two other groups:

- the courts, who sometimes have ruled on the constitutionality of particular budget actions, particularly on proposed administrative actions taken in the absence of a budget when the legislature has been late. They have also had to decide the constitutionality of various budget provisions, like the two-thirds majority requirement for passing the budget or the Proposition 13 limits.

- Moody's, Fitch Ratings, and Standard & Poor's, who rate the ability of the states to repay their bond issues. The rating is one of several factors that influence the cost of selling a bond issue. The lower the credit rating, the higher the interest rate that must be paid to induce investors to purchase the bonds. In 2003, Moody's rating of California's bonds was the lowest rating given for any state. By 2008, California's credit rating had crept up, but it was still the second lowest, next to Louisiana's, among the fifty states. A 2008 campaign by California's former attorney general, Bill Lockyer, to persuade the credit rating agencies to rate public debt on the same scale as corporate debt resulted in Moody's stating that they would revise the system to reflect only the risk of default. In December 2008, however, Standard & Poor's announced the lowering of California's short-term debt rating to reflect the state's continuing budget crisis.

What Is in the Budget?

Every state budget contains the following information:

- economic assumptions—How will the economy respond during the forthcoming fiscal year, and what does that response mean for revenues and expenditures?
- revenues expected in the various categories
- expenditures appropriated by department and program

Revenues

Looking at all sources of revenue, both general funds and special funds, the revenue sources are as follows, according to the governor's budget proposal in January, 2008 and the update provided for the legislature special session in December 2008:

PERSONAL INCOME TAX California's personal income tax ranges from 0 percent to 9.3 percent of income, with a substantial credit per child or dependent. The income tax is considered highly progressive, with the top 5 percent of taxpayers paying about two-thirds of the income tax, while the bottom 40 percent pay less than 1 percent.[5] This is one of the most progressive personal income taxes in the nation. Regular income (salaries and wages) does not vary that much from year to year, but capital gains income (income from selling stock that has appreciated in value, for example) varies considerably from one year to the next, making revenues from the income tax fluctuate considerably one year to the next. The governor's November 2008 revenue estimate for the personal income tax is $48.5 billion, down $7.2 billion or 13 percent in just the six months from the May 2008 estimates.

SALES TAX The state sales tax is 7.25 percent, with counties or taxing districts allowed to add between one-eighth percent and one-half percent per local district

TABLE 8.1 ★ Revenue Sources, 2008–2009 Budget, May 2008 Governor's Revise

REVENUE SOURCES	DOLLARS (IN MILLIONS)	PERCENT OF TOTAL REVENUE
Personal income tax	$ 55,182	43%
Sales tax	33,575	26%
Corporation tax	11,039	9%
Highway users' taxes	3,383	3%
Motor vehicle fees	5,966	5%
Insurance tax	2,029	2%
All others	17,867	14%
Total	129,041	

for local services. In some areas there is more than one district tax in effect. The largest cities in the state have the highest sales tax rates: Los Angeles (8.25%), San Francisco (8.5%), Oakland (8.25%), Sacramento (7.75%), and San Diego (7.75%). Economists consider the sales tax regressive—that is, as individual or household income increases, the proportion of income paid through the tax decreases, because lower-income households spend a higher proportion of their incomes on consumption goods that are taxed compared with higher income households. In California, the state refunds 1.25 percent of its share to the local city and county; this feature has led many cities to search for businesses that are both clean industries and have a high sales volume, such as big-box shopping centers and automobile dealerships.

A state sales tax has existed in California since 1933, with the rate being raised on the average every five years. On January 1, 2002, the state rate went, for example, from 7.0 percent to 7.25 percent. The sales tax base varies considerably with the economy. Within recent five-year periods, gains have ranged from 0 percent to 14 percent per year. The governor's November 2008 revenue estimate for the sales tax is $25.5 billion, down $8.1 billion or 24 percent in just the six months from the May 2008 estimates.

PROPERTY TAX All owners of property pay California's property tax, limited under Proposition 13 to 1 percent of the assessed value in 1975 or the value of a more recent sale. Once acquired, annual tax increases are limited to 2 percent or the amount of inflation, whichever is less. Proposition 13 passed overwhelmingly in 1978 and contains provisions requiring special votes greater than 50 percent for legislators and voters to raise taxes. Proposition 13 rolled back property taxes in California by more than half, and the state has endeavored to make up the difference ever since. Local property tax revenue available for cities, counties, and school districts has been substantially reduced. As a result, all local government entities are more reliant on the state for revenue, and decision-making power has substantially shifted, in the eyes of virtually all observers, from the local level to the state level. School districts are an excellent example of the effects. Whereas California once had some of the best-quality and best-funded schools in the nation, its expenditures per pupil have fallen in comparison to the rest of the nation, its staff per student ratio is now 70 percent of the average for other states, its student achievement levels lag behind the rest of the nation, and a substantially greater proportion of high-income families send their children to private schools compared with the pre-1978 period. At the same time, teacher salaries are relatively high because of the cost of living, in particular housing prices, and the desire to attract good-quality recruits to the profession. The infrastructure discussion in Chapter 10 has more examples.

CORPORATION TAX The corporation tax taxes corporate profits and provides about 8 percent of state revenues. The corporation tax structure is cited favorably by *Governing* magazine in its appraisal of the state's tax system as "tough on the creation of tax-dodge subsidiaries, and the law covers a firm's property and assets, not just its sales."[6] Almost 500,000 corporations filed tax returns in 1999, but "the 1.9 percent with taxable incomes in excess of $1 million paid 80.1 percent of the tax. The ten largest corporations pay 20 percent of the tax in any given year."[7]

The overall tax structure, compared with other states, is more dependent on taxes that are volatile—that is, they go up and down with the economy (income tax, sales tax) and less dependent on taxes that don't vary with the economy (the property tax), because of the Proposition 13 limits. The average state obtains 29 percent of its total state and local tax funds from the property tax, but because of Proposition 13's limits, California obtains only 22 percent.

INDIAN GAMBLING Revenues from Indian gambling operations in California are expected, according to the governor's budget, to produce $430 million in revenues in 2008–2009. This amount represents about 0.3 percent of the budget.

How Well Does the Taxing System Function?

The answer seems to be not very well. Consider *Governing* magazine's February 2003 analysis entitled "The Way We Tax," which gave California one star out of four in the category "Adequacy of Revenue," two out of four in "Fairness to Taxpayers," and two out of four in "Management of System."[8] Only Tennessee received a lower overall rating, and four other states were tied with California. *Governing* cited the following as inadequacies:

- The "highly progressive—and volatile"—income tax is too dependent on capital gains being taxed at the same level as regular income. Thus, when the stock market soared in 2000, tax revenues soared also, but the state received only half this amount the very next year. In 2008 the forecast for the income tax dropped 13 percent in just six months due to the downturn in the economy.

- "The state tax structure is highly elastic and, increasingly, . . . spending is inelastic," according to John Ellwood, a professor at the University of California, Berkeley, cited in the article. An elastic tax structure is one that would vary considerably as the economy expands and contracts, whereas an inelastic structure would not vary in those circumstances.

- The sales tax focuses on goods that are sold, reflecting the manufacturing economy in place when the tax was developed. But the modern economy has shifted toward services, which are not taxed—for example, a doctor's office visit or the labor charge when your automobile is fixed.

- A two-thirds majority is required to pass the California budget, a supermajority required in only two other states (Arkansas and Rhode Island).[9]

- "Ballot measures have imposed rigid spending demands." See the section entitled "Budgetary Limitations," below.

- Tax subsidies have proliferated as the legislature has added them in recent years as inducements to obtain the two-thirds majority necessary to pass the budget.

- Tax administration is split among the Franchise Tax Board, the Board of Equalization, and the Employment Development Department, an inefficient arrangement.

Is California Overtaxed?

In "Cal-Tax: Taxes Are a Heavy Burden in California," the California Taxpayers Association makes the case that "the extraordinary level of taxation in California can provide more than enough in tax revenue to fund police and fire services, education for our children, and public works projects and health and welfare services

CALIFORNIA'S BUDGET PROCESS

A comparison of the fifty states in terms of "spending restraint," "bond rating," and "tax system" has California ranked last. *USA Today* based its June 2003 survey on work done by *Governing* magazine. Each category listed above was rated with one to four stars, with four being the best rating.

USA Today published four categories of states:

- The topmost category, rated Excellent, consists of six states that averaged between ten and eleven stars, that is—three to four stars per category.

- The second category, rated Good, consists of fifteen states that averaged about eight and one-half stars—that is, between two and three stars per category.

- The third category, rated Fair, consists of nineteen states with an average of six and one-half stars—that is, between two and two and one-half stars per category.

- The fourth category, rated Poor, consists of ten states, seven of which have five stars, two of which have four stars, and California, with only two stars.

Why is California rated so low? States in the top category were cited for financial restraint. During the economic boom of the 1990s, these states limited both spending growth and tax cuts. After the economy weakened, they acted swiftly and decisively to limit finances. "California, the worst performing state . . . did the opposite. It approved large spending increases and tax cuts during the boom. When the economy soured, the state began borrowing money and using accounting gimmicks."

A second factor is related to governmental structure. *USA Today* found that spending was more restrained in states in which one party controlled the executive branch and the other party controlled the legislature, or where the houses of the legislature were headed by different parties. California has had a Democratic majority in both houses of the legislature for the last ten years, although during that time the Democrats held the governor's office, only from 1999 until Gray Davis's recall in October 2003.

A 2008 survey of the states by the Pew Center on the States published in the March 2008 issue of *Governing Magazine*, found that the average state was rated B– on money issues, including whether the state had a long-term outlook, the quality of the budget process, the structural balance of revenues and expenditures, contracting and purchasing, and financial controls/reporting. On these issues considered as a whole, California received a D+.

---

for California's poor."[10] Taxes are so high that the state is becoming economically uncompetitive with other states.

- The state is eighth highest "among the states when tax burden is compared on the basis of personal income and seventh highest per capita." No other western state is in that ranking.

- These tax figures do not include local fees imposed "as surrogates for reduced property tax revenue."

- The state's business climate ranks at the bottom of all the states except for Mississippi, according to the Tax Foundation in Washington, DC. This ranking considers both the level of taxes and the tax structure and costs imposed upon business for tax collection.

"Instead of forcing consumers and business in California to underwrite out-of-control spending, the legislature needs to exercise greater care and do a better job managing spending to insure that crucial priorities are met." One analyst puts it this way:

> Many states that rank high on the scale of taxes per $1,000 of personal income are simply low-income states. They are places like North Dakota, Mississippi, and South Carolina. These are states that, because of their low incomes and low tax bases, must exert a higher "tax effort" simply to provide basic services and facilities. California doesn't play in that league. This is a high-income state that must be compared with places like Massachusetts, New Jersey, Connecticut, and New York—places that compete with California for new jobs; places with similar tax bases and can provide an apples-to-apples comparison of tax burden.[11] When compared with these states, California's tax burden is sixth highest, with some of the other high income states ranked much lower.

On the other side of the debate, the *Los Angeles Times* editorial page argues that it is a myth in California that Californians are overtaxed. The editorial makes the following points:

- The tax load from the state and local governments in California is "about average" among the fifty states, and in some categories, it is below average.

- Several times in the last decade, the state has cut taxes, not raised them, as the state received more revenues than it expected. Six of the eight major tax actions in the last decade cut taxes.

- The federal government does not give back to the state in services all that it receives in taxes from California citizens—the last two governors have recommended strongly that the state receive increased reimbursements for the services it provides to undocumented immigrants.

- Even though the state income tax has a top rate of 9.3 percent, the tax is low for middle-class families (one or two adults with children), who pay little or no tax until they earn more than $45,000. The average income tax rate is only 3 percent.

- Although the sales tax of approximately 8 percent is high, it is less than the sales taxes paid in nine other states. Several states have raised their sales taxes, either temporarily or permanently, during the economic downturns.

- The state's gasoline tax is thirty-third in the nation; the wine tax is forty-fifth. Even with the extra fifty cents imposed on each pack of cigarettes in 1998, the cigarette tax is thirteenth in the nation.

- Business has many benefits in the tax system. While the bank and corporation tax is almost 9 percent, there are so many exemptions that the tax rate on the $1 trillion California economy is about two-thirds of 1 percent. Proposition 13 gives businesses relatively low property tax rates, especially since the turnover rate for business and commercial property is much less than the rate for private homes.

In conclusion, states the *Los Angeles Times*, "temporary new taxes cannot be avoided without risking the state's fiscal stability."[12]

Expenditures

Again looking at all expenditures, the following are the major categories for 2008–2009 in the governor's budget proposal, January 2008:

Education (K–12) takes up the largest portion of the state budget, some 40 percent of the general fund. There is a long, gradual upward trend in the proportion of the budget devoted to education, although there is a slight decline in the last two fiscal years because of declining state revenues. With the passage of Proposition 13, a gradually increasing proportion of the state general fund has been spent on K–12 education.

TABLE 8.2 ★ State Expenditures by Category, 2008-2009 Budget*

EXPENDITURES	DOLLARS (IN BILLIONS)	PERCENT OF TOTAL EXPENDITURES**
Education (K-12)	$41.3	32%
Health and human services	37.9	29%
Higher education	11.8	9%
Business, transportation, housing	8.6	7%
Legislative, judicial, executive	5.9	5%
Resources	4.0	3%
Environmental protection	1.2	1%
Corrections and rehabilitation	10.2	8%
General government	7.1	5%
Others	3.1	2%
Total	130.7	

*Includes both the general fund and special funds.
**Total does not add to 100% because of rounding.

The **Health and Human Services** category includes Medi-Cal, California's Medicaid program, which provides health coverage for the poor as well as for senior citizens in nursing homes; the public health system; Healthy Families, California's state children's health insurance program; welfare, Temporary Assistance for Needy Families; and the state contribution to food stamps and the Women-Infant-Children (WIC) supplemental food program, among many others. This category, supplemented by the federal matching funds for Medi-Cal, has been gradually decreasing as a proportion of the general fund, from about 33 percent in 1980–81 to a proposed 29 percent in 2008–2009.

Higher Education includes funding for the community college system (108 campuses), the California State University system (23 campuses), and the University of California system (10 campuses). Since 1980–81 there has been a trend downward in the proportion of the budget devoted to higher education. At one point in the early 1990s, educators feared that their state funding would decline severely, since the Corrections budget was increasing so steeply, but these trends have moderated since the mid-1990s.

The **Corrections and Rehabilitation** category provides funding for the state prisons and youth authorities. This category increased steadily from 1980–81 through the mid-1990s as the public demanded three-strikes laws and similar measures but has since leveled off.

The **Others** category provides funding for everything else in the state budget, from the coastal commissions to the state bureaucracy.

The downturn in the state's economy in 2008 produced major changes in the governor's budget recommendations in November 2008. The governor recommended spending reductions totaling $4.5 billion and revenue increases of $4.7 billion. The legislature in December passed bills by majority vote that would halve the state's eighteen-month shortfall of almost $40 billion, but the governor indicated that he would veto them. The stalemate over the budget continued.

Why Do Revenues Vary So Much?

California's budget goes up and down each year—soaring when the economy is healthy and plunging in even the mildest recessions—because of the following reasons:

- The economy. Revenues from the sales tax and the personal income tax are dependent on how the state economy performs each year.

- Compared with other states, the budget relies more on the personal income tax, the capital gains portion of which varies directly with the economy, than on the property tax, limited in 1978 by Proposition 13.

- Compared with other states, the personal income tax relies more on capital gains than on taxes on wage earners. Wage earners with families have a substantial personal exemption, sufficiently high that families with children do not pay personal income tax until their income is between $40,000 and $50,000. Meanwhile, the capital gain surge of 1999–2000 came from the sales as the stock market surged, and with the recession of the early 2000s, such sales have dwindled.

Budgetary Limitations

In addition to passing bond issues, through initiatives California voters have limited what the state government can do in some very significant areas. Here are the most significant:[13]

- **Proposition 13 (1978)** cut property taxes to the assessed valuation of the property in 1975 and allows reassessment only when the property is sold. If justified by inflation, the tax can rise a maximum of 2 percent in between assessments.

- **Proposition 62 (1986)** requires a vote of the electorate on all taxes that might be used to replace revenues lost under Proposition 13.

- **Proposition 98 (1988)** requires that 40 percent of the general fund be devoted to K–14 education, including community colleges; annual increases are to be at least equal to the increase in school enrollment and the cost of living.

- **Proposition 99 (1988)** mandated a 25-cent tax on cigarettes, with the proceeds to be spent on antismoking campaigns and medical research.

- **Proposition 111 (1990)** increased the gas tax and trucking fees, with the proceeds required to be spent on transportation projects.

- **Proposition 5 (1998)** mandated the state to negotiate a compact to allow tribal casinos in California.

- **Proposition 42 (2002)** requires that the sales tax on gasoline be devoted to transportation-related projects.

- **Proposition 49 (2002)**, supported by actor and (at that point) potential Republican candidate for governor Arnold Schwarzenegger, requires that several hundred million dollars be spent on after-school programs.

- **Proposition 71 (2004)** authorizes the sale of $3 billion in bonds to fund stem-cell research in the state.

- **Propositions 1A, 1B, 1C, 1D, 1E, 84 (2006)** authorizes over $40 billion in bonds to be spent on infrastructure improvements in the state. The interest on these bonds is paid from the budget each year.

Of these, the two that have had the most effect are Propositions 13 and 98. Proposition 13 has made the state budget more reliant on taxes that vary with the economy and less reliant on sources of income that don't vary with the economy, particularly the property tax. Proposition 98 dictated that a certain proportion of the budget, almost half when higher education is included, must be devoted to one policy area.

Recent California Budgets and the Budget Process

In each of the recent years, California lawmakers and the governor have closed the budget gap with the standard techniques used in other states as well—incremental tax increases; cuts in education, health, and social services, the largest portions of the budget; and borrowing through bond issues that are repaid over a five- to ten-year period to cover a portion of the yearly deficit. California Forward, a new bipartisan group aimed at fixing some of California's perennial budget process problems, stated in 2008 that

> the current budget process is largely a relic of the mid-20th Century, with the focus on how much to increase spending (or how much to cut), rather than the value that public services bring to Californians over time. These annual budget decisions often either push California's fiscal systems toward long-term solvency or away from it. The ongoing and chronic imbalance between revenues and expenditures is one indicator of system failure. Changing how budget process decisions are made could enable public leaders to deal with the more intractable and complex problems involving the revenue system and the state-local relationship.

They identify, as we have, the key problems of budgeting:

> The costs of operating state programs are growing faster than the revenue base that supports them. The revenue system is highly sensitive to changes in the economy, producing significant volatility. The single-year budgeting horizon encourages short-term fixes, rather than long-term solutions. The budget does not take a strategic approach to ensure a return on public investments and there is a lack of public and legislative review of how money is spent.[14]

Many commentators noted the cumulative effect of the fees and caps that have been proposed more and more in recent years.[15] Traditionally, California tried to supply sufficient services for all, on the principle that "if you're eligible, we'll serve you." The community colleges guarantee, for example, that any high school graduate can go to college. The Schwarzenegger budget for 2004–2005 in particular had caps on the numbers of persons who can be served in various programs; immigrants in Medi-Cal and the program that supplies drugs for those with AIDS are both capped at the level of January 1, 2004. California's fees for students attending the California State University and the community colleges were among the lowest in the nation; they have increased substantially in recent years. Measures are often proposed as emergency measures, but few emergency measures have ever been repealed in the past. In short, there is a lowered expectation for services that has become particularly apparent in the Schwarzenegger era but has been in the background for the last decade or more.

The California Budgetary Process: Where Are We Now?

As of 2008, the budgetary process needs substantial reform. Dan Walters, a respected California journalist, states that the inability of the legislature to deal with the budget crisis and fiscal matters in general seems to be a reflection of three structural factors:

1. The extremely short term limits on the legislature, meaning that few politicians present in 2002–2003 were also present in the early 1990s during the last budget crisis, that the leadership is inexperienced compared with other states, and that "current members [are relieved] of responsibility for past decisions."[16]

2. The bipartisan gerrymander of legislative districts after the 2000 Census, which seems, by producing so many safe districts, to have reduced the willingness to work for bipartisan solutions and compromise across the two political parties.
3. The two-thirds majority requirement for passing budgets and imposing tax increases.

FOR FURTHER READING

Barrett, Katherine, Richard Greene, Michele Mariani, and Anya Sostek. "The Way We Tax." *Governing* (February 2003): 20.

Baldassare, Mark, and Christopher Hoene. *Local Budgets and Tax Policies in California and U.S. Cities: Surveys of City Officials.* San Francisco: Public Policy Institute of California, December 2004.

Baldassare, Mark, and Matthew Newman. *The State Budget and Local Health Services in California: Surveys of Local Health Officials.* San Francisco: Public Policy Institute of California, September 2005.

California Budget Project. "Who Pays Taxes in California?" Sacramento: California Budget Project, April 2008. www.cbp.org

———. "Governor Releases Proposed 2008–09 Budget." Sacramento: California Budget Project, January 2008.

———. "Budget Backgrounder, A Mini-Primer on Bonds." Sacramento: California Budget Project, February 2006.

California Budget Project. *A Budget for All Californians: Improving the Transparency and Accountability of the State Budget.* Sacramento: California Budget Project, May 2006.

California Taxpayers Association. "Cal-Tax: Taxes Are Heavy Burden in California." www.caltax.org/California.htm

Howard, John. "The Schwarzenegger Budget." *California Journal* (February 2004): 44–47.

Public Policy Institute of California (PPIC). "Just the Facts: California's State Budget." San Francisco: Public Policy Institute of California, June 2008. www.ppic.org

———. "Just the Facts: Proposition 13, 30 Years Later." San Francisco: Public Policy Institute of California, June 2008. www.ppic.org

———. "California's State Budget." San Francisco: Public Policy Institute of California, January 2005.

———. *California's Tax Burden.* www.ppic.org. June, 2003.

——— "PPIC Statewide Survey: Special Survey on the California State Budget, June, 2003." www.ppic.org/main/publication.asp?i=427

ON THE WEB

California Budget Project: www.cbp.org/

California Forward: www.caforward.org/home
California Forward promotes better financial policy and quality public services.

Howard Jarvis Taxpayers Association: www.hjta.org/

Legislative Analyst's Office: www.lao.ca.gov/

State of California, Department of Finance–budget update site: www.ebudget.ca.gov/

State of California, Department of Finance: www.dof.ca.gov/Research/Research.php
California statistics and demographic information site

SUMMARY

The California state budget includes economic assumptions, revenues, and expenditures. Passing the budget involves many difficult decisions and trade-offs; it is at the center of what the state of California does each year.

The budget is formed through four steps:

1. The governor formulates his budget with the help of the Department of Finance. He sends the budget to the legislature each January. Each May he publishes the May revision, which contains any changes made to the budget since its January unveiling.

2. The legislature adopts the budget, passing it and any tax increases by a two-thirds majority in each house. The legislature has its own neutral budget office, the Legislative Analyst's Office. If the Assembly and Senate versions of the budget differ, a budget conference committee, with members from each side and both parties, attempts to iron out the differences. If there still are difficulties, a meeting of the Big 5 will attempt to finalize the process.

3. The governor signs or vetoes the budget. If he signs the budget, he can use his line-item veto to lower any line item, including lowering it to zero.

4. The agencies implement the budget as passed, including any control language with directions for studies that are to be carried out and presented to the legislature.

The courts and the bond review agencies (Moody's et al.) are sometimes involved in the budget process, as well.

California's constitution requires that the governor submit a balanced budget, but it does not require the legislature to pass one, and there are no penalties if the legislature does not meet the June 15 deadline specified in the constitution.

The largest single source of revenue is the personal income tax, which provides almost half the general fund and is highly progressive. The sales tax is the next largest source, providing almost 30 percent of the budget. Local governments are allowed to add one-eighth to one-half percent for local uses to the sales tax. The state returns a portion of the sales tax back to each locality, which has become very significant in the era since Proposition 13, as localities have sought to add sales-tax-producing businesses, such as big box shopping centers and automobile dealerships, to their communities. The corporation tax is the third large source of revenue for the budget. California's tax system is not rated highly, compared to the systems in other states, in part because it is extremely dependent on the economy, producing larger surges than the economy in good times and substantial deficits in poor times.

Education is the largest single expenditure; expenditures for K–14 education are required by Proposition 98 to be 40 percent or more of the general fund. Adding higher education, education constitutes approximately half the state budget. The health and human services category is the next largest, followed by the courts and corrections categories.

The most substantial limitations on the budget have come through initiatives passed by the voters, of which Proposition 13 and Proposition 98 are the most important. The text lists several initiatives that limit the budget, including the recently passed Proposition 49, supported by Arnold Schwarzenegger in 2002, that requires that several hundred million dollars be spent each year on after-school programs.

Recent California state budgets have had huge gaps between revenues and expenditures because revenues plunge when the economy goes into a recession and expenditures stay the same or increase. Therefore, state lawmakers have rolled over part of the debt by borrowing through a bond issue against future revenues. The entire process reflects several factors: the very short term limits, which have left the legislature with few politicians with sufficient experience to deal with these difficult problems; the bipartisan gerrymander after the 2000 Census, which has produced more safe seats and, thus, more partisan politicians who seem unwilling to compromise to pass the budget; and the two-thirds majority requirement, a higher requirement than all but two states.

PRACTICE QUIZ

1. Both the governor and the legislature are obliged by the California state constitution to pass a balanced budget.
   a) True
   b) False
2. The state of California cannot pass its budget each year unless the Assembly and state Senate pass the budget by ___.
   a) 50 percent plus 1 vote
   b) 55 percent
   c) 66.6 percent
   d) 75 percent
3. The state of California cannot raise state taxes unless Assembly and state Senate pass the budget by ___.
   a) 50 percent plus 1 vote
   b) 55 percent
   c) 66.6 percent
   d) 75 percent
4. Proposition 13 requires
   a) property taxes to be lowered to the level when the property was last sold. Property tax values can rise 2 percent per year.
   b) property taxes to be set at 1975 levels; property is reassessed when it is sold. Property tax values can rise 2 percent per year.
   c) property taxes to be lowered to 1945 levels; property is reassessed when it is sold. The level of the tax can rise 3 percent per year.
   d) Property taxes to be raised to the appropriate level when the property on both sides of a house or business has been sold—all the property is then reassessed at current values. The level of the tax can rise 2 percent per year if the property is not sold.
5. Proposition 98 requires education spending to be at least
   a) 50 percent of the entire state budget.
   b) 50 percent of the general fund.
   c) 33.3 percent of the general fund.
   d) 40 percent of the general fund.

6. How do term limits affect the budget process?
   a) More minority and female legislators are elected, and they are more willing to compromise to enact the budget.
   b) Former senior legislators, while not able to hold their current seats, return to the legislature each year to offer their ideas about how to solve the budget crisis.
   c) Term limits have produced majority and minority leaders in both the Assembly and Senate who are willing to compromise and get the job done.
   d) Term limits have produced a less experienced leadership who have found it difficult to compromise and enact the budget.
7. The governor's line-item veto allows
   a) the governor to lower any appropriation item.
   b) the governor, in conjunction with an agency, to veto any bill in its entirety.
   c) the governor to "pencil out" any line or sentence in any bill.
   d) the governor to raise or lower any appropriation item, including lowering the item to zero.
8. The governor's line-item veto, in contrast to his or her regular veto, may be overridden by a 50-percent-plus-one vote in both houses of the legislature.
   a) True
   b) False
9. The credit rating assigned to the state of California by Moody's, Fitch Ratings, or Standard & Poor's is important because
   a) the credit rating influences the size of the deficit or surplus California may have in any given fiscal year.
   b) when the credit rating goes down, the interest rate that the state pays to float its bonds goes up.
   c) when the credit rating goes up, the amount of interest the state pays goes down.
   d) all of the above.
   e) none of the above.
   f) a and b above, but not c.
10. Indian gambling revenues have become an extremely significant source of income for the state of California.
    a) True
    b) False

CRITICAL-THINKING QUESTIONS

1. How might California's tax system be made more predictable and less dependent on the economy than it is now? How might *Governing* magazine rate your proposed changes?
2. How should the budget process in California be reformed, assuming it should be reformed? What goals are important in reforming the process, and what changes in the process might achieve those goals?
3. Should the governor have more authority in the budget process? One of the key differences between California and Georgia was the difference in the power of the governor. Leaving aside the opinion you might have of the current incumbent, what reforms might help with the long-term budget process in California?
4. The other major player in the budget process is the legislature. How might the legislature's consideration of the budget be changed to make California's budget more predictable and timely?

KEY TERMS

At this point you should have a general understanding of the following concepts and terms:

Big 5 group (141)
big-box shopping centers/automobile dealerships (144)
Budget Conference Committee (141)
Department of Finance (141)
governor's budget (140)

Legislative Analyst's Office (141)
line-item veto (141)
May revise (140)
Moody's, Fitch Ratings, Standard & Poor's ratings (142)
personal income tax (143)

progressive (143)
regressive (144)
sales tax (143)
unified budget (140)

9 Local Government

WHAT CALIFORNIA'S LOCAL GOVERNMENTS DO, AND WHY IT MATTERS

Outside the state capital and far from Washington, DC, local governments by the thousands tackle problems, resolve conflicts, make policies, administer programs, maintain public facilities, and provide services that affect all Californians every day and in almost every way. Every person in the state, noted one observer, "is a resident of a dozen or more units of local government."[1] The complexity of the state's local government system makes it hard to generalize about what local governments do. But a short list would include the following:

★ General-purpose local governments, such as cities and counties, do everything from putting out fires to cleaning the streets and seeing that the buses run on time. They protect the health, safety, welfare, and overall quality of life of all who live within their jurisdictions.

★ Limited-purpose governments, such as school districts and other special districts, deliver specific public services such as public education, pest abatement, and irrigation to meet particular needs within defined territorial boundaries.

★ Regional governments address problems such as air pollution and population growth that affect broad areas across many jurisdictions and that require comprehensive study and planning to solve.

★ Many local governments do the actual work involved in implementing state and federal laws, from control of water quality and production of affordable housing to homeland security.

★ Most local governments provide citizens with opportunities to learn about public problems, express their opinions, practice hands-on democracy, and collectively exercise some degree of popular control on issues they really care about close to home.

★ Some local governments experiment and innovate to pioneer new ways of serving citizens better or improving the democratic process. Often these local initiatives spread and can have major impacts in reforming how government works at the state and national levels.

Not all government is local, but all politics is local, as the saying goes. The politicians in Sacramento and Washington, DC would be well advised to care more about the problems facing our local governments, to work harder to fix what's broken, and to give more support to local officials in serving the needs of the citizens who elected them to office. Unfortunately, many state and federal politicians don't care, or care enough, and some of them have paid a political price, as was demonstrated in the 2003 recall election. Local governments do a lot, and all of it matters.

The Legal Framework: Dillon's Rule, Home Rule, and Local Powers of Governance

The U.S. Constitution assigns power and authority to the national and state governments, but it says nothing about local governments. Counties, cities, special districts, and other forms of local government have no inherent rights or powers. What rights and powers they do have are conferred upon them by the state constitution or state legislature.

The constitutional doctrine that gives states ultimate authority over local governments is known as Dillon's Rule. In 1868, Iowa Judge John F. Dillon ruled that "municipal corporations" such as counties and cities are mere "creatures of the state" and may exercise only those powers delegated to them by the state.[2] Upheld by the U.S. Supreme Court in 1903 and again in 1923, Dillon's Rule is firmly established, at least in theory, as the basic legal framework for relations between state and local governments. In practice, however, only a few states like Alabama, Idaho, and Nebraska demand strict obedience to Dillon's Rule and require local governments to seek their permission in order to act. California, like most states, has passed government codes and home-rule laws that allow significant local discretion and autonomy. Within broad limits, county and city residents can select their own form of government, manage their own elections, raise their own revenues, and choose what kinds of functions to perform and at what levels of service.[3]

In California, under the provisions of Article XI, Section 5, of the state constitution and various court rulings,[4] most of the more populous cities and counties have adopted *home-rule charters*, which allow the maximum discretion and autonomy to local governments. The others are designated as *general law* cities and counties that fall more directly under state authority and control. To get an idea of just how far home-rule powers can be taken in asserting local autonomy, see the box on home rule and local autonomy in San Francisco.

A more practical restraint on state meddling in local government is based on the maxim that all politics is local. State legislators, after all, are elected by local constituencies to protect their local interests, and they won't last long if they forget who brought them to the dance. These political realities have shielded local governments from the full blast of arbitrary state authority.[5] Finally, as part of the

As a consolidated city and county, San Francisco has pushed the limits of home-rule powers about as far as they can go. Some examples:

CITY OF REFUGE LAWS

In the early 1980s, San Francisco declared itself a "sanctuary city." It has since passed a number of "city of refuge" laws to protect immigrants from illegal search and seizure by state and federal authorities. In 2001, San Francisco became the first city or county in the nation to require all agencies to honor "matricula consulare" cards offered by undocumented immigrants as legal identification.

LIMITS ON GROWTH AND DEVELOPMENT

Over the years, starting in the 1980s, San Francisco has imposed increasingly severe restrictions on high-rise construction, waterfront development, and land use generally. The city also began charging developer fees to raise new local revenues for affordable housing and public-transit improvements.

GOVERNMENT REORGANIZATION AND ELECTORAL REFORMS

In 1995, San Francisco voters approved a charter amendment that consolidated the city's divided bureaucracy under mayoral authority. The following year, voters decided to change how they elected their Board of Supervisors, rejecting the at-large system in favor of district elections, effective in 2000. Most recently, in 2002, the city adopted instant runoff voting (ranked ballots) for district elections and citywide offices, the first city in the nation to do so.

SOCIAL AND CULTURAL POLICY

In 1996, San Francisco passed its landmark Equal Benefits law, which requires all businesses and nonprofits that have contracts with the city to provide equal benefits to married employees and those with same-sex domestic partners. In February 2004, the city's new mayor, Gavin Newsom, directed that official marriage licenses be granted to same-sex couples. A month later, after more than 4,000 gay and lesbian couples had been married under the new local policy, the California Supreme Court ordered the city to halt the practice, pending judicial review. On May 15, 2008, the court ruled that the state's ban on same-sex marriage was unconstitutional and that such marriages would be legal effective June 2008 for residents and nonresidents. On November 4, 2008, however, the state's voters approved an initiative constitutional amendment, Proposition 8, eliminating the right of same-sex couples to marry. The California Supreme Court is expected to make a final ruling on legal challenges to Proposition 8 in early 2009.

As these examples illustrate, San Francisco often acts as if it were a state unto itself and not merely the creature of one. The decision to certify gay marriages, in particular, created a storm of legal challenge and political controversy across the nation. San Franciscans, however, seem to enjoy sparking conflict by pushing the envelope of their home-rule powers. Where they succeed, others may follow.

SOURCES: Richard Edward DeLeon, *Left Coast City: Progressive Politics in San Francisco, 1975–1991* (Lawrence, KS: University Press of Kansas, 1992).
"San Francisco and Domestic Partners: New Fields of Battle in the Culture War," in *Culture Wars and Local Politics*, ed. Elaine B. Sharp (Lawrence, KS: University Press of Kansas, 1999), pp. 117–36.
Rich DeLeon, "Only In San Francisco?: The City's Political Culture in Comparative Perspective," *SPUR Newsletter*, Report 411 (November 12,2002), www.spur.org/documents/OnlyInSF.pdf
"San Francisco: The Politics of Race, Land Use, and Ideology," in Rufus P. Browning, Dale Rogers Marshall, and David H. Tabb, eds., *Racial Politics in American Cities*, 3d ed. (New York: Longman, 2003), pp. 167–98.
Dean E. Murphy, "San Francisco Mayor Exults in Move on Gay Marriage," *New York Times*, February 19, 2004.

so-called "devolution revolution" that began in the 1970s, federal and state authorities have been only too eager to delegate responsibility to local governments to fend for themselves and solve their own problems, using their own money.

In sum, Dillon's Rule is very liberally construed in California. The state's constitutional and legal framework confers broad formal powers of local governance, especially in charter cities and counties. Home rule on paper, however, does not necessarily translate into home rule in reality. In recent years, as we shall see, the state's chronic budget crises and other financial disasters have been strangling the life out of some local governments and crippling the powers of others to govern. Formal authority minus needed resources equals impotent local government. That equation threatens to reduce the ideal of home rule and local autonomy to a myth.

County Governments

At the first meeting of the California legislature in 1850, lawmakers divided the state into twenty-seven counties for the purpose of administering state laws. Since then many new counties have been created, mostly by subdivision. The state's current fifty-eight counties have been with us since 1907, when the last addition, Imperial County, was carved out of the old San Diego County. (See Figure 9.1.) Political movements have arisen from time to time that attempted to split an existing county to make a new one. An 1894 amendment to the state constitution, however, made it virtually impossible to do so by requiring a favorable majority vote in both the entire county affected and in the territory of the proposed new county.[6]

California's fifty-eight counties vary greatly in their territory, population, and demographic characteristics.

- *Territory:* Just in terms of size, the differences are vast. For example, you could fit 427 areas the size of San Francisco County (47 square miles) within the borders of San Bernardino County (20,053 square miles). The differences in physical geography are equally extreme, ranging from deserts to rain forests, from flat farmlands to tall mountains. Some counties are densely urban and covered with cities, while others are so rural that coyotes outnumber people.

- *Population:* Alpine County's grand total of 1,180 residents could all live comfortably in one San Francisco precinct. Los Angeles County, at the other extreme, is bursting with nearly 10 million people, representing more than 28 percent of the state's entire population. Indeed, if Los Angeles County were a state, it would rank ninth in population size, far above Georgia and just below Michigan. The lowest-ranking twenty-nine counties combined contain only 5 percent of the state's total population; the five most populous counties (Los Angeles, Orange, San Diego, San Bernardino, and Santa Clara) hold about 55 percent of the state's total.

- *Demography:* If you tour the state's fifty-eight counties, you'll discover social and economic worlds as different from each other as Mars is from Venus. The populations of some counties are relatively poor, others relatively rich. Some are mostly white, others mainly nonwhite. Some are dominated by homeowners, others—for example, San Francisco—by renters. In some unemployment is very high, in others very low.

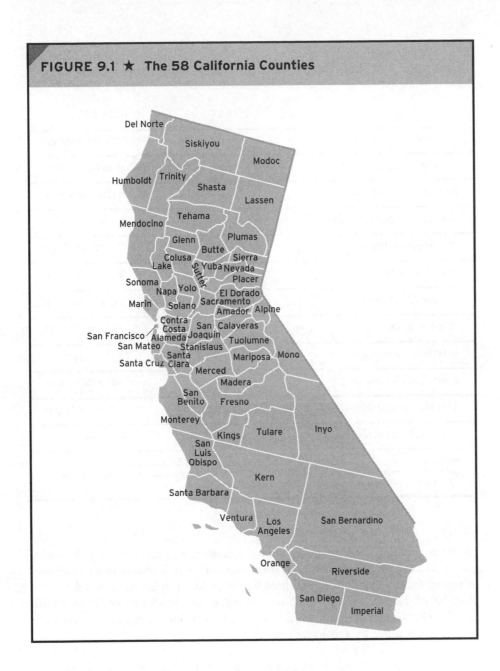

FIGURE 9.1 ★ The 58 California Counties

Table 9.1 reports the lowest- and highest-ranking counties on these and other selected criteria to illustrate the extremes observed among California's counties.

Legal Framework

The state constitution provides a general legal framework for the governing of most counties, which are known as *general-law counties*. It prescribes the number and functions of elected county officials, how they are selected, and what they may or may not do in raising revenue, spending money, delivering services, and so on.

TABLE 9.1 ★ Comparing the Counties of California

	LOWEST	HIGHEST
Total population (2006)	1,180 (Alpine)	9,948,081 (Los Angeles)
Land area (square miles)	47 (San Francisco)	20,053 (San Bernardino)
Population density (2006)	1.6 (Alpine)	15,831 (San Francisco)
% Pop. unincorporated (2008)	0.0% (San Francisco)	100.0% (Alpine, Trinity)
% White **non-Hispanic** (2006)	17.3% (Imperial)	87.2% (Sierra)
% Hispanic (2006)	5.0% (Trinity)	75.7% (Imperial)
% Asian/Pacific Isl. (2006)	0.3% (Sierra)	32.6% (San Francisco)
% Black (2006)	0.1% (Inyo)	15.4% (Solano)
% Homeowners (2000)	35.0% (San Francisco)	78.7% (Calaveras)
$ Per capita income (2005)	$21,465 (Lassen)	$75,884 (Marin)
% Below poverty (1999)	5.8% (Placer)	23.9% (Tulare)
% Unemployment (2008)	4.6% (Marin)	22.6% (Imperial)

SOURCES: U.S. Census Bureau, *USA Counties* (2008); censtats.census.gov/usa/usa.shtml
California Employment Development Department, "California Unemployment Rate Increases to 6.9 Percent,"
July 18, 2008, www.calmis.ca.gov/htmlfile/county/califhtm.htm

Fourteen counties, however, have adopted a *home-rule charter*, which gives voters greater control over the selection of governing bodies and officers, more flexibility in raising taxes and revenues, and broader discretion in organizing to deliver services. All of the state's most populous counties and one small county, Tehama, with its 57,000 residents, are now *charter counties*. Voters can adopt a charter for their county government by a majority vote.

- Long content to live without a charter, the voters of Orange County finally adopted one in March 2002. They did so mainly to prevent the governor from appointing his own choice to fill a vacancy on the county board of supervisors, which he had the authority to do under the general-law provisions.

- San Francisco is an unusual case. It is governed under a single charter as a consolidated county and city, an arrangement that is unique in the state and rare in the country.

County charters vary widely in content and in the range of powers claimed for local control. When a charter does not mention a subject, that subject is governed by the general law.

Government Organization

In all counties except San Francisco, an elected five-member board of supervisors exercises both legislative and executive authority. Given the extremes in the size of county populations, it shouldn't surprise you that small five-member boards yield huge disparities in political representation. For example, each board member in tiny Alpine County represents, on average, only 236 residents. In mammoth Los Angeles County, on the other hand, each board member represents nearly 2 million people, a number greater than the entire population of New Mexico.

County boards of supervisors, whose members are elected by districts for staggered four-year terms, not only pass laws, called *ordinances* at the local level, but also control and supervise the departments charged with administering them. This combination of legislative and executive authority gives county supervisors great power. From time to time, someone suggests a formal separation of powers and greater executive accountability. But nothing has changed in this regard and probably never will.

As always, there is an exception: In the consolidated city and county government of San Francisco, an elected eleven-member board of supervisors has legislative authority. An independently elected mayor has executive authority and some control, shared with many boards and commissions, over the bureaucracy.

In addition to the board of supervisors, other elected county officers required by general law include a sheriff, who enforces the law in areas outside the cities, a district attorney, and an assessor. A 1998 constitutional amendment consolidated municipal and superior trial courts into a single layer of superior court judges elected by county voters. Elections for all offices are nonpartisan. In terms of appointed positions, charter counties have considerable latitude in creating departments and agencies to serve their needs, either by charter provision or by ordinance. Other offices are required or authorized by state law. Some charter counties, like Los Angeles County, have appointed a chief administrative officer to manage their sprawling bureaucracies under board supervision.

Figure 9.2 shows Los Angeles County's organization chart. It illustrates the complexity of local government authority and responsibility that can be found at the county level.

County Government Functions and Responsibilities

County governments have major functions and responsibilities, most of them mandated by state or federal law, especially outside the jurisdictions of cities. County responsibilities include bridges and highways, public safety, public health, employment, parks and recreation, welfare and public assistance, public records, tax collection, general government, court administration, and land use. In the larger counties, the public workforce required to manage all this can be truly massive. Los Angeles County, for example, now has over 102,000 employees. The revenues needed to pay for their efforts can be equally huge. In 2007–2008, for example, Los Angeles County raised and spent over $22 billion. Most of this money was received from intergovernmental transfers ($9.7 billion) and property taxes ($4.6 billion). Most of it was spent on public assistance ($5.4 billion), public safety ($6.0 billion), and health services ($6.3 billion).[7]

Decisions on *land-use policy* are perhaps the most important and controversial ones a county board of supervisors can make. If you're ever in the mood to watch a

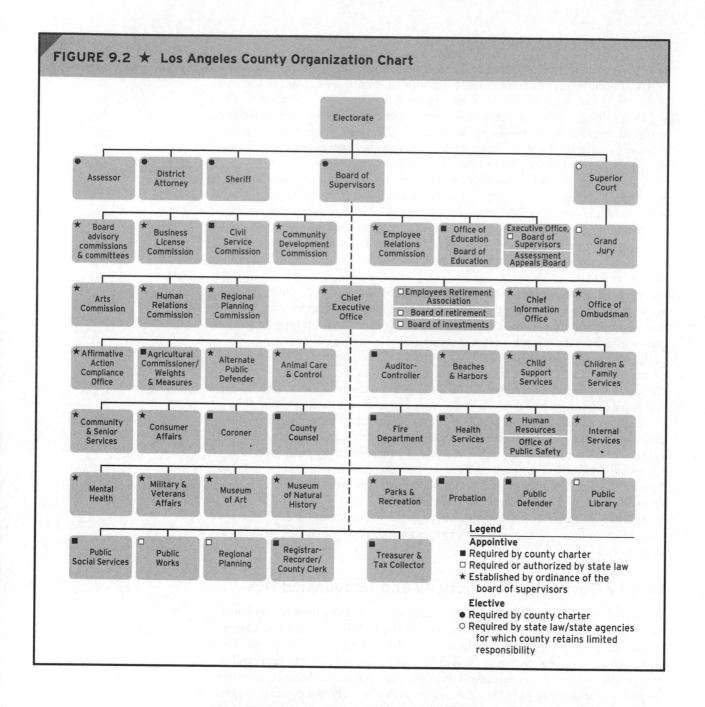

FIGURE 9.2 ★ Los Angeles County Organization Chart

Electorate

Assessor

District Attorney

Sheriff

Board of Supervisors

Superior Court

★ Board advisory commissions & committees

★ Business License Commission

■ Civil Service Commission

★ Community Development Commission

★ Employee Relations Commission

■ Office of Education / Board of Education

Executive Office, Board of Supervisors / Assessment Appeals Board

□ Grand Jury

★ Arts Commission

★ Human Relations Commission

★ Regional Planning Commission

★ Chief Executive Office

□ Employees Retirement Association / □ Board of retirement / □ Board of investments

★ Chief Information Office

★ Office of Ombudsman

★ Affirmative Action Compliance Office

■ Agricultural Commissioner/ Weights & Measures

★ Alternate Public Defender

★ Animal Care & Control

■ Auditor-Controller

★ Beaches & Harbors

★ Child Support Services

★ Children & Family Services

★ Community & Senior Services

★ Consumer Affairs

■ Coroner

■ County Counsel

■ Fire Department

■ Health Services

★ Human Resources / Office of Public Safety

★ Internal Services

★ Mental Health

★ Military & Veterans Affairs

★ Museum of Art

★ Museum of Natural History

★ Parks & Recreation

■ Probation

■ Public Defender

□ Public Library

■ Public Social Services

□ Public Works

□ Regional Planning

■ Registrar-Recorder/ County Clerk

■ Treasurer & Tax Collector

Legend

Appointive
■ Required by county charter
□ Required or authorized by state law
★ Established by ordinance of the board of supervisors

Elective
● Required by county charter
○ Required by state law/state agencies for which county retains limited responsibility

good political fight, attend a typical county board of supervisors meeting in places like Contra Costa County or San Diego County. Places like these still have plenty of open land outside the cities and fast-growing populations that fuel a demand for new housing construction, schools, and public infrastructure (sewers, highways, etc.). Landowners and developers typically badger the county board of supervisors to allow them to build, build, build, often with the result that conservationists, environmentalists, and other groups mobilize in opposition to push them back, back, back.

- In the late 1990s, for example, Contra Costa's board of supervisors, under political pressure from well-organized conservationists and environmentalists, blocked a proposed major housing development that would have paved over large sections of ranch and farm land in the rolling hills of Tassajara Valley.

- More recently, in San Diego County, an aggressive conservation group, Save Our Forest and Ranchlands, collided with the county board of supervisors and its developer-friendly advisory committee on land use. Frustrated by the pace and direction of the process to revise the county's general plan, the group placed a measure called the Rural Lands Initiative on the March 2, 2004, election ballot. That citizen initiative, which was defeated by a two-to-one margin, would have banned nearly all urban development on 700,000 acres of unincorporated county land.

As California's population continues to grow and to spread from the cities into the state's remaining farmlands and rural areas, you can expect to see more land-use battles erupting in the political arenas of county governments.

Local Agency Formation Commissions

All fifty-eight California counties have a Local Agency Formation Commission (LAFCo), whose members are appointed by the county board of supervisors. These commissions play a critical role in resolving conflicts among the many local governments that often compete with one another for power and resources within their county jurisdictions. A county's LAFCo is responsible for

- reviewing and approving the incorporations of new cities, the formation of new special districts, and any proposed changes of jurisdictional boundaries, including annexations and detachments of territory, secessions, consolidations, mergers, and dissolutions;

- reviewing and approving contractual service agreements between local governments and between local governments and the private sector;

- defining the official spheres of influence for each city and special district;

- initiating proposals for consolidation, dissolution, mergers, and reorganizations if such changes seem necessary or desirable.

These powerful commissions are especially busy in counties that are rocked by large-scale land-use battles, such as San Diego County and Contra Costa County, or that teem with masses of people, multitudes of governments, and major secession movements, such as Los Angeles County.

City Governments

Legal Framework

Like counties, California's cities derive their powers as municipal corporations from the state constitution and state legislature. Within that legal framework, as of

April 2005, the state's 478 incorporated cities fell into three categories: general-law cities (370), charter cities (107), and the unique case of San Francisco's consolidated city and county. The state Government Code, enacted by the legislature, specifies the general powers and structure of *general-law cities*. Broader home-rule powers are granted to *charter cities*, giving citizens more direct control over local affairs. Under these different arrangements, all cities have the power to legislate, as long as their local policies don't conflict with state or federal law. They have the power to raise revenues, levy taxes, charge license and service fees, and borrow. They may also hire personnel as needed; exercise police powers to enforce local, state, and federal laws; and condemn property for public use.

Incorporation: How Cities Are Born

The state grants powers to cities, and in that sense cities are indeed creatures of the state. But cities themselves are created only by the request, and with the consent, of the residents in a given area. In California, this process of *municipal incorporation* is typically initiated by a citizen petition or by a resolution of the county board of supervisors. Landowner petitions are also possible but rare. Some of the more important reasons that motivate residents to seek incorporation are

- to limit population growth, or perhaps to accelerate it;
- to provide more or better-quality services than those provided by the county;
- to prevent annexation by a nearby city;
- to create a unit of government more responsive to local needs and concerns.

A petition for municipal incorporation must be submitted to the county's LAFCo. The LAFCo panel reviews the proposed plans for the new city, its boundaries, service provisions, governing capacity, and financial viability. The LAFCo also studies the likely financial and other impacts of the proposed incorporation on neighboring local governments, including the county itself. If the petition for incorporation survives this initial review and a later public hearing and possible protests, it moves to an election. If a majority of voters living within the boundaries of the proposed new city approve, a new city is legally born.

New cities are created by incorporation quite frequently. Between 1962 and 2008, for example, the number of cities in the state grew from 373 to 480.[8] One of the most recent additions is Rancho Cordova, a formerly unincorporated community of 57,000 located in Sacramento County. Following a majority vote for incorporation, Rancho Cordova achieved formal cityhood on July 1, 2003. No longer ruled in most matters by the Sacramento County Board of Supervisors, the new city's residents now control their local affairs through their own newly minted city government. Thus empowered, the city's pro-growth leaders immediately welcomed proposals by developers to build new housing projects within the city limits. That same prospect of rapid growth and development, however, scared many of the 57,000 residents of sleepy Castro Valley. In November 2002, they voted three to one against incorporation. They were happy to remain northern California's largest unincorporated community and to continue being governed locally by the Alameda County Board of Supervisors.

City Government Functions and Responsibilities

City governments provide a wide range of services and facilities that directly affect the lives of their residents: fire and police protection; street construction and maintenance; sewage and waste disposal; health, social, and recreational programs; and planning and zoning to determine land use consistent with a community's needs and values. Most city governments provide water, and some run public transit systems. A few, like Los Angeles and Sacramento, own and manage municipal electricity or natural gas utilities.

Residents in most cities are content if the basic services, such as police, fire, and waste management, are provided reliably and efficiently, either directly by the municipality itself or, as in many smaller cities, by contracting services from other local governments and the private sector.[9] In some places, however, residents demand more from their city government than just the basics. In some cities, for example, business leaders and entrepreneurs often pressure city hall to promote rapid economic growth and development. In other cities, such as Berkeley and San Francisco, community activists often pressure city hall to limit growth and development and to pursue ambitious social agendas on the world stage.

City Government Revenues and Expenditures

As shown in Table 9.2, the typical city budget in California relies most heavily on current service charges and taxes for most of its revenues. Most of what it spends goes for public safety, community development and health, public utilities, and transportation. We will have more to say about city finances later in this chapter in the context of the state's continuing budget crisis.

Forms of City Government and the Legacy of Progressive Structural Reforms

The overall vision and structural reforms advanced by the Progressives nearly a century ago have had an enduring impact on the form of municipal government in California. Progressive reformers sought to replace government by corrupt bosses running partisan, ward-based, big-city political machines with government by reputable civic leaders and nonpartisan experts managing local affairs in the public interest. The structural reforms implementing that vision called for

- strong managers and weak mayors;
- nonpartisan elections;
- at-large council elections;
- nonconcurrent elections;
- the tools of direct democracy (the initiative, referendum, and recall).

Other Progressive reforms included civil service (merit-based) systems of municipal employment and, especially in the larger cities, professionally run city planning commissions and departments.[10] Reformers were particularly successful in the southwestern states, where populations were growing fast and new cities were

TABLE 9.2 ★ Typical Sources and Uses of Municipal Funding

REVENUES		EXPENSES	
Taxes	30.88%	Public safety	26.22%
Current service charges	40.24%	Community development and health	22.04%
Intergovernmental agencies	12.56%	Public utilities	19.01%
Revenues from use of money and property	4.86%	Transportation	15.22%
Special benefit assessments, licenses and permits, fines and forfeitures	3.64%	Culture and leisure	8.58%
		General government	7.87%
Other revenues and other financing sources	7.82%	Other	1.06%
	100%		100%

SOURCE: California Governor's Office of Planning and Research [CGOPR], *A Guide to the LAFCO Process for Incorporations: Appendices* (Sacramento, CA: OPR, October 2003), Appendix G. www.calafco.org/docs/inc-studies/Incorp_appendices.pdf

popping up everywhere, isolated from the influence of eastern-style partisanship and urban machine politics.[11] Municipalities that have all or most of these institutional features are known as *reform governments*. Most medium-sized American cities and nearly all of California's cities qualify for that label.

THE COUNCIL-MANAGER PLAN VS. THE MAYOR-COUNCIL SYSTEM

Under the *council-manager* form of government, the voters elect a city council, which in turn appoints a professionally trained city manager to run the administration. The city manager directly controls the bureaucracy and supervises the performance of department heads. The council restricts itself to legislative policy making, while retaining the ultimate authority to fire or replace the appointed manager. Fully 96 percent of the 456 California cities surveyed in 2002 are governed by the council-manager plan,[12] including some big ones like San Diego and San Jose. Mayors are directly elected in about a third of these cities, but with few exceptions (e.g., San Jose) they perform mainly ceremonial duties and have no independent executive powers, such as the veto or budgetary control.

The rest of California's cities are governed by *mayor-council systems*. Most are very small cities that can't afford a professional city manager. In the larger cities that have mayor-council systems, like San Francisco and Los Angeles, the voters elect a mayor and a city council in separate elections. The mayor serves as the city's overall chief executive and exercises independent veto and budgetary powers. The council (or, in the case of San Francisco, the board of supervisors) is responsible for legislative policy making. Typically, as in Los Angeles and San Francisco, various appointive boards and commissions set overall policy and supervise administration of important city departments, such as police and fire, thus limiting the mayor's direct control of the bureaucracy.

In practice, formal and informal power arrangements vary markedly across both systems. In recent years, many council-manager cities have strengthened mayoral authority to become more responsive to their political environments.[13] Some mayor-council cities, on the other hand, have hired professional managers to achieve greater administrative control and efficiency. One study of both forms of government in California cities shows that informal factors such as personal ambition, political skill, and leadership style are key factors that determine just how powerful a given mayor or manager really is in running things and shaping public policy.[14]

NONPARTISAN ELECTIONS California law requires that all local elections be officially nonpartisan. In nonpartisan elections, no information about a candidate's political party membership is shown on the ballot. Unofficially, of course, many local contests are fiercely partisan, especially since the courts some years ago permitted political party organizations to endorse candidates in local races. For example, in San Francisco's 1999 mayoral runoff election between Willie Brown and Tom Ammiano, the local Republican Party reluctantly endorsed the state GOP's archenemy, Democrat and former Assembly Speaker Willie Brown. Shocked and humiliated by this action, some outraged GOP warlords sought to expel the local chapter from the state party organization.[15]

AT-LARGE VERSUS DISTRICT COUNCIL ELECTIONS A recent survey found that nearly all California cities (93 percent) conduct at-large council elections, in which voters elect council members citywide rather than by districts or wards.[16] Under the *at-large system*, for example, if a number of candidates compete for one of the three vacant seats on the council, all of the city's voters have the opportunity to vote for any three of them, and the top three vote-getters are declared the winners. About 5 percent of cities use the *district election method*, which divides the city into districts and requires the voters in each district to elect one of the candidates running in that district to represent them on the council. The remaining cities—Oakland is an example—use some hybrid combination of at-large and district elections to elect their councils.

Some cities, most prominently San Francisco in 2000, have changed from at-large to district elections. San Francisco's switch to the district system was a response to voter demand for greater representation of neighborhoods and minority groups, reduced influence of big money on elections, and a wider field of candidates who otherwise could not afford to run citywide campaigns.[17] Of course, the district system by itself doesn't guarantee a more neighborhood-oriented council, less costly campaigns, or political life on a smaller scale. The fifteen members of the Los Angeles City Council, for example, are elected by districts. But each council member represents nearly a quarter of a million residents on average and must run expensive campaigns over vast territories to get elected.

NONCONCURRENT ELECTIONS Progressive reformers sought to insulate local government from the corrupting influence of national partisan politics. One way they accomplished this goal was to require many cities to conduct nonconcurrent elections for council seats. That is, they scheduled local elections in nonpresidential election years or at odd times, deliberately out of sync with the national election calendar. A recent survey found that only about 19 percent of California cities hold council elections concurrently with the presidential general election or presidential primaries.[18] Forty-five percent hold them at the same time as the gubernatorial election, and 37 percent hold them in odd-year November elections or at other times, usually in spring. As discussed below, nonconcurrent elections have been blamed as the number one structural cause of the dismally low voter turnout rates in California cities.

DIRECT DEMOCRACY At the local level of government, just as at the state level, ordinary citizens have access to the tools of direct democracy (the initiative, referendum, and recall) bequeathed to them by Progressive Era reformers. Specifically, if citizens gather the required number of valid signatures on formal petitions, they can

- initiate direct legislation, including proposed ordinances and charter amendments, by placing such measures on the ballot for voter approval;

- suspend implementation of council legislation until the voters approve it at a referendum election;

- subject incumbent elected officials to a recall vote and possible dismissal prior to the next scheduled regular election.

Local referenda are quite rare. Local recall elections are even rarer, except in places like the contentious little town of Pacifica, where voters have successfully petitioned for five recall elections over the last thirty years. The use of local ballot initiatives, however, is much more frequent and widespread, although not nearly to the extent observed at the state level. Direct legislation by citizen initiative has become almost routine in some cities, such as San Francisco, especially around land-use issues. A recent study, however, found that only forty-three of 387 cities surveyed (11 percent) had even one citizen initiative on their most recent ballot.[19]

LOCAL VOTER TURNOUT AND POLITICAL REPRESENTATION Voter participation is low and still falling at all levels of government in California. At the local level, a recent survey revealed that only 48 percent of a city's registered voters, on average, cast ballots in the most recent council elections. That same survey found that "California residents who are highly educated, wealthy, old, and white are much more likely to participate than residents who are poor, young, less educated, and nonwhite."[20] The political exclusion of the state's large and growing noncitizen immigrant population only adds to the problem of achieving democracy for all (see Box 9.2). Clearly, at least at the local level, California's active electorate is not very large and is demographically not representative of the state's population.

Certain institutional reforms could boost voter turnout and eventually produce more representative and responsive local government. One electoral reform in particular would likely have a major impact: the rescheduling of local nonconcurrent elections to coincide with high-turnout presidential elections. Doing so in a given city "could well mean a doubling of voter turnout."[21] A number of California cities

BOX 9.2

The Case of Noncitizens: Does Political Exclusion Create Political Apartheid?

California's large noncitizen population poses a particular challenge to local leaders who seek to increase political participation, fair representation, and government responsiveness in their communities. According to the 2000 U.S. Census, the state has at least 85 cities where noncitizens comprise more than 25 percent of the adult population. Noncitizens are the majority in twelve of these cities. In Los Angeles, noncitizens make up an astounding 32 percent of the adult residents. Noncitizens are constitutionally banned from voting in elections, denied formal political representation, and excluded from the policy-making process. Even in San Francisco, the self-proclaimed "sanctuary city," the voters rejected a local ballot initiative in 2003 that would have allowed noncitizen parents of public school children to vote in school board elections. Some critics argue that the exclusion of noncitizens from the political process violates the democratic principle of rule by the consent of the governed. Joaquin Avila contends that the "ultimate product of such exclusion is a political apartheid." What do you think?

SOURCES: Joaquin Avila, "Political Apartheid in California: Consequences of Excluding a Growing Noncitizen Population," Latino Policy & Issues Brief No. 9, UCLA Chicano Studies Research Center (December 2003). Ron Hayduk, *Democracy for All: Restoring Immigrant Voting Rights in the United States* (New York: Routledge, 2006).

have recently moved to concurrent elections, partly as a cost-saving measure. As noted earlier, however, 81 percent of the state's cities still hold council elections in nonpresidential election years. Without such electoral reform or some kind of new political mobilization of the inactive electorate, the unrepresentative active electorate will continue to choose who governs at the local level.

Special Districts

Special districts are limited-purpose local governments. They fill the need or desire for services that general-purpose governments such as counties and cities can't or won't provide. If residents or landowners desire new or better services, they can take steps to establish a special district to pay for them. As a popular guide to special districts notes: "Special districts *localize* the costs and benefits of public services. Special districts allow local citizens to obtain the services they want at a price they are willing to pay."[22] Examples of special districts include fire protection districts, cemetery districts, water districts, recreation and park districts, storm water drainage and conservation districts, irrigation districts, and mosquito abatement districts.

School and Community College Districts

California's school and community college districts are a unique type of special district. As of 2008, there were 1,050 K–12 school districts in the state, a number whittled down, mostly by consolidation, from the 1,630 districts that operated in 1962.[23] School districts derive their authority from the state Education Code and are governed by locally elected school boards. Each board sets general policies and appoints a superintendent as chief executive officer, who serves at the pleasure of the board. The superintendent has overall responsibility for managing the system and its various schools and programs. In 2008, the state's community college system of two-year public institutions had 110 colleges organized into seventy-two districts. Serving more than 2.5 million students, it is the largest system of higher education in the world. Each community college district is governed by a locally elected board of trustees that sets general polices and appoints a chancellor as chief executive officer. As discussed elsewhere in this book, the state of the state's K–14 public education system and especially the financial crises that surround it continue to be a major focus of policy debate and political battle.

Nonschool Special Districts

Excluding the school districts, the state had 2,765 special districts in 2007, according to the most recent U.S. Census of Governments.[24] These special districts can be classified in three different ways: single-purpose versus multiple-purpose special districts; enterprise versus nonenterprise special districts; and independent versus dependent special districts.

- About 85 percent of the state's special districts perform a single function, such as fire protection or mosquito abatement. The others are multifunctional, such as the state's nearly 900 County Service Areas (CSAs), which provide two or more services, such as enhanced recreation services and extended police protection.

- About one in four special districts are enterprise districts, which are run like businesses and charge user fees for services. Nearly all water, waste, and hospital districts are enterprise districts of this sort. The state's many nonenterprise districts provide public services such as fire protection and pest control that benefit the entire community, not just individual residents. Typically, property taxes rather than user fees pay the costs.

- About two-thirds of the state's special districts are independent districts. An independent district is governed by its own separate board of directors elected by the district's voters. Dependent districts are governed by existing legislative bodies. All CSAs, for example, are governed by a county board of supervisors.

These three ways of classifying special districts are not mutually exclusive, and examples of all possible combinations exist.

Legal Framework

Like all local governments in the state, special districts must conform to the state constitution and the legislature's Government Code. Statutory authority for special districts derives either from a principal act or a special act of the state legislature. A *principal act* is a general law that applies to all special districts of a given type. For example, the Fire Protection District Law of 1987 in the state Health and Safety Code governs all 386 fire districts. About sixty of these principal law statutes are on the books and can be used to create a special district anywhere in the state. Another 120 or so *special acts* have been passed by the legislature to adapt a special district's structure, financing, and authority to unique local circumstances. The Alameda County Flood Control and Water District, for example, was formed under such a special act.

How Special Districts Are Created

To form a special district, the voters in the proposed district must apply to their county's LAFCo. After the LAFCo reviews and approves the proposal, it moves to an election in which only the voters residing inside the proposed district boundaries may vote. A simple majority is required for approval in most cases. A two-thirds majority is required if new special taxes are involved. New special districts are hard enough to create. Getting rid of them once they are established, however, is almost impossible. As of 2006, thirty-three of the state's eighty-five health care districts no longer operated hospitals. Yet all thirty-three continued to exist and to collect property tax revenues.[25] Given this institutional ratchet effect, it is not surprising that 803 new special districts were created in California between 1962 and 2007.[26]

The Advantages and Disadvantages of Special Districts

The advantages claimed for special districts include

- the flexibility that such districts allow in tailoring the level and quality of service to citizen demands;

- the linking of costs to benefits, so that those who don't benefit from a district's services don't have to pay for them;

- the greater responsiveness of special districts to their constituents, who often reside in smaller geographic areas of larger city and county jurisdictions.

The disadvantages of special districts include

- the overlapping of jurisdictions and the resulting duplication of services already provided by cities and counties or by other special districts;

- the reduced incentives for needed regional planning, especially in providing water, sewer, and fire protection services, which are typically offered by a host of special districts governed by independent boards without any central coordination;

- the decreased accountability that results from the sheer multiplicity of limited special districts, which overwhelms the average citizen's ability to find out who is in charge of delivering specific services.

These critics would abolish most special districts and centralize their functions in established general-purpose city and county governments. One contends that special districts "make a mockery of the natural connections that people have with a specific place. Special districts lie beyond the commonsense experience of most citizens; their very purpose is to divorce a narrow element of policy from the consideration of those charged with the maintenance of the common interest."[27]

Regional Governments

A number of regional governments have formed in California to cope with problems such as air pollution, waste management, growth control, affordable housing production, and transportation gridlock—problems that affect large geographical areas and millions of people living in many different city and county jurisdictions. Some of these regional bodies have strong regulatory powers. Others are mainly advisory in function.

Regulatory Regional Governments

Examples of state regional governments that have strong regulatory powers include the California Coastal Commission, the South Coast Air Quality Management District, and the San Francisco Bay Conservation and Development Commission.

CALIFORNIA COASTAL COMMISSION (CCC) Appointed by the governor and the state legislature, the twelve-member CCC has state-empowered regulatory authority to control all development within the 1,000-yard-wide shoreline zone along the entire California coast. Exercising its powers to grant or withhold permits for development, the CCC has succeeded over the years in opening public access to beaches, protecting scenic views, and restoring wetlands.

SOUTH COAST AIR QUALITY MANAGEMENT DISTRICT (SCAQMD) The twelve-member SCAQMD board has state-granted regulatory authority to control emissions from stationary sources of air pollution (e.g., power plants, refineries, gas stations) in the state's South Coast air basin. This region encompasses all of Los Angeles and Orange counties and parts of Riverside and San Bernadino counties, an area of 12,000 square miles and home to more than 12 million people, nearly half the state's total population. This area also has the worst smog problem in the nation. Over the years, the board, which is appointed by city governments in the basin area, has conducted many studies, monitored air pollution levels, developed regional pollution abatement plans, and vigorously enforced federal and state air pollution laws. In large part thanks to its efforts, the maximum level of ozone in the basin has been cut to less than half of what it was in the 1950s, despite the tripling of population and quadrupling of vehicles in the region over that same period.

SAN FRANCISCO BAY CONSERVATION AND DEVELOPMENT COMMISSION (BCDC) The twenty-seven-member BCDC was created by the state legislature in 1965 in response to growing public concern about the future of San Francisco Bay, which was rapidly being dredged and polluted at an alarming rate by landfill projects. The commission includes members appointed by the governor, legislature, and various state and federal agencies, as well as four city representatives appointed by the Association of Bay Area Governments, and nine county supervisors, one from each of the nine bay area counties. The commission is charged with regulating all filling and dredging in the bay; protecting the Suisun Marsh, the largest wetlands in California; regulating proposed new development within the first 100 feet inland from the bay to insure maximum public access; enforcing the federal Coastal Zone Management Act; and other regulatory functions. By exercising its permit powers, BCDC not only stopped development that eventually could have reduced the bay to a pond, but also actually added hundreds of acres of new open water.

Advisory Regional Governments

In addition to regional regulatory bodies, the state also has a number of regional planning, research, and advisory institutions. The most important are various regional *councils of government* (COGs). COGs are assemblies of delegates representing a region's counties and cities who join voluntarily and meet regularly to discuss common problems and regional issues. The state's two most prominent COGs are the Southern California Association of Governments (SCAG), the nation's largest COG, and the Association of Bay Area Governments (ABAG).

SCAG's regional jurisdiction encompasses 15 million people living in an area of more than 38,000 square miles, while ABAG's boundaries include 6 million people living in an area of 7,000 square miles. Both SCAG and ABAG have general assemblies that represent the broad membership of counties and cities located in each region. In both COGs, the serious work is done by smaller executive committees, a seventy-five-member regional council in the case of SCAG, and a thirty-eight-member executive board in the case of ABAG. Like most COGs, both SCAG and ABAG have professional staffs that conduct extensive research and planning studies of regional problems. Both regularly host regional conferences and forums on a range of substantive issues. And both have been designated by the federal government as metropolitan planning organizations for their regions, with the mandate to draw up plans for regional transportation, air quality, growth management, hazardous waste management, and production of affordable housing.

Both SCAG and ABAG have raised public awareness of regional problems and issues. They have also encouraged more regional planning and collaborative decision making. Neither COG, however, has the effective power or authority to enforce its policy recommendations on other local governments in their regions. Many Bay Area local officials, for example, pay lip service to ABAG's recommended fair-share quotas for production of affordable housing but then routinely ignore them when making decisions.

Occasionally, a serious organized effort is made to create a truly comprehensive regional government with broad regulatory authority and strong enforcement powers. In the early 1990s, for example, an attempt was made to establish a powerful Bay Area regional government under the banner of BayVision 2020.[28] That proposal failed, like all the others, because most of the region's local governments were unwilling to surrender local autonomy and delegate some of their powers to a new, higher authority.

California's Local Political Cultures from Left to Right

Political culture is difficult to define and quantify. However, we can offer at least a few statistics to show how three of the state's most populous counties differ in terms of political partisanship, political ideology, political activism, political tolerance, and voting tendencies on important issues. Table 9.3 compares and contrasts San Francisco City/County, Los Angeles County, and San Diego County on those selected indicators of local political culture.

Political Party Registration and Voter Turnout

As of May 2008, registered Democrats outnumbered Republicans in San Francisco by nearly six to one, and by two to one in Los Angeles County. In San Diego County, however, Republicans had the advantage by a 38 percent to 36 percent margin. In the November 4, 2008, general election, voter turnout as a percent of those registered was 77 percent in Los Angeles County, 79 percent in San Francisco County, and 84 percent in San Diego County.

Political Ideology

Based on community surveys conducted in late 2000, about one in five San Franciscans identify themselves politically as "very liberal" and only 4 percent as "very conservative." In both Los Angeles County and San Diego County, conservatives outnumber liberals by about two to one. [29]

Political Participation

Those same surveys show that San Francisco citizens are much more politically active than their counterparts in Los Angeles County and San Diego County. Fifty-one percent scored "high" on a nationally normed electoral activity index, as compared with only 33 percent in Los Angeles County and 30 percent in San Diego County. Moreover, 47 percent of San Francisco citizens scored "high" on a nationally normed political protest activity index, as compared with only 30 percent in both Los Angeles and San Diego counties.

Support for Proposition 13

Proposition 13, the 1978 initiative that rolled back property tax rates and limited the government's ability to raise local property taxes in the future, regarded by some observers "as one of the most significant political events in California's history,"[30] won by a landslide vote nearly everywhere throughout the state, including a 67 percent yes vote in Los Angeles County and a 60 percent vote in San Diego County. In San Francisco, however, it mustered only 47 percent, not even a majority.

Political Tolerance and Support for Racial and Cultural Diversity

Table 9.3 reports county voting results on six different statewide ballot propositions over the period 1994–2008. All six can be viewed as indicators of political tolerance and support for racial and cultural diversity.

- Proposition 187 was a 1994 initiative constitutional amendment that made undocumented immigrants ineligible for various public social services. The state's voters approved it by a wide margin, with 56 percent voting yes in Los Angeles County and 68 percent in San Diego County. Only 29 percent voted for it in San Francisco.

TABLE 9.3 ★ Regional Political Cultures: Three California Counties Compared from Left to Right

INDICATOR	SAN FRANCISCO	LOS ANGELES	SAN DIEGO
1. % Democrats (2008)	56	51	36
2. % Republicans (2008)	10	25	38
3. % Voter Turnout (Nov. 4, 2008)	79	77	84
4. % Very Liberal (2000)	21	8	6
5. % Very Conservative (2000)	4	15	14
6. % High Electoral Activity (2000)	51	33	30
7. % High Protest Activity (2000)	47	30	30
8. % Yes on Prop. 13 (1978)	47	67	60
9. % Yes on Prop. 187 (1994)	29	56	68
10. % Yes on Prop. 209 (1996)	29	45	63
11. % Yes on Prop. 215 (1996)	78	56	52
12. % Yes on Prop. 22 (2000)	32	59	63
13. % Yes on Prop. 8 (2008)	25	50	54
14. % Yes Recall Gov. Davis (2003)	20	49	66
15. % Vote Schwarzenegger (2003)	19	45	60
16. % Vote Bustamante (2003)	63	38	24
17. % Vote Camejo (2003)	6	3	2
18. % Vote Obama for President (2008)	84	61	54

SOURCES: Indicators 1-3, 8-18: California Secretary of State, various official statements of vote. Indicators 4-7: Analysis of sample survey data obtained from the Social Capital Benchmark Survey 2000.

- Proposition 209 was a 1996 initiative constitutional amendment that prohibited state and local government agencies from giving preferential treatment to any individual or group on the basis of race, sex, color, ethnicity, or national origin. Widely viewed by friends and foes alike as an attack on affirmative action, this measure also passed in the statewide vote, with 63 percent support in San Diego County. It received only 45 percent in Los Angeles County, however, and a mere 29 percent in San Francisco.

- Proposition 215 was a 1996 initiative statute that permitted the medicinal use of marijuana. This measure passed in the statewide vote, but only barely in San Diego County with 52 percent, more comfortably in Los Angeles County with 56 percent, and by a landslide 78 percent vote in San Francisco.

- Proposition 22 was a 2000 initiative statute declaring that only marriage between a man and a woman is valid or recognized in California. This measure was approved by a landslide statewide vote, with 59 percent support in Los Angeles County and 63 percent in San Diego County. In San Francisco, however, a resounding 68 percent voted no.

- Proposition 54 was a 2003 initiative constitutional amendment that would have banned state and local government agencies from classifying any individual by race, ethnicity, color, or national origin. The measure failed by a wide margin in the statewide vote, receiving only 20 percent support in San Francisco, 29 percent in Los Angeles County, and 40 percent in San Diego County.

- Proposition 8 was a 2008 initiative constitutional amendment that eliminated the right of same-sex couples to marry. Backers of the proposition placed it on the ballot as a direct challenge to the California Supreme Court's ruling in May 2008 affirming the constitutionality of same-sex marriage. The measure was approved 52 to 48 percent in the statewide vote. Only 25 percent of San Francisco County's voters voted yes, however, compared with 50 percent in Los Angeles County and 54 percent in San Diego County. (Responding to a lawsuit challenging the validity of the Proposition 8 vote, the California Supreme Court will decide in 2009 whether the measure was in fact an "amendment" or, as the lawsuit claims, a more fundamental "revision" of the state constitution, in which case a two-thirds vote of both houses of the legislature would be required for approval.)

The Statewide Recall Election of 2003

The 2003 recall vote revealed the sharpest contrast in the state's regional political cultures, especially in terms of partisan loyalties and voting behavior. Exercising their power to recall elected officials, the voters fired Governor Gray Davis, a Democrat, and elected Republican Arnold Schwarzenegger as his replacement. Fully 66 percent of voters in San Diego County supported the recall, falling to 49 percent in Los Angeles County, and a mere 20 percent in San Francisco. In the separate replacement election, candidate Schwarzenegger received 60 percent of the vote in San Diego County, 45 percent in Los Angeles County, and only 19 percent in San Francisco.

The Gubernatorial Election of 2006

The regional differences were nearly as stark three years later in the 2006 contest between the incumbent Schwarzenegger and major challenger Phil Angelides. Schwarzenegger crushed his Democratic Party rival 66 percent to 30 percent in San Diego County. Angelides edged Schwarzenegger 49 percent to 46 percent in Los Angeles County, however, and thrashed him 63 percent to 30 percent in San Francisco. Although Green Party candidate Peter Camejo won only a tiny fraction of the statewide vote and barely made a dent in Los Angeles County or San Diego County, he received a respectable 5 percent of the votes in San Francisco.

The Presidential Election of 2008

In the November 4, 2008, presidential election, California voters supported Barack Obama in a landslide over John McCain by 61 to 37 percent. Majorities in all three counties voted for Obama, with San Francisco County leading the pack with 84 percent for Obama, followed by Los Angeles County at 61 percent and San Diego County at 54 percent.

To Sum Up

The statistics in Table 9.3 show that political life varies dramatically in California from region to region. If you happen to reside in San Francisco, you live in one of the nation's most liberal, tolerant, and activist political cultures.[31] The political environment in San Diego County, on the other hand, is more conservative, less tolerant, and more passive. Los Angeles County falls somewhere between these two extremes. These three counties reflect the range of political cultural differences that exist across the state. You can easily see why local representatives in the state legislature fight so much and so fiercely and have a very hard time agreeing on anything.

Two Case Studies in Local Government Revolt

The following two mini-case studies dramatically illustrate how California's local governments have coped with recent crises that have threatened to tear cities apart and undermine home rule. The first looks at what happened when the citizens of San Fernando Valley attempted to secede from the city of Los Angeles in 2002. The second examines the successful revolt of local officials against the state government in 2004 when Sacramento legislators tried, one last time, to balance the state budget by grabbing property tax money from the cities, counties, and special districts.

Breaking Up Is Hard to Do: The San Fernando Valley Secession Movement

Nearly all of California's local governments have developed stress fractures of one kind or another from trying to cope with growing populations, increased demands for service, shrinking financial resources, and a state government that seems determined to make things worse rather than better. On top of all that, the state's largest city, Los Angeles, has been beset by internal conflicts that threaten to tear it apart. On November 5, 2002, that city's voters rejected a citizen referendum that would have allowed the San Fernando Valley and its 1.35 million residents to secede from Los Angeles and become a separate city. If the measure had passed, the new city would immediately have ranked as America's sixth-largest city, while what remained of Los Angeles south of the Santa Monica mountains would have fallen from second- to third-largest in terms of population.

This secessionist revolt did not come out of the blue. It was only the latest in a long string of failed secession attempts that began thirty years earlier with the predominantly white Valley's opposition to Los Angeles's school integration and busing policies. Since then, however, the Valley's population has grown in size and diversity—it is now 40 percent white and 45 percent Latino. Its political and business leaders have become more organized and sophisticated. And its list of grievances against Los Angeles city hall, codified in a latter-day "Declaration of Independence," have expanded to include complaints and demands which can no longer be easily dismissed by Los Angeles power elites as narrow, selfish, or racist.

Encouraged by a 1997 state law that prevented city councils from simply vetoing secession attempts, Valley Voters Organized toward Empowerment (Valley VOTE) and other secession groups gathered over 100,000 signatures to place the referendum on the ballot. They secured LAFCo approval based on studies showing that both cities, old and new, would be economically viable following the split. They argued their case that Valley residents paid more in taxes than they received in services from the distant, unresponsive politicians and bureaucrats who ruled Los Angeles city hall. And key leaders, including many developers and business owners, most of them white, appealed to Los Angeles voters to "Free the Valley!" by giving Valley residents control of their own city government—presumably more friendly to small businesses, more inclined to cut taxes and improve services, and more responsive to the Valley's needs and aspirations.

Los Angeles mayor James Hahn and other city officials were slow to take this latest secession attempt seriously and respond to it. Alarmed, downtown business leaders, city hall lobbyists, and public service employee union chiefs organized "LA United Together" to fight the Valley secession referendum and another one by Hollywood, on the same ballot. They raised over $7 million for the antisecession campaign, outspending the Valley and Hollywood cityhood advocates by more than two to one. They unleashed a blitz of TV ads declaring that secession would not solve any problems and would only make things worse. In the middle of a statewide economic downturn and budget crunch, Mayor Hahn warned, Valley secession would cause a citywide financial disaster of "biblical proportions." Among other complications of the proposed "divorce," Valley kids would still belong to the Los Angeles Unified School District, Los Angeles city departments and agencies would have to provide a wide range of contractual services to Valley residents until the new city established its own bureaucracy, and the new city would also be required to pay Los Angeles an "alimony" totaling $2 billion over twenty years under LAFCo-arranged compensation for lost revenue. Leading up to the referendum vote, these arguments gave pause to many Valley residents, especially Latinos who depended on jobs and services dispensed by Los Angeles city hall.

Under the 1997 state law, formal secession required majority approval both from the entire Los Angeles city voter population and from the breakaway subpopulation of Valley voters themselves. The referendum passed narrowly in San Fernando Valley, achieving at least a moral victory. The measure failed by a wide margin in the citywide vote, however, thus squelching this latest secession attempt. Nonetheless, the stresses and strains that had given rise to the movement in 2002 were still active in 2008 and could erupt once again in the years ahead.[32]

The State Budget Crisis and Local Government Revolt

By February 2004, the state's budget deficit had grown massive and out of control. Many observers had trouble even finding the words to describe it. Herb Wesson, Jr., Speaker of the State Assembly, offered one of the more dramatic word pictures of the crisis that Californians faced. Commenting on the current deficit as it stood in

February 2003—a staggering $34.8 billion—he wrote: "That's a hole so deep and so vast that even if we fired every single person on the state payroll, we would still be billions short."[33]

The story of how that hole was dug starts in 1978, when the state's voters passed Proposition 13. Most of the state's fiscal misery, short-term and long-term, branches out from there (see Chapter 8). Surveying the damage that Proposition 13 had caused over the last twenty-five years, Peter Schrag recited the familiar list: reduced public services at all levels of government; the declining quality of public education; the neglected and rotting infrastructure; and so on. But as bad as that was, Schrag wrote, the biggest California impact "was the seismic shift in California's governmental structure, accountability and power: from local to state government; from representative democracy to direct democracy through the initiative process: from a communitarian ethic in how we paid for public services to a fee ethic."[34]

The next major chapter in this story was written in 1988, when the state's voters passed Proposition 98, which required the state's annual budget to allocate approximately 40 percent of the general fund to the schools. When the state later faced serious revenue shortfalls, the legislators found a way to balance the state budget while also complying with Proposition 98. They deposited a major portion of the collected local property tax revenues into "educational revenue augmentation

BOX 9.3 | **An Unfunded Mandate: California Cities and the Clean Water Act**

Like all cities with storm drains that flow to rivers and oceans, the small City of Bellflower (population 73,000) must comply with the federal Clean Water Act. That law prohibits municipal storm water discharges without a National Pollutant Discharge Elimination System (NPDES) permit. In California, the NPDES permit program is administered by the State Water Resources Control Board and nine regional water quality control boards. To obtain the needed permit, a city must at minimum develop and implement storm water pollution prevention plans that include management and monitoring programs, controls on industrial runoff, and public education. In recent years, the state regional boards have imposed even more stringent and costly requirements on municipal storm drain operators. The Los Angeles regional board, for example, required Bellflower and other cities seeking NPDES permits to eliminate all litter—repeat, all litter—from their storm drains. "If a single Styrofoam cup should reach the ocean, these agencies would be in violation of federal law." While imposing this new mandate with the best of intentions, the federal and state governments have refused to fund it. Local governments must pay for it out of their own hides. For many cities, the effects of this unfunded mandate have been "financially devastating." In October 2002, for example, the City of Bellflower was forced to cut $358,000 from its limited budget to comply with the new regulations. To prevent that Styrofoam cup from reaching the ocean, Bellflower residents paid the price in terms of one less gang specialist deputy probation officer ($24,013); one less recreation staff position ($54,500); reduced law enforcement overtime ($15,000); reduced sidewalk, curb, and gutter improvements ($40,791); postponed purchase of an emergency generator ($55,000); and slashed funding for other important local services.

SOURCE: Institute for Local Self Government (ILSG), *The Fiscal Condition of California Cities: 2003 Report* (Sacramento, CA: The Institute for Local Self Government, 2003), p. 23.

funds" (ERAFs) and directed that those funds be spent on schools to meet the obligations imposed by Proposition 98. But what about the financial needs of other local governments, whose property tax revenues (thanks to Proposition 13) were now placed under state government control and being handed out to the schools? In what can only be described as a shell game, the state tried to solve that problem by giving some money back to local governments from other funds. That solution might have worked, except that most of those other funds had strings attached, including paying for state-mandated programs that had little or nothing to do with local priorities. To make matters worse, the state and federal politicians continued to crank out new mandated programs for local governments to administer with no additional funding at all—so-called "unfunded mandates."

By 2002, according to one study, only a handful of cities received more back from the state than they lost. The net minus for the others added up to $616 million in 2002.[35] California's cities and counties had become "net donors to the state general fund" and were "at the mercy of the state as long as the Legislature is in session." Alarmed, they declared that the state budget process had been lowered to the level of a "fiscal street mugging."[36] To some critics these trends spelled doom for effective home rule.[37]

To adapt and survive, many local governments were forced to slash public services, lay off employees, defer infrastructure maintenance, and charge new user fees wherever they could. Many also pursued the "fiscalization of land use."[38] That is, they changed their economic development and land-use policies to discourage new residential housing (whose property taxes now go to the state, not to the local governments) in favor of attracting new businesses, such as shopping malls and automobile dealerships, that would capture sales-tax revenues for starved local treasuries.

In January 2004, the state's new governor, Arnold Schwarzenegger, tackled the growing budget crisis he had inherited by first making it worse. By executive order, he rolled back the tripling of car registration fees imposed by Governor Gray Davis in 1998. This action kept a campaign promise and pleased the voters, but it also slashed $4 billion from the vehicle license fee (VLF) funds, which many local government officials had counted on to backfill some of the $6 billion of local property tax revenues just diverted to ERAF accounts. Then the governor released his 2004–2005 budget, which proposed to shift an *additional* $1.3 billion in property tax revenues from cities, counties, special districts, and redevelopment agencies to the ERAF accounts to help cover the state's remaining obligation to the schools.

For many local officials, the governor's budget demands were the final straw. Indeed, even before the October 2003 recall election, some outraged local officials had already begun to take political action—not as lobbyists skulking to Sacramento to plead their case, but as street-level agitators of mass citizen revolt. In June 2003, for example, Bakersfield city officials blocked off a city street and held a combination press conference and rally. They were angered and alarmed by reports that state legislators had just met behind closed doors to take more than a billion dollars from local governments to help cover the state's massive deficit. The city's mayor declared that "everyone must fight this impending crisis."[39] In September 2003, the *Long Beach Press-Telegram* blasted state legislators for "plundering their hometown treasuries." Commenting that state politicians are "always looking for the easy way out of financial disasters of their own making," the editors exulted that "finally, their hometowns are fighting back."[40] Local governments are indeed "creatures of the state," but now these creatures were banding together politically, grabbing torches and pitchforks, and marching toward the capitol with bared teeth.

Responding to cries for action and reform, the League of California Cities, the California State Association of Counties, the California Special Districts Association, and other local government organizations formed the Californians to Protect Local Taxpayers and Public Safety coalition to place an initiative constitutional amendment on the November 2004 statewide ballot. Endorsed by more than 160 cities, this ballot measure, Proposition 65, would almost immediately require voter approval before the state used local government revenues for state, rather than local, purposes; ban the state from taking local tax dollars that fund local services such as police and fire, emergency and trauma care, parks, roads, libraries, and water delivery; require that the state pay the costs of any mandates requiring local governments to provide new programs and services; and require voter approval on any future state legislative actions that would reduce funding sources for essential local services.

Faced with this political and financial threat, Governor Schwarzenegger and a bipartisan majority of the state legislature proposed a more limited and flexible alternative measure, Proposition 1A, in return for local government acceptance of two more years of reduced funding to help balance the state budget. Under the provisions of legislative constitutional amendment Proposition 1A, the state cannot reduce local sales tax rates or alter the method of allocation; shift property taxes from local governments to schools or community colleges; decrease VLF revenues without providing replacement funding; and enforce unfunded mandates. Dropped was Proposition 65's harsh requirement of voter approval of state use of local government revenues. Starting in 2008–2009, however, Proposition 1A would require a declared fiscal emergency, a two-thirds vote of both houses of the legislature, and the governor's approval in order to shift local government property tax revenues to the schools. Further, those diverted revenues would have to be repaid, with interest, within three years.[41]

The leaders of the local government coalition agreed to this deal. Joined by the governor and state legislators, they endorsed Proposition 1A and withdrew their support from Proposition 65. Backed by a broad alliance of local government officials, police and fire departments, and public-sector labor unions, Proposition 1A passed overwhelmingly with 84 percent of the vote, and the discarded Proposition 65 was defeated. Many of California's local government officials celebrated Proposition 1A as the new Magna Carta of state-local fiscal relations. Local government finance expert Michael Coleman called it a "landmark" constitutional amendment that would "restore predictability and stability to local government budgets."[42]

Local Government: Where Are We Now?

In December 2008, multiple specters haunted California's thousands of local governments. These included natural disasters, economic recession, the subprime mortgage collapse, yet another state government budget crisis, partisan deadlock in the state legislature, and the continuing neglect by a federal government preoccupied with war and other costly misadventures. Despite the hard times, however, some local government leaders seized the opportunity found in crisis to adapt, innovate, and inspire new movements of political and social reform.

Persistent drought caused water shortages in many counties and prompted the governor to declare a state of water emergency. The drought conditions also contributed to the unprecedented number of wildfires raging across the state, leading to more emergency declarations and also a proposed surcharge on property taxes to deal with it. In a robust and growing state economy, these challenges would have been manageable. But jobs and economic opportunities, like the land, were drying up, too. In October 2008, the state's unemployment rate had increased to 8 percent from 5.4 percent the year before. Imperial County, with an unemployment rate of 27.6 percent, was especially hard-hit.[43] Even worse, as the nation's mortgage crisis deepened, California had the highest total of foreclosures of any state—nearly 250,000 in 2007 alone, more than triple the number in 2006. Projected to cost Californians an estimated $67 billion in lost property values, these foreclosures also chopped about $4 billion from expected property, sales, and transfer tax revenues. Seeking rescue from dire financial straits, the League of California Cities urged the state's congressional delegation to support legislation giving the nation's cities $4 billion to purchase foreclosed properties and to help low- and moderate-income families become home buyers.[44] These cries for help were likely to grow louder. By the end of September 2008, in the grip of recession, the state's mortgage crisis worsened as 3.9 percent of all home loans were in foreclosure.[45]

Meanwhile, faced with an $11.2 billion revenue shortfall for FY 2008–2009, and an astounding $28 billion total projected deficit over the next two years, state legislators battled one another to a standstill over how to fill the gap. As usual, the Democrats pushed for higher taxes and the Republicans insisted on hard cuts and limits on spending. Also as usual, members of both parties once again began plotting yet another raid on local government property tax revenues to bail themselves out of their jam.[46] Governor schwarzenegger quickly put a stop to that by invoking the provisions of Proposition 1A and his pact with the state's city and county governments. Addressing the state legislators in July 2008, he said: "What message does it send that you have spent too much and don't have a rainy day fund to cover yourself and then you go to the cities and counties where they do have a rainy day fund set aside for emergencies and now grab their money?"[47] Two months later, in a speech to the League of California Cities, the governor promised to enforce both the letter and the spirit of Proposition 1A by moving local government funds "off the table" of budget negotiations at the state capitol. He also called upon the League's city and county officials to mobilize politically and support his stand.[48] The League responded by urging city and county officials to demand that state legislators "cut up" the local government credit card and leave their money alone.[49] With local government revenues (except for local redevelopment agency funds) placed off limits, the state's budget crisis intensified and the partisan gridlock got even worse. On December 8, 2008, Governor Schwarzenegger declared a fiscal state of emergency, giving the legislature forty-five days to thrash things out and come up with a solution. Whatever the outcome in early 2009, it probably won't damage city and county budgets too severely thanks to the local government revolt behind Proposition 1A in 2004 and the governor's strong support of it at the end of 2008.

Overall, with nature, economics, and politics all conspiring to brew a perfect storm of trouble, 2008 has not been a good year for local government in California.

On the brighter side, and despite the hard times, California's local government officials and community activists have taken positive steps to solve their own problems while also trying to clean up the various messes made by the state and federal governments.

For example, the mayors of 125 California cities have now signed the U.S. Conference of Mayors Climate Protection Agreement. This initiative was launched by Seattle mayor Greg Nickels on February 16, 2005, the day the Kyoto Protocol became law for the 141 countries that had ratified it by that date. President Bush had rejected the Protocol and dismissed the science of global warming that had prompted it. But these California mayors, along with 725 others from across the country, took matters into their own hands. They pledged to meet or beat the Kyoto Protocol targets in their own cities and to urge their state governments and the federal government to do the same.[50] Two of those mayors, Gavin Newsom of San Francisco and Antonio Villariagosa of Los Angeles, have moved their cities to the front by thinking globally and acting locally to reduce greenhouse emissions on their own turf. Under their leadership, San Francisco and Los Angeles are now competing for the title of "greenest" city in the land.[51] The competition won't end there; both mayors are also planning to run for governor in 2010.

San Francisco, in particular, has arguably become the nation's vanguard city of progressive reform and social change. A few examples. In July 2007, Mayor Newsom and Supervisor Tom Ammiano initiated the city's pioneering universal health-care program, called Healthy San Francisco, which aims at covering the city's 73,000 uninsured residents. "Cities shouldn't have to do this, but I'm very proud that our city is doing it," Newsom said.[52] San Francisco has served as the West Coast center for mobilizing popular opposition to the Iraq War and is the nation's leading Sanctuary City, protecting and serving undocumented immigrants at a time of widespread fear and xenophobia. San Francisco has also been a major leader of the democracy reform movement. In 2002, San Francisco became the first big U.S. city to adopt instant runoff voting (IRV) for supervisorial and city-wide elections. Many other local governments have followed suit in the state and across the nation, including the California cities of Berkeley, Oakland, Davis, and San Leandro. A group of elected officials and community activists in Los Angeles are now seriously considering IRV and may propose it for voter adoption soon.[53] Most recently and famously, Mayor Newsom's bold move to authorize same-sex marriages in 2004 ultimately led to the California Supreme Court's decision on May 15, 2008, declaring that the state's ban on gay marriages was unconstitutional. The story did not end there, however. On November 4, 2008, a slim majority of the state's voters approved an initiative constitutional amendment, Proposition 8, eliminating the right of same-sex couples to marry. And the battle goes on. The California Supreme Court is scheduled to hear arguments on legal challenges to Proposition 8 in March 2009.

In sum, where most of the state's local governments are now, especially economically and financially, is in a very bad place. But many local government leaders and community activists have taken the initiative and pointed the way toward greater success, if not salvation. If America does become more peaceful, prosperous, and just under new presidential leadership, major credit can be given to California's local governments for preparing the ground and moving things along in a better direction.

FOR FURTHER READING

Baldassare, Mark. *A California State of Mind: The Conflicted Voter in a Changing World*. Berkeley: University of California Press, 2002.

Bridges, Amy. *Morning Glories: Municipal Reform in the Southwest*. Princeton, NJ: Princeton University Press, 1997.

DeLeon, Richard Edward. *Left Coast City: Progressive Politics in San Francisco, 1975–1991*. Lawrence, KS: University Press of Kansas, 1992.

Hajnal, Zoltan L., Paul G. Lewis, and Hugh Louch. *Municipal Elections in California: Turnout, Timing, and Competition*. San Francisco: Public Policy Institute of California, 2002.

Rodriguez, Daniel B. "State Supremacy, Local Sovereignty: Reconstructing State/Local Relations under the California Constitution." In Bruce E. Cain and Roger G. Noll, eds., *Constitutional Reform in California: Making State Government More Effective and Responsive*. Berkeley, CA: Institute of Governmental Studies Press, University of California, 1995; pp. 401–29.

Sonenshein, Raphael J. *Politics in Black and White: Race and Power in Los Angeles*. Princeton, NJ: Princeton University Press, 1993.

ON THE WEB

California Department of Finance/Research: www.dof.ca.gov/Research/Research.php

The Department of Finance produces detailed and up-to-date statistical reports and studies on local government finances, the state budget process and its impacts on localities, and a wide range of demographic and economic information on cities and counties.

California Employment Development Department: www.edd.ca.gov/

Valuable source of up-to-date statewide and county-level information on employment and labor market conditions.

California Secretary of State: www.sos.ca.gov/elections/

Excellent source of information on county-level election results for statewide candidate races and ballot propositions.

California Special Districts Association: www.csda.net/

California State Association of Counties: www.csac.counties.org/

Useful source of wide-ranging news and information on California's counties, with a main focus on policy and administration.

Institute for Local Government: www.cacities.org/index.jsp?zone=ilsg

The research arm and affiliate of the League of California Cities and the California State Association of Counties. Very good source of in-depth studies of key policy issues facing the state's local governments.

League of California Cities: www.cacities.org/index.jsp

An excellent source of news, information, and data on all aspects of governing California's cities.

U.S. Conference of Mayors: www.usmayors.org/

SUMMARY

California has more than 4,000 local governments of various types. These include general-purpose governments such as counties and cities, specific-purpose governments such as school districts and special districts, and regional governments. Local governments provide essential services, ranging from law enforcement and fire protection to waste management, street maintenance, and air and water quality control.

The state has ultimate authority over local governments. Under a doctrine called Dillon's Rule, local governments are "creatures of the state" and have no inherent rights or powers except those given them by the state constitution or legislature. California, like most states, gives counties and cities significant powers to govern themselves, make policies, enforce laws, raise revenues, borrow, and generally control local affairs as long as their decisions don't conflict with state or federal laws. Most of the more populous cities and counties have adopted home-rule charters that allow maximum local autonomy in self-governance. The others operate as general-law counties and cities, which have to abide more strictly to the state legislature's local government code.

California's fifty-eight counties are extremely diverse in terms of territorial extent, population size, demographic characteristics, and political culture. Except for the unique case of San Francisco's consolidated city and county government, all are governed by five-member boards of supervisors that exercise both legislative and executive powers. Counties perform many important functions, many of them required by state government laws and mandates. Counties also provide many essential services, especially in areas outside the cities and other jurisdictions, and they are major arenas for making large-scale land use and development policies. Each county also has a Local Agency Formation Commission (LAFCo), which plays a critical role in creating, merging, or dissolving new local governments, such as cities and special districts, and resolving disputes among competing jurisdictions.

The state has 478 cities, most of them general-law cities, the rest charter cities that have significant home-rule powers and local autonomy. Cities are legally created through a process of municipal incorporation that requires LAFCo review and approval and final majority vote of the community seeking formal city status. Nearly all cities have a form of government modeled on the vision of Progressive Era reformers: strong city managers, weak mayors, nonpartisan elections, at-large council elections, nonconcurrent elections, and direct democracy, including the initiative, referendum, and recall. Important exceptions include cities such as Los Angeles and San Francisco, which have strong mayor systems and, in the case of San Francisco, district elections. Voter turnout in city elections has been steadily declining in recent years, and those who vote tend to be whiter, older, richer, and more educated than those who don't. The state's growing population of noncitizens, in particular, has little political voice or formal representation in local government. Certain electoral reforms, such as a shift from noncurrent to concurrent elections, could markedly increase voter turnout levels.

Special districts are limited-purpose local governments. Excluding the state's 1,044 K–12 school districts and 72 community college districts, there are nearly 3,000 special districts that provide a range of services—such as irrigation, pest abatement, parks and recreation, water, fire protection—that are not provided at all, or in sufficient amounts, by general-purpose governments like counties and cities. Created by a LAFCo-approved citizen petition and majority vote, most special districts are independent agencies that provide one type of service received and paid for by residents in smaller territories of larger jurisdictions, like counties. Some are enterprise districts that charge individual user fees for service, but most are funded by taxes or special assessments from service recipients.

The advantages of special districts include greater flexibility and responsiveness in tailoring service and the levels of cost and benefits to citizen demands. The disadvantages include duplication of services, lack of coordination, and unclear structures of authority and accountability.

The state's regional governments address problems such as air pollution and population growth that affect large areas and multiple local government jurisdictions. Some regional governments, such as the San Francisco Bay Conservation and Development Commission and the California Coastal Commission, have strong regulatory authority and enforcement powers. Others, such as the Southern California Association of Governments, the Association of Bay Area Governments, and other councils of government (COGs), perform mainly research, planning, and advisory functions and have little or no power or authority to impose their decisions on local jurisdictions.

Three major kinds of problems confront California's various local governments. One is the extreme polarization in regional political cultures across the state that makes legislative compromise and consensus building difficult, as illustrated by the stark differences in partisanship, political tolerance, and voting tendencies observed in San Francisco, Los Angeles County, and San Diego County. The second is the challenge posed by internal conflicts and secessionist movements in some local jurisdictions, as illustrated by the recent attempt of the San Fernando Valley to secede from Los Angeles. The third is the crisis in local government finance and the threat to effective home rule caused by the worsening state budget deficit and the state government's efforts to solve it by seizing property tax revenues from county and city governments.

PRACTICE QUIZ

1. Cities and counties that have home-rule charters have the authority to make their own laws even if they violate state and federal laws.
   a) true
   b) false
2. The U.S. Constitution gives local governments inherent rights and powers which cannot be taken away by state governments.
   a) true
   b) false
3. County boards of supervisors have both legislative and executive authority.
   a) true
   b) false
4. Most cities are governed by manager-council systems.
   a) true
   b) false

5. At the local government level, citizens cannot petition for a referendum or recall election.
   a) true
   b) false
6. Which of the following is not a characteristic of reform government at the local level?
   a) at-large council elections
   b) nonpartisanship
   c) city manager plan
   d) concurrent elections
7. Which of the following counties operates under a single charter as a consolidated city and county?
   a) Los Angeles
   b) Sacramento
   c) San Francisco
   d) Orange

8. Which of the following is *not* a tool of direct democracy?
   a) referendum
   b) incorporation
   c) initiative
   d) recall
9. Which of the following elected officials will be found only in county governments?
   a) sheriff
   b) mayor
   c) council member
   d) manager
10. The fiscalization of land use is one way some local governments have found to
    a) encourage the construction of new affordable housing.
    b) prevent the building of new shopping malls.
    c) promote new businesses that will return a local share of state-collected sales taxes.
    d) raise property taxes to pay for new schools and sewage systems.

CRITICAL-THINKING QUESTIONS

1. Do you think the Progressive Era reform vision for local governments is still a good one today and that the state's local governments should continue to be run by professional managers and insulated as much as possible from state and national party politics? Why or why not?
2. Should local governments, such as cities, be given more home-rule powers and greater local autonomy free of state interference? Test case: Would it be okay with you if all California cities asserted their home-rule powers and local autonomy to the extent that San Francisco has? Why or why not?
3. Do you agree with some critics that most special districts should be abolished and their functions centralized under the control of county and city governments? Why or why not?
4. Do you agree with some observers that California needs more and stronger regional governments? Why or why not? If you agree, what are some of the problems facing those who seek to form such governments, and what steps would you take to create them? How would you balance your recommendations with the principles of home rule and local autonomy?
5. Do you think communities such as those in San Fernando Valley should be allowed to secede from established jurisdictions and form their own cities? If so, do you think it should be easier or harder for them to do so than it is now?
6. Do you support or oppose the rebellion of local governments against the state as a response to the state's attempt to use local government property tax revenues to solve its budget deficit problem? Why or why not?

KEY TERMS

At this point you should have a general understanding of the following concepts and terms:

advisory regional governments (173)
at-large elections (167)
charter cities and counties (164)
cities (164)
council-manager plan (166)
councils of government (COGs) (173)
counties (158)
Dillon's Rule (156)
direct democracy (168)
district elections (167)
Educational Revenue Augmentation Funds (ERAFs) (179)

enterprise districts (168)
fiscalization of land use (180)
general-law cities and counties (156)
home rule (156)
independent districts (170)
Local Agency Formation Commissions (LAFCo) (163)
mayor-council plan (166)
municipal incorporation (164)
noncurrent elections (167)
nonpartisanship (167)
ordinances (161)

political culture (173)
property taxes (180)
recall (176)
referendum (168)
reform governments (164)
regional governments (172)
regulatory regional governments (172)
school districts (169)
secession (177)
special districts (169)
unfunded mandates (180)
user fees (170)

10 Public Policy in California

WHAT CALIFORNIA GOVERNMENT DOES, AND WHY IT MATTERS

Consider the following problem: The state highway system consists of highways, bridges, overpasses, and the like built and maintained by the state. To build and maintain this system, we have a state highway department, which in California is called Caltrans. Caltrans can design the highways and bridges itself or contract this work out to the private sector. Who should design and build these highways?

You would not think this would be a complicated public-policy problem. In fact, this problem is so complicated that not only do we not have a definitive answer, we also have a continuing political controversy that has involved interest groups, the legislature, the governor, the courts—and ultimately the voters—since competing initiatives have been submitted in the last six years for voter approval.

The 13,000 engineers, architects, surveyors, and related professionals who work for Caltrans and other agencies are represented by their union, Professional Engineers in California Government. According to Daniel Weintraub, *Sacramento Bee* columnist, Governor Pete Wilson obtained the ability to contract out highway engineering work in the 1990s. The Professional Engineers in California Government responded with Proposition 224, placed on the June 1998 primary election ballot. The proposition would have amended the California constitution to ban contracting "where performance of work by civil service employees is less costly unless urgent need for contract." It would also have prohibited contracting out if the awarding agency found that "the quality of work would be lower than civil service work." These provisions favored the public-sector engineers. The voters rejected the measure by a vote of 62 percent against and 38 percent in favor.

The legal battle continued, according to Weintraub. "The state engineers sued to try to stop the private contracts, and the private-sector firms fought back." The private-sector firms sponsored Proposition 35, which, again quoting ballot pamphlet language, would have eliminated "existing restrictions on state, local contracting with private entities for engineering, architectural services." This initiative passed 55 percent to 45 percent.[1]

The public engineers responded with a provision in their union contract in 2002 that would have limited the ability of state agencies to contract out architectural and engineering work. The legislature's lawyers decided the provision was unconstitutional, and the administration withdrew the contract. In the last days of the 2003 legislative session, with the recall election of Governor Davis in full swing, the administration approved another contract, this one with a provision for a labor-management committee to review all proposed private contracts. Lawsuits from both the private sector and the public engineers continued over these provisions into the next year.

Should we care? In the third section of this chapter, on the state's infrastructure, we will find a recent study that finds the state's roads are among the worst in the nation. And, at the same time, the groups that should coalesce to support an increase in funding for transportation purposes are instead fighting among themselves over who will do highway engineering and construction work.

Public policy involves the end results of government, not the process of the legislature, or of the bureaucracy, or the courts, but the results of what government actually does. In the case of transportation, the end result is the quality and quantity of highways produced. In the paragraph above we illustrated an all-too-typical occurrence in California government, one that probably results over time in fewer highway miles being constructed or repaired than if the public- and private-sector interests cooperated instead of battling each other.

In this chapter on public policy in California, we could not possibly cover the gamut of policy areas or results. Instead, we are going to use some of the controversies that are in the newspapers to illustrate some aspects of public policy. Here are the policy areas or problems we will discuss:

- workers' compensation;

- immigration and the policy problems associated with high immigration;

- the state's infrastructure and its deterioration;

- Indian gaming and the associated policy problems.

Workers' Compensation

The object of the workers' compensation law is to protect both workers and employers. Workers are protected, in theory, by being promptly and fairly compensated for work-related injuries. Employers are protected, again in theory, because workers, in return for receiving fair and prompt compensation, give up their right to sue the employer for "pain and suffering" or "punitive damages." The laws originated in the Progressive Era, just after 1900, and California was one of the first states to adopt workers' compensation legislation. The system is funded by an insurance policy that employers are required to purchase, either through a state fund (the State Compensation Insurance Fund—SCIF, the insurer of last resort) or from the private sector. Insurance companies are free to offer such policies or not. The rates vary depending on the occupation of the employee and the risk of injury.

One would think that this system would be as uninteresting as the question of who designs highways, but in fact, employers have cited workers' compensation costs as the single most expensive feature of doing business in California. In fact, some businesses have left the state rather than pay what they consider to be outrageous insurance rates. Meanwhile, the system has been found, by national standards, not to do very well at compensating employees who are injured, and to compensate lawyers and doctors very well indeed. The cost of this system is approximately $24 billion per year. This cost is outside the state budget but heavily regulated by government.[2]

The issues in workers' compensation involve

- the cost to employers, which employers contend is too high;

- the kind of coverage required, which employers contend is too broad;

- who determines whether an incident has resulted in an injury, which falls under the workers' compensation system, or an illness, covered by the worker's health insurance;

- the benefit amount;

- the cost of rehabilitation, if appropriate;

- fraud on the part of any of the several players;

- the timeliness of a decision;

- attorneys' fees.

Over time the workers' compensation system has become increasingly expensive and complex because of inflation, benefit increases, fraudulent injury claims, and fluctuations in economic and business cycles. Why did costs increase? There have been, in the words of California State Insurance Commissioner John Garamendi, "sharp increases in claim costs which include . . . medical payments and indemnity claim payments."[3] These costs reflect the substantial increases in medical costs seen in recent years.

Another important factor is that many insurance companies that used to provide workers' compensation insurance have left the market. At least twelve have been declared insolvent and either liquidated or merged since 2000, including the biggest workers' compensation insurer in the state, which found that costs were substantially higher than estimated. The carriers left in the market have increased their premiums to compensate for the increased costs. The result has been that one company, SCIF, had increased its share of the workers' compensation marketplace to 54 percent in 2003, although that proportion subsequently fell as a result of the governor's 2004 reform package.[4]

The insurance commissioner, an elected officer, is an important player in workers' compensation costs. The commissioner can challenge the rates that the insurers plan to charge if they seem too low to cover their costs, and he approves or disapproves proposed rate increases.

A substantial cost of the workers' compensation system is the more than $1.5 billion per year spent for litigation, mostly for legal and medical expenses for reports to prove or disprove a claim. The Los Angeles District Attorney's Web site describes "organized workers' compensation fraud involving doctors and lawyers":

> Fraud rings have made a practice of recruiting people to file phony work injury claims by appealing to laid-off employees who were unhappy in their jobs. They advertise in newspapers and on television and use special recruiters known as "cappers" who frequent unemployment offices and even workplaces. The workers are sent to medical clinics or legal referral centers (commonly known as "claim mills"), which in turn refer them to a doctor or lawyer who is in on the scheme. Regardless of the legitimacy of the claim, many mill operators maximize the number of medical/legal reports and referrals in each case to maximize the amount they can bill. These mills operate on a volume basis. Because there are few limits on the number of medical/legal reports, unscrupulous lawyers often team up with unscrupulous doctors to generate fraudulent claims. By preparing multiple medical/legal reports—whether they are needed or not—mill operators increase the cost of a claim by thousands of dollars.[5]

The result of all of these factors is that

- the premiums that employers paid for workers' compensation coverage in California were among the highest in the nation in 2004, double the national average (premiums fell substantially between 2004 and 2008 as a result of the governor's 2004 reform package).

- benefit payments for injured workers were only average for the nation and, until they were raised recently, were among the lowest in the nation.[6]

Three key issues that separate the Democrats and Republicans on workers' compensation are

- Regulating the insurance companies that offer workers' compensation insurance. The Democrats want to make sure that insurance companies are not making excessive profits; Republicans want to keep the system deregulated.

- Which doctor workers should see when an injury occurs. Employers want to pick the doctors, while workers' groups have argued that the right to pick one's own doctor is fundamental to workers' rights.

- Eliminating permanent partial disability payments. These are given for injuries that are not obvious or easily measured, such as back pain or mental stress.[7]

The issue is intensely partisan. Republicans, supported by business groups, have generally supported reforms restricting benefits, while Democrats, supported by labor unions and the attorneys who represent the applicants, have talked of regulating the workers' compensation system. Insurance-commissioner candidates, however, have found that their major source of campaign funds is the insurance industry.

Reforms were enacted in 2003, resulting in a small decrease in premiums and costs, but business groups still contended in 2004 that the issue is the number one reason why businesses leave California for other states and that the high cost of workers' compensation is one reason businesses don't hire more employees. Governor Schwarzenegger brokered an agreement among the various groups in April 2004, involving compromises around the key issues. These included his policies on insurance rates, that they should not be regulated, and the selection of doctors—workers must select doctors from a pool approved by employers and insurers. The eligibility requirements for permanent disability payments were tightened, and temporary disability could no longer continue for more than two years. The results of both the 2003 and 2004 reforms were that premiums fell by more than 50 percent in the next two years and insurers earned high profits on their workers' compensation business. But injured workers and their advocates complained strongly that insurers were delaying or denying medical treatment, and the benefits under workers' compensation were among the lowest in the nation. Senator Don Perata (D), State Senate majority leader, sent legislation to the governor in 2006 and 2007 that would have raised benefits substantially, but the governor vetoed the bill each year, stating that his own reviews were under way and were not completed as yet. In 2008, a study showed that premiums had fallen by over 40 percent as a result of the governor's reform plan, a major source of Schwarzenegger's strong business support.[8] Employee groups, meanwhile, contend that benefits have been cut too far and cite numerous examples of severely injured workers who cannot receive sufficient rehabilitation to return to work.[9] The issue continues to be strongly partisan and contentious.

Immigrants in California

When a large proportion of a state's population is born in other countries and a substantial proportion of that population is not in the United States legally, there are many public-policy implications. In Chapter 1 we noted that

- 27 percent, or 9.9 million people, of the state's population in 2006 was born outside the United States. Of those, almost half are from Mexico.

- of the 38 million people in California, 2.8 million, almost one-fourth of the foreign-born population, are undocumented.

What issues arise from immigration?

Campaign Issues

Immigration itself is an issue in many state campaigns. Governor Pete Wilson ran for re-election in 1994 in part on a stance opposing illegal immigration. Recent governors have actually sent bills to the federal government for extra payments that they allege arise from the level of immigration, which is a federal-government responsibility.

School Issues

Immigrants tend to have more children than those who have lived in this country for several generations, and consequently areas that have more immigrants need more schools. Schools entail both construction costs and ongoing expenses for teachers and supplies. In six of California's largest cities, immigrants comprise a majority: Glendale, Santa Ana, Daly City, El Monte, Union City, and Alhambra. Santa Clara (36 percent), San Francisco (36 percent), and Los Angeles (35 percent) are the counties with the highest percentages.

Costs of State Welfare and Health Programs

Since immigrants tend to be poorer than those born in the United States, the state's costs for welfare, Medi-Cal, and public health programs are substantially higher than they would be otherwise. The immigrant population's poverty rate is 18 percent, compared with 12 percent for those born in the U.S.[10] These costs are the basis for the state's asking the federal government for assistance because of the disproportionate impact of immigration, a federal-government responsibility.

Driver's Licenses

Should noncitizens, particularly those who are not legally in this country, receive driver's licenses? A decision by the legislature and the Davis administration to grant driver's licenses to undocumented immigrants in 2003 was a major issue in the vote to recall Governor Davis in October of that year. The law required applicants to have other forms of identification, such as a federal individual taxpayer identification number, with the DMV given discretion to specify the type of identification required. After the recall in 2003, Governor Schwarzenegger asked the legislature to repeal the law, and it did.

Voting

A policy issue that could arise in the future is the question of whether noncitizens should be allowed to vote in any elections at the state or local level. The options include all state and local elections, city elections only, neighborhood councils within cities, or something similarly restricted. While federal law and the U.S. Constitution do not allow noncitizens to vote in federal elections for president, U.S. senator, or congressional representative, the state could change its constitution and laws to allow noncitizens to vote in state and local elections, using the differences between the total population and the voting population as justification. Maryland allows noncitizens to vote in state and local elections, and the question was debated in 2004 in New York, another large state with a substantial immigrant population. UCLA's Chicano Studies Research Center issued a policy paper in 2003 stating that immigrants were more than 25 percent of the population in over eighty-five California cities and calling for efforts to increase their political participation.[11]

It is not immigration per se that has led to these public-policy problems. What makes immigration such a difficult issue is the concentration of immigrants, both legal and illegal, in certain border states, producing costs that are far beyond those of the average state. These costs are a result of federal immigration policies over which the states have little control. Although the federal government formulates and implements immigration policy, it does not reimburse states for costs that are above the average level of other states as a result of those policies.

California's Infrastructure

Infrastructure is the part of government that citizens come into contact with the most—highways, schools, universities, commuter buses, and rail. California's infrastructure deteriorated significantly into the mid-2000s, but the five bond issues approved by the voters in November 2006, totaling over $40 billion, for infrastructure improvements to transportation systems, housing, public education, higher education, and disaster/flood control should make a significant difference in these systems over time as the bonds are issued and construction takes place. One factor that makes the maintenance of the state's infrastructure difficult is what Bruce Cain of University of California, Berkeley's Institute of Governmental Studies calls California's "infrastructure ambivalence." On the one hand, Californians want modern facilities and infrastructure, but "we don't want what often comes with those things. There are, for instance, unavoidable environmental costs. Water projects can endanger fisheries in the Delta. New roads and housing can separate and destroy ecosystems."[12] Consider these examples:

Highways

California's public road system is worth approximately $300 billion. The Federal Highway Administration database that shows the proportion of each state's roads that are unacceptably rough, based on a federal standard, indicates the national average at 8 percent of the roads; California's percentage is 26 percent. Only Massachusetts has a higher percentage of unacceptably rough roads. A 2008 survey of the nation's bridges found 25 percent of them structurally deficient or functionally obsolete, with some 6,977, or 29 percent, of California's bridges falling into the deficient/obsolete category. With Californians reducing their driving somewhat in 2008 and the major source of highway and bridge repair being the 18.4 cents per gallon gasoline tax, the prospects for increased repair work are not good.[13]

Fire Prevention

In early March 2004, voters in San Diego County considered seven attempts to raise more money for fire prevention and to "beef up fire departments that were overwhelmed in the deadly wildfires of last fall."[14] The city of San Diego is a good example. The proposal was to increase the hotel room tax, what is often called the "tourist tax," from 10.5 percent to 13 percent of the price of a hotel room, a rate similar to what is charged in other large tourist-oriented cities in California. It attracted a 61 percent positive vote, a landslide in most elections, but the state constitution and laws, as amended by Proposition 13 and its follow-up legislation and constitutional amendments, require any new tax or increase in any existing local tax to be approved by two-thirds of the voters. The increase would have provided an extra $8 million for the Fire Department, $3 million for the police, and $7 million for tourism promotion projects.

Meanwhile, in the unincorporated areas of the county, many now served by volunteer fire departments that were overwhelmed by the fires of fall 2003, three tax increases failed. In one of them, the ballot statement opposing the $50 a year per parcel increase read: "Taxes won't stop. Next year, another tax. Taxing will continue until they break you financially." After the fires in fall 2003, the consensus was that the poor communications, volunteer fire departments, lack of coordination among agencies, and poor training had been major contributors to the quick spread of the fires and to the hundreds of homes lost. In spite of that, supporters could not muster a two-thirds vote.

In 2008, San Diego County remained the only county in the state *without* a unified countywide fire department, and the county needed more than twenty additional fire stations and 800 additional firefighters to meet national fire-service accreditation standards. A *Los Angeles Times* series in mid-2008 pointed out that not only were fire departments across the state short of firefighters and equipment, but that a major factor in the increased losses from forest fires was the tendency of new developments to be located adjacent to wildlands. The state Department of Forestry and Fire Protection now estimates that "about 40% of the more than 12 million homes in the state are on land with a high or extreme threat of wildfire."[15] In wealthier areas, the recent tendency is to pay a private firefighting service a premium of "at least $10,000 per year . . . [to protect] homes with a value of at least $1 million."[16]

The California State University (CSU)

CSU has a yearly budget of approximately $2.5 billion, which, along with an additional $1 billion in student fees, supports the enrollment and instruction of about 400,000 students. The system has approximately $800 million in deferred maintenance: unpainted walls and classrooms; damaged floors and windows; unrepaired heating, ventilation, and air-conditioning systems; old and damaged desks and chairs; and projection equipment for classrooms not replaced—all the things that should be done to maintain the property that the state has spent billions to construct. The amount of deferred maintenance has stayed about the same for over a decade and a half. Almost no progress has been made on reducing the amount, because each year the governor eliminates this item from his budget proposal with no explanation, just as previous governors have done during the entire decade of the 1990s, including budget-surplus years. The clear implication is that the state is deliberately neglecting its infrastructure, presumably because the infrastructure doesn't vote.

Elementary and Secondary School Buildings

In late 2002, the state released a study finding that 7,537 school buildings, about 10 percent of the total school buildings in California, failed to meet the Field Act standard for performance in earthquakes. The Field Act, passed in the wake of the 1933 Long Beach earthquake, mandates standards for K–12 public school buildings, but not for private schools or institutions of higher education. However, in order not to worry citizens and school officials, the findings for individual schools were not published in the comprehensive study. School districts had to ask for the results for their own individual school district. A year and a half after the study was released, only thirty (3 percent) of the state's 1,000 school districts had even asked for their results. The Northern California Chapter of the Earthquake Engineering Research Institute published a fact sheet in 2003 indicating that over 1,000 school buildings in the Bay Area "provide questionable resistance to earthquakes and require additional study to determine if they meet a 'life safety' standard."[17]

Levees

In 1986, a levee broke along the Yuba River and inundated the small town of Linda in the Central Valley, causing several hundred million dollars' worth of damage. In 2004, eighteen years later, the state Supreme Court ratified a Court of Appeal decision that found the state of California liable because it had not repaired the stretch of levee that broke. While the state resisted liability for the break and its consequences, the courts have found that the state will have to pay for the consequences of its neglect.[18]

The *Sacramento Bee* recently published a series of articles that detailed the several governmental agencies that were responsible for flood control and maintenance of the levees along the Sacramento River. While the agencies have not been able to find the funds to repair over 150 sites where the levees could fail during a major flood, builders and developers have continued to construct large developments in the Central Valley near Sacramento in areas where levees hold back rivers that are capable of flood damage to thousands of homes and businesses.[19]

In mid-2004, just after the publication of the *Sacramento Bee* series, a dirt levee broke suddenly in the Delta region, instantly changing 12,000 acres of farmland into a 12,000-acre lake. Officials found that a second levee was in danger of breaking, and a third needed to be shored up in order to prevent a road from being flooded, cutting the only connection to two islands with their 178 residents.[20] Total damage: $35 million to buildings and crops, plus another $36.5 million to fix the levees.

The Future of California's Infrastructure

The neglect of the state's infrastructure in these instances is obvious. The reasons why infrastructure repair and upkeep are not a higher priority are less obvious. One is that infrastructure is a long-term problem, and our political system, based on two- and four-year terms of office, thinks short-term. This factor is magnified by the term limits imposed on the legislature, traditionally a body where legislators spent several decades on their careers and could think in longer terms than the governor and the executive-branch officials, who are elected for only one or two four-year terms. Now with term limits, the members of the legislature are subject to the same short-term time constraints.

A second factor is the impact over time of the public employee unions, who represent potential votes for politicians and whose emphasis, as one would imagine, is on maintaining or increasing personnel in the public sector, not on fixing infrastructure.

All of this changed with the destruction wreaked by Hurricane Katrina on the Gulf Coast and the subsequent failure of government in many places to fulfill its emergency responsibilities. The public-works package of bond issues approved by the voters in November 2006 included Proposition 1E, the Disaster Preparedness and Flood Prevention Act of 2006, which authorized $4.1 billion in bonds to rebuild flood-control structures, including the delta levees. The money authorized will provide a solid start toward rebuilding the eroding facilities.

Every governor in recent years has appealed to the federal government for extra help. Except for the Clinton administration's response to the Northridge earthquake in 1994, the federal government has not responded with anything out of the ordinary. California remains a relatively wealthy state that pays more to the federal government in taxes than it receives in federal benefits. In December 2008, Governor Schwarzenegger presented President-elect Barack Obama with a list of California infrastructure projects ready to break ground immediately, urging Obama to fund nearly $44 billion of work as part of the effort to stimulate the national economy and create jobs.

Indian Gaming in California

In 1931 the first casino opened in Nevada. Only Nevada had gambling casinos until 1976, when New Jersey voters legalized gambling in Atlantic City. Nine more states legalized gambling between 1989 and 1998, and there are now over 400 nontribal casinos in eleven states. In the early 1980s, Indian tribes in Florida and California began to operate bingo games with larger prizes than state regulators allowed. The cases in both states went to court; the result was a Supreme Court decision in 1987 and in 1988 the passage by Congress of the Indian Gambling Regulatory Act. The act requires tribes to have a compact with the state specifying the type of gambling permitted on their lands. Today, at least 198 of the 561 federally recognized Indian tribes run more than 325 gambling casinos and other facilities, "generating about $10 billion per year in revenue, or one-seventh of all gambling proceeds."[21]

In California, former Governor Pete Wilson negotiated the first compact in 1998. It placed such severe restrictions on slot machines that the tribes qualified an initiative, Proposition 5, for the November 1998 ballot, taking the issue to the voters. The campaign was the most expensive in California at that time, with $90 million spent by both sides, and Proposition 5 was approved by a substantial majority. It required the governor to approve any tribal casino proposal. It placed no limits on the number of casinos statewide or the number of gambling machines or tables each casino could operate. It lowered the gambling age to eighteen and allowed the tribes to continue using the video slot machines that the state and federal governments had deemed illegal. Tribal casinos would be self-regulated, governed by a tribal-appointed gaming board. There would be no direct state or local involvement in casino operations.[22] The California Supreme Court struck down Proposition 5 in 1999.

The tribes, however, found Wilson's successor, Gray Davis, more willing to negotiate compacts. He negotiated with sixty tribes, "allowing them to expand current gambling operations, allowing Nevada-style gambling . . . , legalizing video slot machines, [and] allowing casino employees to unionize." The compacts depended on the approval of Proposition 1A on the March 2000 ballot; it passed with a 65 percent majority. At this point, it is estimated that the tribes are generating revenues of at least $5 billion per year, and they have become major contributors to California election campaigns. "Gaming has become so lucrative that hundreds of Native Americans are petitioning the Bureau of Indian Affairs for recognition of fifty-four new California tribes in order to buy land, often in urban areas, and build casinos."[23]

One policy issue is the percentage of gaming revenues that should be returned to the state of California. At present, the tribes pay approximately $400 million per year, about 8 percent of their total revenues, to the state to help other tribes that do not have gaming operations. They also make voluntary contributions to the local governments in the area of their casinos to offset increased expenses that may result from the casino. Connecticut receives 25 percent of the revenues from the Foxwoods Casino in that state; other states receive less.

Another casino-related issue is the lack of knowledge of the odds of winning at the various kinds of gambling available in California. In other states, non-Indian gambling operations must reveal their odds, but among the states with Indian gaming, only Connecticut requires the tribes to reveal the odds of winning.[24]

Tribal casinos are not required to address environmental problems, such as "damage to local roads, animal and plant life, and over demands . . . casinos placed on water supplies and public services." On his last day in office, after being recalled, Governor Davis wrote a letter releasing the tribes from any obligation to negotiate over these issues.[25]

Another contentious issue is the exclusion of hundreds of persons who thought they were members of Indian tribes and thus entitled to receive the substantial annual payments generated from casino profits that go to lawful members. Several tribes in recent years voted former members out of membership on the grounds that they were not lineal descendants of the original members of the tribe. The governor has been urged to investigate the disenrollments, which in some cases are contravened by DNA evidence, and the disenrolled members have threatened to sue in state, federal, or Bureau of Indian Affairs courts, although none of these courts normally takes on membership issues.

Indian gaming, then, raises a host of issues about whether private entities that profit from public infrastructure and legal rights granted by state government have any obligation to support the state in return. These are difficult issues, particularly given the history of the treatment of Native Americans in California, and they promise to be in the news for years to come.

Conclusion

Intense interest-group activity is obvious and exists in most public-policy areas. Our political system seems unable to cut through the intensely held feelings of various groups in order to make policy for the public as a whole. In his first year, Governor Schwarzenegger showed that a strong leader who continually appeals to the public as a whole and uses the threat of initiatives can coax the legislature into making policy that benefits the entire state, but whether that characteristic alone is sufficient to produce public-policy results over the long run is uncertain. The threat of the initiative permeates every area and is used as a weapon by all sides. California finds it difficult to make policy for all of the reasons we began with in this book: the two-thirds requirement for passing the budget, which prolongs budget negotiations to the exclusion of other policy areas that may need attention, and the interest-group impasse demonstrated so well in this chapter.

We began this book with a series of reform suggestions from State Senator John Vasconcellos, a liberal with a long record of thoughtful suggestions for improving the operation of state government. We conclude with the suggestions of *The Economist* from its recent survey of California. The similarities between *The Economist*'s diagnosis and Senator Vasconcellos's diagnosis of the problems are striking, while their solutions are somewhat different. *The Economist*:

- Establish an independent commission for redistricting to produce more competitive electoral districts for Assembly, Senate, and congressional districts.

- Reduce the size of the districts by considering a unicameral legislature of 120 members, limited to terms of fourteen years, which would liberalize the current term limits of six years in the Assembly and eight in the Senate.

This change would keep the same number of legislators, reduce the size of legislative districts, and strengthen the role of expertise in the legislature by allowing legislators to stay in office longer.

- Hold open primaries in which a party's voters could vote for the candidates of the other party.

- Reallocate state and local taxes so that different taxes go to different levels of government—income tax to the state, property tax to localities, sales tax split.

- Allocate state governmental functions so that the state is responsible for the universities, water, and welfare, for example; regional authorities are responsible for transportation, the environment, and planning; and cities and counties are responsible for police and schools. Consider removing counties and school districts as unnecessary layers of government.

- Increase the number of signatures necessary to place an initiative on the ballot.

- Consider placing a time limit on the laws enacted through the initiative so that the legislature makes an explicit decision to renew the measure after a decade or more.

No reform plan, however, can succeed without certain prerequisites. Leadership is needed to form a group of prominent citizens and politicians who can agree on a limited number of measures that the public might accept. Funds are needed to develop the measures in the appropriate language and collect sufficient signatures to put the initiatives on the ballot. Leadership is then needed even more than before to convince skeptical and distrusting citizens that changing the state constitution in these ways will make a difference in how California is governed. And citizens need to pay attention and be interested in change. In the past, most of these factors have been lacking.

Anyone, from *The Economist* to John Vasconcellos, can put together a reform package, and many of the proposed packages will overlap. The hard work begins with focusing on a limited number of measures that will actually make a difference, measures that a leadership group can argue for with conviction. Our own candidates for reform would be three measures:

- a commission to do reapportionments of legislative districts;

- open primaries along the lines of Washington or Louisiana, in which voters vote for one candidate from a single list and then the top two candidates regardless of party go on the November ballot (producing more moderate legislators ideologically);

- lowering the threshold to pass the budget to 55 percent or 60 percent. Ideally, the threshold should be 50 percent and should include the ability to raise taxes, but the California public has made it very clear over the years that it will not vote for a 50 percent rule.

The hardest part, however, is not agreeing on the measures but convincing a skeptical public that they should be adopted.

FOR FURTHER READING

"Arnold's Big Chance: A Survey of California." *The Economist*, May 1, 2004, 1–16.

Light, Steven Andrew, and Kathryn R. L. Rand. *Indian Gaming and Tribal Sovereignty: The Casino Compromise*. Lawrence: University Press of Kansas, 2005.

Neumark, David. *The Workers' Compensation Crisis in California: A Primer*. California Economic Policy vol. 1, no. 1. San Francisco: Public Policy Institute of California, January 2005.

Schrag, Peter. *California: America's High-Stakes Experiment*. Berkeley: University of California Press, 2006.

Simmons, Charlene Wear. *Gambling in the Golden State, 1998 Forward*. Sacramento: California Research Bureau, California State Library, May 2006.

State of California, Legislative Analyst's Office. *A Primer: The State's Infrastructure and the Use of Bonds*. Sacramento: Legislative Analyst's Office, January 2006.

ON THE WEB

American Association of State Highway and Transportation Officials: www.transportation.org

California Progress Report: www.californiaprogressreport.com
A daily briefing on politics and policy.

Center on Policy Initiatives, San Diego: www.onlinecpi.org/index.php

Public Policy Institute of California: www.ppic.org

UCLA Chicano Studies Research Center: www.chicano.ucla.edu/center.htm

University of California, Berkeley, Institute of Governmental Studies Library, "Hot Topics": http://igs.berkeley.edu/library/hot_topics/HTINDEX.html
Provides concise but thorough information on California elections and public policy.

SUMMARY

Five cases of how public policy is made and implemented in California are presented in this chapter. The first deals with the continuing battle between the state highway engineers represented by their union, the Professional Engineers in California Government, versus the private-sector highway engineers. The battle centers over how much state highway work is to be contracted out to the private sector.

Workers' compensation insurance is designed to compensate workers when they are injured at work. The system is complicated by high insurance rates for employers, the involvement of elements of both the medical and legal profession, a much higher proportion of litigated claims than in other states, partisan and opposing views on the system by members of the Republican and Democratic parties in the legislature, fraud, and the involvement of many groups.

California has a much higher proportion of immigrants than other states, and one-quarter of the immigrants, it is estimated, are undocumented. The high proportion of legal and illegal immigrants makes immigration a continuing campaign issue, a school issue because of the number of immigrant children in the schools, and an issue in the state budget because of the higher costs of Medi-Cal and public-health programs compared with those of other states. There is the further controversy over whether immigrants without documentation should be issued driver's licenses.

California's physical infrastructure is deteriorating, as noted in the sections on highways, the CSU, K–12 school buildings, and levees. More important, the support that is needed to maintain adequate public services can sometimes be lacking, in particular where support is needed at the level of a two-thirds vote to increase fees and taxes to support, for example, fire protection services. The San Diego and San Bernardino fires of 2003 provided evidence that the volunteer fire departments are not up to the task in some areas.

Indian gaming is a major issue in California. Caught between tribes that desire to host casinos and a public that is relatively supportive of gambling in Indian casinos, California State government has negotiated compacts that return very small proportions of the revenues to the state. The tribes are also heavy campaign contributors, which complicates the negotiations.

PRACTICE QUIZ

1. Employers cite workers' compensation costs as a major factor in deciding whether to locate new businesses in California because
   a) costs are too high in the view of many.
   b) litigation is involved in many claims, driving up costs.
   c) fraud mills put forward many false claims, which must be disputed.
   d) all of the above
   e) none of the above
2. The results of the workers' compensation reform of 2004 included all of the following *except*
   a) regulation of the workers' compensation insurance industry.
   b) the question of who selects the doctor to evaluate the worker who claims to be injured.
   c) restrictions on both temporary and permanent disability payments.
   d) proposals designed to lower rates for employers.
3. Most immigrants in California are from Mexico.
   a) true
   b) false
4. Just as immigrants are spread throughout California, they are also spread throughout the United States on a roughly equivalent basis.
   a) true
   b) false
5. California's infrastructure has been neglected for all of the following reasons *except*
   a) most recent budgets have had to cut expenses, and infrastructure is among the easier items to cut.
   b) the state legislature does not put a high priority on infrastructure issues because infrastructure does not vote.
   c) most politicians in California have time horizons that are relatively short.
   d) public employee unions have emphasized their members, who are voters, rather than infrastructure issues.
6. Indian gaming in California operates under the same general set of rules as the casinos in Nevada do.
   a) true
   b) false
7. Indian gaming issues in California have involved which of the following:
   a) tribal-sponsored initiatives
   b) federal court decisions over the legality of Indian casinos in California

   c) compacts negotiated by the governor and ratified by the State Senate
   d) substantial gaming revenues received by local governments in California
8. The war between the Caltrans engineers and surveyors and those employed in the private sector is primarily about
   a) the ability of both to use Indian casinos without allegations of conflicts of interest.
   b) contracting out the design of state highways.
   c) enforcing rules that require privately employed engineers to subsidize those working in the public sector.
   d) how substantial the decline in California's infrastructure is.
   e) whether state-employed engineers and surveyors will be able to have pay comparable to the private sector.
9. Workers' compensation premiums, paid by employers, declined by almost 50 percent after Governor Schwarzenegger's reform in 2003 because
   a) the governor was able to enact a substantial reform over the objections of both employers and employees.
   b) the governor's reform reduced waste and duplication in the administration of the workers' compensation system.
   c) benefits to workers were cut, in some cases justifiably and in others perhaps not.
   d) benefits to workers were actually increased but the total number of eligible workers was reduced, resulting in substantial savings.
   e) all of the above
10. According to the book, California voters are unwilling to support sufficient fire protective services in some counties because
    a) voters are opposed to paying increased taxes for this purpose.
    b) private fire protective services have largely replaced those in the public sector in these counties.
    c) about 40 percent of existing housing in California is located in areas classified as "high" or "extreme" fire danger.
    d) the increased majorities required to raise taxes under Proposition 13 require majorities that are higher than have been obtained in these areas.
    e) a) and d)

CRITICAL-THINKING QUESTIONS

1. Discuss the condition of California's highways, both in your experience and as presented in the book. What does the condition of our highway system have in common with the other infrastructure problems mentioned, such as fire prevention, the California State University, city swimming pools, school buildings, and levees?

2. The involvement of many different groups makes Indian gaming a significant public-policy problem. Indicate the different groups that are involved; their goals, which may be different or conflicting; and something about their success thus far.

3. Discuss the ways in which undocumented immigration is a problem for localities (counties, cities, towns, unincorporated areas) in California. What in general can be done to solve these problems?

4. Discuss the groups involved in the workers' compensation system and whether and how their goals conflict.

KEY TERMS

At this point you should have a general understanding of the following concepts and terms:

Caltrans (189)
"claim mills" (192)
Field Act (196)
fraud rings (192)
independent commission for redistricting (199)
Indian Gambling Regulatory Act (198)
infrastructure (194)

levels of government (200)
nontribal casinos (198)
odds of winning (198)
open primaries (200)
permanent partial disability (192)
Professional Engineers in California Government (189)
Proposition 5 (198)

public policy (193)
redistricting (199)
tribal casinos (198)
tribal membership (199)
unicameral legislature (195)
workers' compensation law (190)

Notes

Chapter 1

1. "California in Crisis," *California Journal* (August 2003), p. 20.
2. Dan Walters, "Ex-Governors Miss Chance to Discuss Complexities," *Santa Barbara News-Press*, February 21, 2004, p. A11.
3. James Q. Wilson, "A Guide to Schwarzenegger Country," *Commentary* (December 2003), pp. 45–49; Field Institute, *Legislation by Initiative vs. through Elected Representatives* (San Francisco: Field Institute, November 1999), field.com/fieldpollonline/subscribers/COI-99-Nov-Legislation.pdf
4. "Just the Facts: Immigrants in California," PPIC (Public Policy Institute of California), July 2002.
5. Jeffrey S. Passel, Randy Capps, and Michael Fix, *Undocumented Immigrants: Facts and Figures* (Washington, DC: Urban Institute Immigration Studies Program, January 12, 2004), www.urban.org/UploadedPDF/1000587_undoc_immigrants_facts.pdf
6. California Department of Finance, *Census 2000 California Profile* (Sacramento: Department of Finance, August 2002), www.dof.ca.gov/html/demograp/Census2000CA_profile.doc

Chapter 2

1. Amanda Meeker, "An Overview of the Constitutional Provisions Dealing with Local Government, Report of the California Constitutional Review Commission" (1996), www.library.ca.gov/CCRC/reports/html
2. Carl Brent Swisher, *Motivation and Political Technique in the California Constitutional Convention 1878–79* (New York: Da Capo Press, 1969).
3. Spencer C. Olin, Jr., *California's Prodigal Sons: Hiram Johnson and the Progressives, 1911–1917* (Berkeley: University of California Press, 1968), p. 70.
4. John M. Allswang, *The Initiative and Referendum in California, 1898–1998* (Stanford: Stanford University Press, 2000), p. 15.
5. Richard Hofstadter, *The Age of Reform* (New York: Washington Square Press, 1988), p. 23.
6. George E. Mowry, *The California Progressives* (Chicago: Quadrangle, 1963), pp. 12–13.
7. Kevin Starr, *Inventing the Dream: California through the Progressive Era* (New York: Oxford University Press, 1985), pp. 242–43.
8. Dean R. Cresap, *Party Politics in the Golden State* (Los Angeles: The Haynes Foundation, 1954), p. 12.
9. Mowry, *The California Progressives*, p. 12.
10. Ibid., p. 15.
11. Quoted ibid., p. 65.
12. Starr, *Inventing the Dream*, p. 254.
13. California Secretary of State, *A History of California Initiatives, 2002*, and listing of initiatives for years 2003–2008.
14. Allswang, *The Initiative and Referendum*, p. 33.
15. Ibid., p. 75.
16. David Broder, *Democracy Derailed: Initiative Campaigns and the Power of Money* (New York: Harcourt, 2000), p. 5.
17. William A. Niskanen, in "Do Ballot Initiatives Undermine Democracy?" *Cato Policy Report* (July/August 2000), pp. 6, 7, 9, www.cato.org/pubs/policy_report/v22n4/initiatives.pdf
18. California Secretary of State, *California Referenda: 1914–Present* November 6, 2007, www.sos.ca.gov/elections/referenda_history.pdf
19. Jim Puzzanghera, "History of Recall Gives Fuel to Both Sides," *The San Jose Mercury News*, June 18, 2003, www.mercurynews.com/mld/mercurynews/news/6113858.htm

Chapter 3

1. Jay Michael and Dan Walters, with Dan Weintraub. *The Third House: Lobbyists, Money and Power in Sacramento* (Berkeley: Berkeley Public Policy Press, 2002), p. 13

2. Carey McWilliams, *California: The Great Exception* (Berkeley: University of California Press, 1999), p. 198.

3. Arthur H. Samish and Bob Thomas, *The Secret Boss of California: The Life and High Times of Art Samish* (New York: Crown, 1971), p. 13.

4. California Secretary of State, "History of Political Reform Division Office," 2004, www.ss.ca.gov/prd/about_the_division/hostory.htm

5. Ibid.

6. Sam Delson, "Some Call Spending Money to Get Money Respectable but Necessary for Inland Cities and Schools," *Riverside Press-Enterprise*, July 6, 1997, p. A2.

7. California Secretary of State, "Top 10 Lobbying Firms," 2003, www.ss.ca.gov/prd/lobreport00_8qtr/chart6.htm

8. McWilliams, *California: The Great Exception*, p. 198.

9. "California Lobbyist Control Gets a C," *Silicon Valley/San Jose Business Journal*, May 23, 2003.

10. Mark Sappenfield, "Why Clout of Lobbyists Is Growing," *The Christian Science Monitor*, July 22, 2003, news.corporate.findlaw.com/csmonitor/s/20030723/23jul2003084412.html

11. Donald R. Roach, "Carpenter Is Sentenced to Prison for Seven Years," *CaltaxNewsletter* (January 1995), www.caltax.org/member/taxletter/vol8-03.htm

12. California Secretary of State, "Lobbying Expenditures and the Top 100 Lobbying Firms: January 1, 1999 through December 31, 2000," 2003, www.ss.ca.gov/prd/lobreport00_8qtr/lobmainpage.htm

13. California Secretary of State, *Lobby Activity: Lobbying Firms*, 2003, cal-access.ss.ca.gov/lobbying/firms

14. American League of Lobbyists, 2003, www.alldc.org

15. American League of Lobbyists, "Lobbying as a Career," 2003, www.alldc.org

16. Ron Faucheux, "The Grassroots Explosion," *Campaigns & Elections* (December/January 1995), p. 20.

17. Stephen Ansolabehere, James Snyder, Jr., and Mickey Tripathi, "Are PAC Contributions and Lobbying Linked? New Evidence from the 1995 Lobby Disclosure Act," econ-www.mit.edu/faculty/snyder/files/contribs_&_lobbying_6.pdf

18. Center on Juvenile and Criminal Justice, "California Prison Politics," 2002, www.cjcj.org/pdf/cal_prison_politics.pdf

19. Mark Martin and Pamela J. Podger, "Prison Guards' Clout Difficult to Challenge," *San Francisco Chronicle*, February 2, 2004, p. A-1.

20. Daniel Macallair, "Prisons: Power Nobody Dares Mess With." *The Sacramento Bee*, February 29, 2004, p. A-16.

21. Nancy Vogel, "Two Bills Target Capitol Consultant-Lobbyist," *Los Angeles Times*, July 17, 2003.

22. Larry L. Berg and C. B. Holman, "The Initiative Process and Its Declining Agenda-Setting Value," *Law and Policy* 11, no. 4 (1989), pp. 451–65.

23. Mark Baldassare, "The California Initiative Process—How Democratic Is It?" Public Policy Institute of California (February 2002), p. 3.

24. Elisabeth R. Gerber, *Interest Group Influence in the California Initiative Process* (San Francisco: Public Policy Institute of California, 1998), p. 13, www.ppic.org/content/pubs/R_1198EGR.pdf

25. Baldassare, "The California Initiative Process," p. 3.

26. Susan F. Rasky, "Covering California: the Press Wrestles with Diversity, Complexity, and Change," in *Governing California: Politics, Government, and Public Policy in the Golden State*, ed. Gerald C. Lubenow and Bruce E. Cain (Berkeley: Institute of Governmental Studies Press, University of California, 1997), pp. 157–88.

27. Ibid., p. 182.

28. Jim Rutenberg, "Working to Spin Distrust of Media into Votes," *New York Times*, October 12, 2003.

Chapter 4

1. Spencer C. Olin, *California's Prodigal Sons: Hiram Johnson and the Progressives, 1911–1917* (Berkeley: University of California Press, 1968).

2. A. James Reichley, *The Life of the Parties: A History of American Political Parties* (New York: Free Press, 1992).

3. Michael Finnegan, "The Race for the White House," *Los Angeles Times*, September 8, 2004, p. A1.

4. Sherry Bebitch Jeffe, "California's Primary Kept Clinton Going," *Washington Independent*, June 2, 2008, http://washingtonindependent.mypublicsquare.com/view/californias-primary

5. "The Mormon Money Behind Proposition 8," Oct. 3, 2008, http://andrewsullivan.theatlantic.com/the_daily_dish/2008/10/the-mormon-fact.html.

6. S. Rasky, Introduction to "An Antipolitician, Anti-establishment Groundswell Elected the Candidate of Change," in *California Votes: The 2002 Governor's Race and the Recall That Made History*, ed. G. Lubenow, (Berkeley: Berkeley Public Policy Press, 2003).

7. Ibid.

8. Ibid.

9. Ibid., p. 175.

10. Bruce E. Cain, "The California Recall" (interview), Brookings Institution, October 8, 2003.

11. Decker, C., "State's Shifting Political Landscape," *Los Angeles Times*, November 6, 2008, p. A1.

12. Rasky, Introduction.

13. William Booth, "In Calif. Governor's Race, It's Ads Infinitum," *Washington Post*, May 29, 1998, p. A1.

14. Cecilia Rasmussen, "When Voters Were Identified by Goiters, Missing Fingers and Tattoos," *Los Angeles Times*, September 14, 2003, p. B5.
15. Carol A. Cassel, "Hispanic Turnout: Estimates from Validated Voting Data," *Political Research Quarterly* 55, no. 2 (June 2002), pp. 391–408; Michael A. Jones-Correa and David L. Leal, "Political Participation: Does Religion Matter?" *Political Research Quarterly* 54, no. 4 (2001), pp. 751–70.
16. Megan Garvey, "Candidates Targeting State's Absentee Voters," *Los Angeles Times*, September 8, 2003, p. A19.

Chapter 5

1. Emily Bazar, "A Mad Dash into Confusion: As Lawmakers Race to Wrap Up for the Year the Public Often Gets Left in the Dark," *Sacramento Bee*, September 16, 2001.
2. Peter Schrag, *Paradise Lost: California's Experience, America's Future* (New York: New Press, 1998), p. 244.
3. Institute of Governmental Studies, "IGS Goes to Sacramento to Assess Ten Years of Term Limits," *Public Affairs Report* 42, no. 3 (Fall 2001).
4. National Conference of State Legislators, www.ncsl.org
5. Schrag, *Paradise Lost*, p. 143.

Chapter 6

1. Richard E. Neustadt, *Presidential Power and the Modern Presidents: The Politics of Leadership from Roosevelt to Reagan* (New York: Macmillan, 1990).
2. Thomas E. Cronin and Michael A. Genovese, *The Paradoxes of the American Presidency* (New York: Oxford University Press, 1998).
3. State of California, Department of Finance, *2006 California Statistical Abstract* (Sacramento: Department of Finance, downloaded March 2008), pp. 263 and 264, Tables P-26 and P-27.

Chapter 7

1. 2008 Court Statistics Report www.courtinfo.ca.gov/reference/documents/csr2008.pdf
2. U.S. Census Bureau, Annual Population Estimates 2000–2008. www.census.gov/popest/states/NST-ann-est.html
3. www.courtinfo.ca.gov/jc/tflists/documents/minutes_jcfTaskForce_091107.pdf
4. California *Official Voter Information Guide*. Available at: www.voterguide.sos.ca.gov/argu-rebut/argu-rebutt8.htm
5. 2008 Court Statistics Report.

Chapter 8

1. Marla Dickerson, "State Fiscal Woes Threaten Cities' Budgets and a Leading Job Engine," *Los Angeles Times*, January 17, 2003, pp. C1, C4.
2. California Department of Finance, "History of Budgeting," February 24, 1998, www.dof.ca.gov
3. George Skelton, "The 'Budget Nun' Earns Her Pay and Bipartisan Respect," *Los Angeles Times*, May 26, 2003, p. B5.
4. California, Department of Finance, "California's Budget Process," October 10, 2000, www.dof.ca.gov/fisa/bag/process.htm
5. Public Policy Institute of California (PPIC), "California's Tax Burden," 2003, www.ppic.org
6. Katherine Barrett, Richard Greene, Michele Mariani, and Anya Sostek, "The Way We Tax," *Governing* (February 2003), p. 20.
7. California Budget Project, "Who Pays Taxes in California?" 2002, www.cbp.org/2002/qh020415.htm
8. Barrett et al., "The Way We Tax," p. 20.
9. Dennis Cauchon, "1 State Gets Fiscal Discipline, 1 Gets a Disaster," *USA Today*, June 24, 2003, p. 7A.
10. California Taxpayers Association, "Cal-Tax: Taxes Are Heavy Burden in California," www.caltax.org/California.htm
11. Stephen Kroes, "Californians Carry Heavy Tax Burden," *Cal-Tax Digest* (September 1999).
12. "You Don't Have It So Bad," *Los Angeles Times*, May 27, 2003, p. B12.
13. James D. Savage, "California's Structural Deficit Crisis," *Public Budgeting and Finance* 12, no. 2 (Summer 1992), pp. 82–97.
14. http://caforward.org/files/CA%20FWD%20Budget%20Principles.pdf
15. Peter Nicholas and Virginia Ellis, "Budget Signals Narrowed Ambitions," *Los Angeles Times*, February 18, 2004, p. A1.
16. Dan Walters, "California's Crisis of Governance Undermines Democratic Theory," *Sacramento Bee*, July 4, 2004, p. A16.

Chapter 9

1. Brian P. Janiskee, "The Problem of Local Government in California," *Nexus, a Journal of Opinion* (Spring 2001), p. 230.
2. Bernard H. Ross and Myran A. Levine. *Urban Politics: Power in Metropolitan America*, 6th ed. (Itasca, IL: F. E. Peacock, 2001), p. 90.
3. Dale Krane, Platon N. Rigos, and Melvin B. Hill, Jr., *Home Rule in America: A Fifty-State Handbook* (Washington, DC: Congressional Quarterly Press, 2001).
4. Daniel B. Rodriguez, "State Supremacy, Local Sovereignty: Reconstructing State/Local Relations under the California

Constitution," in Bruce E. Cain and Roger G. Noll, eds., *Constitutional Reform in California: Making State Government More Effective and Responsive* (Berkeley: Institute of Governmental Studies Press, University of California, 1995), pp. 401–29; Krane, Rigos, and Hill, *Home Rule in America*; Melvin B. Hill, *State Laws Governing Local Government Structure and Administration* (Washington, DC: U.S. Advisory Commission on Intergovernmental Relations [ACIR], 1993).

5. Ross and Levine, *Urban Politics*, p. 91.

6. John Taylor, "What Happened to Branciforte County?" (Sacramento: California State Association of Counties, 2000), www.csac.counties.org/defaultasp?id=52

7. *County of Los Angeles Annual Report 2007 to 2008*, http://lacounty.info/budget.htm

8. U.S. Census Bureau, *2007 Census of Governments* (Washington, DC: Government Printing Office, 2007); and League of California Cities, report December 10, 2008.

9. Zoltan L. Hajnal, Paul G. Lewis, and Hugh Louch, *Municipal Elections in California: Turnout, Timing, and Competition* (San Francisco: Public Policy Institute of California, 2002), pp. 23–24.

10. Ross and Levine, *Urban Politics*, pp. 165–78.

11. Amy Bridges, *Morning Glories: Municipal Reform in the Southwest* (Princeton, NJ: Princeton University Press, 1997).

12. International City/County Management Association (ICMA), "Officials in U.S. Muncipalities 2,500 and Over in Population," in ICMA, *The Municipal Year Book 2003* (Washington, DC: ICMA, 2003), pp. 195–200.

13. H. George Frederickson and Gary Alan Johnson, "The Adapted American City: A Study of Institutional Dynamics," *Urban Affairs Review* 36, no. 6 (2001): 872–884; Susan A. McManus and Charles S. Bullock III, "The Form, Structure, and Composition of America's Municipalities in the New Millennium," in ICMA, *The Municipal Yearbook 2003*, pp. 3–18.

14. Bruce E. Cain, Megan Mullin, and Gillian Peele, "City Caesars?: An Examination of Mayoral Power in California," presented at the 2001 annual meeting of the American Political Science Association, August 29–September 2, San Francisco.

15. Richard Edward DeLeon, *Left Coast City: Progressive Politics in San Francisco, 1975–1991* (Lawrence: University Press of Kansas, 1992).

16. Hajnal et al., *Municipal Elections*, p. 25.

17. DeLeon, *Left Coast City*.

18. Hajnal et al., *Municipal Elections*, p. 19.

19. Ibid., p. 26.

20. Ibid., p. 3.

21. Ibid., p. 64.

22. Senate Local Government Committee, *What's So Special about Special Districts?: A Citizen's Guide to Special Districts in California*, 3d ed. (Sacramento: California State Senate, 2002), p. 3.

23. U.S. Census Bureau, 2007 and 2008, *Census of Governments*.

24. Ibid.

25. Margaret Taylor, *California's Health Care Districts* (Oakland, CA: California HealthCare Foundation, April 2006).

26. U.S. Census Bureau, *2007, Census of Governments*.

27. Janiskee, "The Problem of Local Government in California," pp. 219–33.

28. Gabriel Metcalf, "An Interview with Joe Bodovitz," *SPUR* report no. 378 (September 1999).

29. Roper Center for Public Opinion Research, *Social Capital Community Benchmark Survey: Methodology and Documentation*, February 17, 2001, www.ropercenter.uconn.edu/scc_bench.html

30. Mark Baldassare, *A California State of Mind: The Conflicted Voter in a Changing World* (Berkeley: University of California Press, 2002), p. 47.

31. DeLeon, *Left Coast City*.

32. For more information on the secession movement and its outcome, see Tom Hogen-Esch, "Urban Secession and the Politics of Growth: The Case of Los Angeles," *Urban Affairs Review* 36, no. 6 (2001): 783–809; Martin Kasindorf, "L.A. Secession Drives Faltering as City Hall Warns about Risks," *USA Today*, October 30, 2002, p. 3A; William Booth, "L.A. Secession Campaign Tests Hahn's Mettle," *Washington Post*, September 22, 2002, p. A4; David Devoss, "Secession Is Dead, but Self-Rule Dream Lives," *Los Angeles Times*, November 9, 2002, p. 3.

33. Herb J. Wesson, Jr., "Cutting to the Bone," *Western City* (February 2003).

34. Peter Schrag, "25 Years Later," *San Diego Union-Tribune*, June 22, 2003, p. G1.

35. Institute for Local Self Government (ILSG), *The Fiscal Condition of California Cities: 2003 Report* (Sacramento: ILSG, 2003), p. 23

36. Michael Coleman and Bob Leland, "State Intrusion Creates Fickle Fiscal Future for Cities" *Western City* (April 2003).

37. Michael Coleman and Michael G. Golantuono, "Local Fiscal Authority and Stability: Control and Risk in California City Revenues," *Western City* (August 2003).

38. Dean J. Misczynski, "The Fiscalization of Land Use," in John J. Kirlin and Donald R. Winkler, eds., *California Policy Choices*, Vol. 3 (Los Angeles: University of Southern California, 1986); Paul G. Lewis and Elisa Barbour, "The Quest for Retail Development: Do Local Governments Make Land Use Decisions Based on the Need to Generate Revenue?" *California County* (May/June 2000), www.csac.counties.org/

39. James Burger, "Municipal Nerves Left Frayed by Fiscal Woe," *Bakersfield Californian*, June 19, 2003.

40. "End the Plunder," *Long Beach Press-Telegram*, September 14, 2003.

41. For a detailed analysis of Proposition 1A, see League of Women Voters of California Education Fund, *Nonpartisan Analysis of Proposition 1A*, November 2004, at ca.lwv.org/lwvc/edfund/elections/2004nov/pc/prop1A.html

42. Michael Coleman, "A Primer on California City Finance," *Western City*, March 2005.

43. Employment Development Department, State of California "Monthly Labor Force Data for Counties: October 2008 Preliminary," November 21, 2008. (www.labormarketinfo.edd.ca.gov/?pageid=131).

44. League of California Cities, "League of California Cities Supports Federal Legislation to Help Cities Recover from Effects of Mortgage Crisis," July 2, 2008.

45. E. Scott Reckard, "Record 10% of U.S. Homeowners in Arrears or Foreclosure," *Los Angeles Times*, December 6, 2008.

46. Evan Halper, "Legislature Considers Raiding Voter-Approved Funds," *Los Angeles Times*, July 18, 2008.

47. Quoted in the *Sacramento Bee*, July 16, 2008.

48. Governor Arnold Schwarzenegger, "Governor Delivers Remarks at the League of California Cities 2008 Annual Conference," State of California, Office of the Governor, September 25, 2008. Source: http://gov.ca.gov/index.php?/speech/10623/.

49. Details of the League's "cut up the card" campaign can be viewed at www.cutupthecard.com

50. U.S. Conference of Mayors, "U.S. Conference of Mayors Climate Protection Agreement," http://www.usmayors.org/climateprotection/agreement.htm (accessed on July 19, 2008).

51. Margot Roosevelt, "L.A. and San Francisco Vie for Title of 'Greenest City,'" *Los Angeles Times*, April 22, 2008.

52. Wyatt Buchanan, "734 Businesses Sign Up for S.F. Health Program," *San Francisco Chronicle*, May 2, 2008.

53. For more information on IRV and its use, see http://www.fairvote.org

Chapter 10

1. Daniel Weintraub, "Highway Robbery: Another Davis Legacy Bites the Dust," *Sacramento Bee*, March 18, 2004.

2. For a general description of the program and issues, as well as links to important articles, see the library overview at the Institute of Governmental Studies at the University of California, Berkeley, www.igs.berkeley.edu/library/

3. Institute of Governmental Studies, University of California, Berkeley, "Hot Topic, Workers' Compensation in California," March 2004, www.igs.berkeley.edu/library

4. California Restaurant Association, "Rising Premiums and the Workers' Comp Crisis: What's Up?" 2003, www.calrest.org/newsinfo/risingpremiums.asp

5. Los Angeles County District Attorney's Office, "Workers' Comp Fraud Is No Paid Vacation," March 1996, da.co.la.ca.us/pdf/workcomp.pdf

6. George Skelton, "Workers' Comp Reform Requires Action, Not Just Talk," *Los Angeles Times*, January 22, 2004, p. B-6.

7. Daniel Weintraub, "State Workers' Comp That Really Works," *Santa Barbara News-Press*, February 18, 2004, p. A11.

8. Dan Walters, "Dems Want to Roll Back Schwarzenegger's Changes in Workers' Comp," *Sacramento Bee*, July 7, 2008.

9. Marc Lifsher, "Workers' Comp Changes Ease Pains but Don't Work for All," *Los Angeles Times*, October 17, 2006, pp. A1, A16.

10. Public Policy Institute of California, "Just the Facts, Immigrants in California," July 2002, www.ppic.org

11. Joaquin Avila, "Political Apartheid in California: Consequences of Excluding a Growing Noncitizen Population," Latino Policy and Issues Brief, No. 9, (UCLA Chicano Studies Research Center, December 2003).

12. Bruce E. Cain, "Searching for the Next Pat Brown: California Infrastructure in the Balance" in *California's Future in the Balance*, California Policy Issues Annual, special ed. (Los Angeles: Edmund G. "Pat" Brown Institute of Public Affairs, November 2001).

13. P. J. Huffstutter and DeeDee Correll, "Bridge Urgency Has Buckled," *Los Angeles Times*, August 1, 2008, p. A8. American Association of State Highway and Transportation Officials, *Bridging the Gap: Restoring and Rebuilding the Nation's Bridges* (Washington, DC: American Association of State Highway and Transportation Officials, 2008).

14. "Penny-Wise, Fire-Foolish" (editorial), *Los Angeles Times*, March 8, 2004, p. B10.

15. Bettina Boxall, "A Santa Barbara Area Canyon's Residents Are among Many Californians Living in Harm's Way in Fire Prone Areas," *Los Angeles Times*, July 31, 2008, p. A1.

16. Kimi Yoshino, "Buying a Quick Response," *Los Angeles Times*, October 26, 2007, pp. A1, A21.

17. Earthquake Engineering Research Institute, Northern California Chapter, "K–12 Public Schools Fact Sheet" (n.d.), www.quake06.org

18. Stuart Leavenworth, "Logjam May Break on Mending Levees," *Sacramento Bee*, April 2, 2004.

19. Stuart Leavenworth, "Defenses Decayed: Neglected Levees Pushed Past Limits," *Sacramento Bee*, March 28, 2004.

20. Sara Lin and William Wan, "Crews Shore Up Levees as Concerns Rise over Upkeep," *Los Angeles Times*, June 10, 2004, pp. B1, B8.

21. Craig Lambert, "Trafficking in Chance," *Harvard Magazine* (July–August 2002), p. 40.

22. "Indian Gaming in California," Hot Topic, Library, Institute of Governmental Studies, University of California, Berkeley (Spring 2005), www.igs.berkeley.edu/library/index.html

23. Ibid.

24. Paul Pringle, "Players at Indian Slots Have No Clue on Payout," *Los Angeles Times*, February 10, 2003, p. B1.

25. Ibid.